VICTORIAN INTERIOR DESIGN

JOANNA BANHAM
SALLY MACDONALD
JULIA PORTER

CASSELL

Cassell
Villiers House
41–47 Strand
London WC2N 5JE

First published in the UK 1991 by Cassell

Created, designed and produced by Studio Editions Limited
Princess House, 50 Eastcastle Street
London W1N 7AP

ISBN 0 304 34051 0

Distributed in Australia by
Capricorn Link (Australia) Pty Limited,
PO Box 665, Lane Cove, NSW 2066

Printed and bound in Hong Kong

CONTENTS

Acknowledgements   7

1   The Victorian Revival   9

2   Victorian Values   27

3   The Battle of the Styles   45

4   The Reformed Home   63

5   Morris & Co.   81

6   The Aesthetic Movement   107

7   Palaces of Art   131

8   Cottage Style   157

9   New Art   177

10   Revivalism Revisited   195

Bibliography   213

Selected Biographies   215

Index   222

ACKNOWLEDGEMENTS

Like many publications this book is not the outcome of its authors' efforts alone. Many people have also given generously of their knowledge and time, and we should like to thank firstly the staff of those libraries and museums who have patiently and cheerfully provided material for research. These include the British Library, the Geffrye Museum, the National Art Library, the National Monuments Records Office, the Royal Borough of Kensington & Chelsea Libraries, the Whitworth Art Gallery, the Victoria & Albert Museum Print Room, the Victorian Society and Warners Archive. Secondly, thanks are also due to certain individuals who have provided invaluable advice and practical help: Sheila Ayres, Dorothy Bosomworth, Dorian Church, Charlotte Gere, Norah Gillow, Paul Hardy, Robert Howley, Richard Jeffries, Juliet Kinchin, Patricia de Montford, Charles Newton, Rob Pryce, Keith Sugden, Mark Turner, Clive Wainwright, Christine Woods, and Hilary Young. In addition, we are grateful to John Rogers and Terry Thorpe for their assistance with photography and to Sara Waterson who has far exceeded her brief as picture researcher to help unearth some little-known and fascinating images. Finally, special thanks are due to Harriet Dover for all her speedy suggestions and help, and to Peggy Vance and Sarah Sears for their unfailing enthusiasm and support as editors of the book.

PICTURE ACKNOWLEDGEMENTS

American Museum in Britain, Bath: 55
Art Institute of Chicago: 158 (Friends of American Art Collection)
Birmingham City Art Gallery: 108
H Blairman & Co., London: 79
Boston Museum of Fine Arts: 40 (M & M Karolik Collection of American Watercolours and Drawings)
Bradford City Art Gallery: 92
Bridgeman Art Library: 85, 170, and
    Bonhams, London: 16
    British Museum, London: 59
    Cheltenham Art Gallery and Museum: 177
    Forbes Magazine Collection: 53
    Guildhall Art Library: 110
    Kelmscott Manor, Lechlade: 87, 94
    Private Collections: 2, 18, 32, 33, 35, 47, 54, 127, 213
    Roy Miles Fine Art: 47, 127, 138
    Townley Hall Art Gallery and Museum: 25, 57, 78, 86, 96, 98, 183, 199
    University of Glasgow: 192
    Victoria and Albert Museum: 25, 57, 78, 86, 96, 98, 183, 199
    Christopher Wood Gallery: 45, 70, 137, 141
British Library, London: 144, 145, 152, 155
Brooklyn Museum, New york: 22 (Gift of John D. Rockefeller Jr & John D. Rockefeller III), 208 (Gift of Miss Gwendolen O.L. Conckling)
Cheltenham Art Gallery and Museum: 178
Christie's Colour Library, London: 49, 80, 95, 182, 186, 189, 200
Colonial Williamsburg Foundations: 36 (Abby Aldrich Rockefeller Folk Art Center), 56
Country Life Magazine: 88, 167
John Donat Photography: 168
English Heritage Photo Library: 46
First Garden City Heritage Museum, Letchworth: 172, 173
Fischer Fine Art: 68
Free Library of Philadelphia, Picture and Print Department: 14
Freer Gallery of Art, Smithsonian Institution, Washington D.C.: 123
Geffrye Museum, London: 28, 30, 39, 41, 176, 212, 216, 224
Haggin Museum, Stockton, Calif: 207
Hammersmith and Fulham Public Libraries: 90
Hatfield House, Courtesy of the Marquess of Salisbury: 37
Hunterian Museum and Art Gallery, Glasgow: 120, 193, 194
AF Kersting: 89, 100
Lambeth Archives Department, Minet Library: 43, 50
London Borough of Hackney Archives Department: 7
London Borough of Hounslow Library Services: 171

London Transport Museum: 161
Lyman Allen Art Museum, New London, Conn: 206
Manchester City Art Gallery: 198
Mark Twain Memorial, Hatfield, Conn: 9
Maryland Historical Society, Baltimore: 9
Metropolitan Museum, New York: 8 (Gift of Frederic H. Hatch 1926), 210 (Gift of the Estate of Ogden Codman Jr. 1951)
Museum für Angewandte Kunst, Vienna: 188
Museum of Decorative Arts, Copenhagen: 187
Museum of the City of New York: 209, 217
National Gallery of Art, Washington: 143 (Chester Dale Fund)
National Portrait Gallery, London: 153
National Trust Photo Library: 29 (Michael Boys), 101 (Jonathan Gibson), 169 (J. Whitaker), 132 (Charlie Waite)
National Trust for Scotland, Photos Glyn Slatterly Book: 190, 191
New York Historical Society: 52
Old Sturbridge Village, Mass.: 51
Philadelphia Museum of Art: 113 (John G. Johnson Collection)
Private Collections: 63, 154
Royal Academy of Arts, London: 136
Royal Borough of Kensington and Chelsea Library Services: 102, 103, 104, 121, 142, 139, 148, 149, 151, 157, 159, 160, R.B.K. & C. Courtesy of the Victorian Society: 4, 23, 130
Royal Commission on the Historical Monuments of England: 3, 11, 66, 76, 105, 106, 107, 114, 126, 166, 174, 202, 203, 211, 214, 218, 219, 220
Royal Institute of British Architects: 147, 150 (Drawings Collection), 75 (Library)
Royal Library Windsor Castle (by Gracious Permission of Her Majesty the Queen): 34
Salisbury and South Wiltshire Museum: 42
A. Sanderson & Co Archives: 10, 12, 27
Society for the Preservation of New England Antiquities: 48 (Photo E. Marr & Sons)
Sotheby's New York: 26
Tate Gallery, London: 73, 74
Courtesy of Traditional Homes Magazine: 204
By Courtesy of the Trustees of the Victorian and Albert Museum: 6, 15, 17, 19, 20, 31, 38, 58, 61, 62, 65, 67, 71, 72, 73, 77, 81, 82, 83, 91, 93, 99, 109, 111, 112, 115, 118, 119, 122, 124, 129, 131, 133, 135, 156, 162, 163, 164, 165, 179, 180, 181, 184, 184, 195, 196, 197, 201, 205, 215, 222, 223, 225, 226
Watts Gallery, Guildford: 140
Westminster City Archives: 13
Whitworth Art Gallery, Manchester: 1, 21, 60, 69, 84, 97, 116, 117, 125, 128, 134
Unlisted photos were provided by the Publisher.

THE VICTORIAN REVIVAL

*His room was filled with a strange jumble of objects – a harmonium in a gothic
case, an elephant's foot wastepaper basket, a dome of wax fruit, two
disproportionately large Sèvres vases, framed drawings by Daumier – made all the
more incongruous by the austere college furniture and the large luncheon table.
(Evelyn Waugh,* Brideshead Revisited, *1945)*

THE STORY OF the Victorian era is a rich, complex, paradoxical, fascinating and topical one. Monumental changes took place during the reign of Queen Victoria (1837–1901) which have many bizarre parellels with today. Popular interest in the Victorian design which mirrored these changes has boomed in recent decades, and Victorian styles of furnishing are once again fashionable.

Victorian furniture and furnishings have been collected since the middle of this century, when young people, unable to afford eighteenth-century antiques, first began to appreciate "Victoriana". By the late 1960s the Victorian revival was in full swing. Many people in Britain and America now choose to live in nineteenth-century houses, in surroundings which provide a link with the past. The fashion for authentic décor, which has grown steadily since the early 1980s, has further fuelled popular interest in Victorian style.

"Victorian" interiors are typically densely patterned and cluttered with masses of ornaments. The "Victorian Parlour" displays, so often seen in museums of social history, film sets for Victorian costume dramas such as *The Forsyte Saga* and period style publications, reinforce this view.

Closer study of the period reveals a far more complex situation. There is no such thing as Victorian style; a myriad of different styles co-existed at the time, each carrying subtle social connotations. The terminology is confusing. Different names were applied to broadly similar styles. Twentieth-century design historians have added to the confusion by grouping things differently and inventing new labels. Most modern books about Victorian design present various styles as distinct and successive, even if they include a chapter on mid-Victorian eclecticism, and concede that different views on style could exist at the same time. Part of the problem with this approach lies in trying to explain stylistic diversity and development in a social and economic vacuum, or with very little contextual information.

A further distortion has been caused by the tendency to emphasize progressive developments such as Art Nouveau and the Arts and Crafts Movement, at the expense of traditional forms and revival styles which were far more prevalent at the time. Nikolaus Pevsner's *Pioneers of Modern Design* (1936) was one of the first and most influential books to apply this approach. One of the results was to place undue stress on the importance of individual design heroes, few of whom were afforded such stature in their own time. Simon Jervis in *High Victorian Design* (1983), Peter Thornton in *Authentic Decor* (1984) and other more recent writers have made scholarly attempts to redress the balance.

This book provides a chronological survey of what is now regarded as Victorian interior design from its beginnings in the early nineteenth century to its demise sometime during the First World War (1914–18). Interspersed with information on those designers whose work has been traditionally viewed as influential, is a discussion of the main styles of furnishing and decorating, the circumstances in which they were employed and the reasons for their popularity, or lack of it.

Victorian design is not peculiar to Britain. Many designers were successful abroad, both in Europe and North America, some more so than in their native country. British goods, as well as British talent, were

---

1. **AN AMERICAN WALLPAPER SHOWROOM, c.1895.** *By this date the buyer or customer could choose from a huge range of new art, naturalistic and revivalist styles.*

2. *John Ballantyne*, PORTRAIT OF DAVID ROBERTS RA IN HIS STUDIO. *Artists' houses were often at the forefront of fashionable taste. Their studios were much admired. Roberts, a painter of Middle Eastern landscapes, clearly favoured furniture in the Jacobean and Renaissance styles, but his many souvenirs, collected on his travels to the East, add an exotic touch to this room.*

marketed throughout the British Empire and the Western world. The United States were, with South Africa and Australia, one of the largest importers.

An awareness of style permeated every class of Victorian home. But the majority of working-class people in both Britain and America could not afford to decorate and furnish their homes with new and fashionable products. Few writers wrote for working-class readers, or bothered to describe working-class homes. Few artists or photographers chose to record them. Surviving interiors, even individual items of furniture, are relatively rare; in poorer homes most things were used until they were worn out. So while mantelpiece ornaments from middle-class parlours have been treasured and handed down, rag rugs from one-room tenements have been thrown away. Source material for a study of Victorian domestic design mainly relates to middle- and upper-class homes, and any view of nineteenth-century period style must therefore be highly selective.

New Money and New Markets

There has been a constant rising and falling in society going on – new families taking the place of the old, which have subsided in many cases into the ranks of the common people (Samuel Smiles, *Self-Help with Illustrations of Character and Conduct*, 1859).

The early years of the nineteenth century saw a vast expansion in the number of consumers able to exercise choice when buying products for the home. The reasons for the growth, in the decades following the Industrial Revolution, of new middle-class markets is outside the scope of this book. But the economic and social mobility of this period, the diversification of the market for consumer products, and the economic reasons for the multiplication of new styles are key factors in understanding the period.

For the new rich, home was a very important symbol. During the nineteenth century, urbanization and suburbanization took place on a large scale. London's population more than doubled in the first forty years of the century. Other manufacturing and commercial centres, like Manchester, grew even faster. The new urban population needed homes, and most major cities expanded rapidly outwards. In 1850, the reporter Henry Mayhew commented in the *Morning Chronicle* that:

Since 1839 there have been 200 miles of new streets formed in London, no less than 6,405 new dwellings have been erected annually since that time; and it is but fair to assume that the majority of these new homes must have required new furniture.

The majority of houses during the period were rented rather than owned; in England before 1900 nine out of ten houses were privately rented. The cost of buying a house varied enormously, from £300 to £400 for a modest suburban villa to over £2,000 for a large house in the town or country. Flats were cheaper, and "mansion" blocks were built in fashionable parts of London, but, unlike in continental Europe, they were usually regarded as less desirable than houses. Building societies were still relatively undeveloped and borrowing large sums to buy houses or flats was not easy. Renting was comparatively cheap. In the 1890s a five- to six-bedroom house could cost as little as £20 to £40 a year. With prices as low as this, the cost of painting and papering a newly occupied house represented no deterrent. Writers and design critics like Lewis F. Day deplored the decoration of the standard speculatively built rented house. In his book, *Every Day Art* (1882) he commented that: "Before the tenant ever came into possession the walls were hung with paper selected by the builder, in whose eyes those patterns are most

3. THE INDIAN ROOM AT 7 CHESTERFIELD GARDENS, LONDON, *1893. The furnishings of the "Indian" room included items from all over Asia juxtaposed with European imitations to create a Westerner's vision of an Eastern bazaar.*

beautiful on which the largest trade discount is allowed."

As a result, many writers, like the one who maintained, "it is only people in very straightened circumstances who accept, in these artistic days of ours, the landlord's scheme of decoration", actually recommended redecoration as a cheap and easy means of personalizing and improving the appearance of a rented home.

The new middle classes mostly wanted home and furniture which reflected their aspirations. People who had had to live with cheap, utilitarian, or second-hand furnishings were keen to acquire things which, while affordable, looked new, colourful, stylish and expensive. Home furnishing and decoration had always been, for the aristocracy, a potent means of expressing wealth and good breeding. For the new "self-made" urban middle classes, often living close to working-class areas, social positioning and the need to demonstrate status and taste were even more crucial.

The manner in which a room could be made to express the refinement or some other aspect of the inhabitant's personality had, by the late nineteenth century, become a matter of status. An American or English middle-class woman was judged by her sensibility in much the same way as fifty years earlier she had been measured by her moral scruples. As the New

Yorker, Elsie de Wolfe, wrote in her influential book *The House of Good Taste* (1913):

A house is a dead-give-away . . . We are sure to judge a woman in whose house we find ourselves for the first time, by her surroundings. We judge her temperament, her habits, her inclinations, by the interior of her home. We may talk of the weather, but we are looking at the furniture.

The earlier Victorians had furnished their homes to last a lifetime. During the middle years of the century, style dictated the use of opulent materials and finishes, such as carved and inlaid wood, gilt decoration on tableware, cut glass and damask, which could not be easily discarded and replaced. Obsolescence had not yet been built in. Mrs J. E. Panton, daughter of the popular Victorian painter, W. P. Frith, observed in 1919 that:

Fifty years ago, if carpets and curtains were bought at all, it was after high and long debates in the family, and heavens how they wore! At this moment I could put my hand on amber coloured damask curtains bought more than sixty years ago, and pieces of carpet bought more than eighty years since.

By the end of the century the conventions regarding visiting and entertainment had led to a slightly more flexible use of the home. The Arts and Crafts Movement had encouraged women to extend the sphere of management within the home to include its decoration. Some women went further and put their taste and practical expertise on a professional footing. This happened first in America, where possibly the Puritan ethic of self-sufficiency made it more acceptable for a woman

to find independent work, and only later in England, where women such as Syrie Maugham and Sibyl Colefax made names for themselves decorating the houses of wealthy and fashionable friends.

Elsie de Wolfe, in *The House of Good Taste*, explained the role of women as decorators:

I . . . wish to trace briefly the development of the modern house, the woman's house, to show you that all that is intimate and charming in the home as we know it has come from the unmeasured influence of women. Man conceived the great house with its parade rooms, its *grand apartments* but woman found eternal parade tiresome, and planned for herself little retreats, rooms small enough for comfort and intimacy. In short, man made the house: woman went one better and made of it a home.

New Technology

Speculative builders, furnishing manufacturers and retailers were anxious to satisfy the new middle-class market, its aspirations and prejudices. Profit provided an incentive to develop new products; new technology a means. Mechanization took place in a piecemeal way, and there were many trades where traditional handwork continued to play an important part. But in almost every area of production, methods were found of producing a wide range of expensive-looking goods, in larger quantities, more cheaply.

At the forefront of change was the textile industry. The Jacquard loom, which could be programmed using punched cards, was widely used from the mid-1820s onwards. It allowed a single weaver, working without an

4. (*opposite*) THE DRAWING-ROOM AT LINLEY SAMBOURNE HOUSE, LONDON. *An almost completely preserved example of an artistic interior of the 1870s, the house reflects the tastes of Linley Sambourne, a cartoonist and illustrator, and the preoccupations of the affluent and fashionable city-dwellers of the mid-Victorian period. There is almost no spare space. The walls are crammed with pictures, the rooms with a mixture of different furnishing types and styles: the fruits of Sambourne's passion for collecting old furniture.*

5. (*above*) *Charles Spencelayh,* HIS FAVOURITE, c.1895.

assistant and therefore more cheaply, to mass-produce complex patterns. From 1810 onwards, new, fast, mechanically driven roller printers began to replace the hand block printing of cotton. Experiments with natural and synthetic dyes produced a new range of brighter colours; cochineal pink (1818), manganese "bronze" (1822–3), chrome yellow (early 1820s).

Developments in the pottery industry included the refinement of bone china clay bodies and the introduction of Parian ware, or "statuary porcelain". Cheap versions of hard paste porcelain, both of these ceramic bodies were well adapted for mass-production and moulding. Likewise in the glass industry, the press-moulding method (invented in 1827) provided a means of mass-producing a hand-made cut-glass effect. Transfer-print decorating methods were improved and polychrome printing was introduced in the 1840s. With the increasing use of cheap water-gilding methods, and an expanding palette, tablewares and ornaments could be more colourful and more decorative.

In the furniture trade, the introduction, during the 1830s, of machines to cut veneers had a dramatic effect on production. The new saws could cut veneers more than twice as thinly as a skilled hand sawyer. This not only cost less in skilled labour, it used less good wood. A high quality veneer on a deal base could make a cheap piece of furniture look expensive. Wood as a material, though, was not well suited to mechanization, and furniture manufacturers consequently sought other materials which could be moulded or cast. Moulded papier-mâché furniture, painted, gilt and inlaid with mother-of-pearl, was made in large quantities from around 1830. Cast iron furniture, which likewise offered possibilities for mass-production, was made in even greater quantities and marketed for use in halls and gardens. The upholstery process also underwent changes in the early part of the century with the patenting, in the 1820s, of springing. This gave a greater depth, softness and curvature to the upholstery of seat furniture, without the skill and expense involved in traditional stuffing.

Dramatic changes also took place within the wallpaper industry. Until the 1830s, most wallpapers were produced by hand, using traditional block printing methods on hand-sorted rag paper, the whole process subject to a tax which put 1¾d. on a yard of patterned paper. With the invention of machinery to produce continuous wove paper from wood-pulp, at a fraction of the cost of hand-made paper, came a major breakthrough. In 1836 the tax was repealed, and three years later a machine was patented which could roller-print eight-colour patterns in a single operation on to the continuous roll of paper. Within a generation the price of wallpaper dropped to ¼d. a yard and what had formerly been a luxury item became a widely available commodity.

Together with the changes in the market and in the various industries producing goods for the home, went developments in how those products and services were marketed and sold to the consumer.

New Professionals: Decorators and Furnishers

The task of painting and decorating was traditionally undertaken by a professional firm. At the luxury end of the market were companies like J. G. Crace & Son, who could undertake complete furnishing and decorating schemes. Less wealthy clients were catered for by local firms. The Arrowsmiths' *The House Decorator's and Painter's Guide*, one of the leading trade manuals, lists an

6. THE DRAWING-ROOM AT EATON HALL, CHESHIRE, *late nineteenth century. The opulent and crowded drawing-room of the Duke of Westminster, one of the richest men in England. Fifty indoor servants were employed to maintain this degree of splendour.*

impressive range of skills which include (in addition to paperhanging) marbling, stencilling, graining, gilding and staining, as well as more mundane techniques, such as distempering and varnishing.

Although the quantity of wallpapers produced after 1860 was enormous, the absence of retail outlets made the choice of decorations appear more limited than it does today. Larger manufacturers such as Essex & Co. had extensive showrooms in London, in which their goods were displayed, but these existed primarily to serve the trade. Department stores that sold a complete range of household goods, such as Liberty's and Shoolbred's, were pioneers in this area. The ordinary consumer purchased wallpapers from the decorator who kept a number of pattern books in store from which the customer could make a choice. Some writers were critical of this situation, as it gave considerable power to the decorator, who was more likely to be concerned with the profit margin than with the artistic value of the works he sold. Lewis F. Day, for instance, claimed that the decorator rarely offered the public a selection that was not either excessively expensive or inappropriately fashionable and he advised his readers to "find out the names of the best paper stainers and to insist upon seeing their books" as the only means of giving their choice "fair play". The cost of furnishing and decorating always, of course, included the fee paid to the decorator.

The paperhanging and upholstery trades were related – and separate from decorating and painting – because the origins of wallpaper lay in fabric wall-hangings, and traditionally these were designed to be in keeping with the draperies and soft furnishings of the

7. (*above*) SPECULATIVE BUILDERS IN LONDON, *1882. Only a tiny proportion of Victorian houses were designed by architects. The vast majority of homes, especially in the new industrial areas, were designed and built by speculative building firms, using a combination of local vernacular styles and standardized decorative elements, like the leafy column capitals on the terrace on the left.*

8. (*opposite, above*) *J. Eastman Johnson*, THE FAMILY OF ALFREDERICK SMITH HATCH, *1871. During the Victorian period, 'home' came to embody an ideal of privacy, comfort, warmth and family stability.*

9. (*opposite, below*) THE LIBRARY AT MARK TWAIN'S HOUSE, HARTFORD, CONNECTICUT. *Despite the ornate carving and sumptuous red plush upholstery, the library, and the conservatory beyond, are clearly spaces for informal family use. The library is separated from the dining-room only by a curtain, allowing vistas through to the conservatory during the day.*

10. (*left*) *William Morris,* PIMPERNEL, *block-printed wallpaper, 1876.*

11. (*below*) SHOWROOM OF J. WARNROP & SONS, LIVERPOOL, *1890, photograph by Bedford Lemere. The nineteenth-century decorator was expected to master a range of techniques and media and his skill could sometimes rival that of the fine artist. This showroom illustrates some of the more elaborate effects available for 'artistic' rooms and includes a fine 'Aesthetic' dado and painted panels, as well as examples of more conventional work such as marbling and graining.*

12. (*opposite*) *Walter Crane,* SLEEPING BEAUTY, *machine-printed wallpaper, 1876. This nursery wallpaper was designed for mass-production and is surface-printed by roller. During the 1880s, amid the growing preoccupation with health in the home, it was specially promoted as a sanitary paper; unlike earlier wallpapers these were washable and, more importantly, contained no arsenic. As one contemporary put it, "with our walls covered by such papers, we can gratify our artistic taste and at the same time rest assured that we are not being slowly poisoned."*

room as a whole. In the early part of the century, wallpaper was subject to duty, was expensive and was therefore not widely used. But one upholsterer, James Arrowsmith, remarked in his book, *The Paper Hanger's and Upholsterer's Guide* (1854), that since the removal of tax, paperhanging had been "entrusted to persons of various callings and entire strangers to the business". These people, referred to by Arrowsmith as "slap bang innovators" were unfamiliar with the tools and preparatory techniques – pasting and sizing – of proper paperhanging. Arrowsmith nevertheless aims his book at these beginners, giving recipes, directions and hints.

Upholstery as a trade traditionally encompassed a range of activities, including the making up of curtains, draperies, hangings and seat upholstery, the selection and supply of carpets and even ornaments, and, on occasion, undertaking, valuing and house-letting. The upholsterer to the eighteenth-century gentry and aristocracy could supervise the furnishing of an entire room, choosing appropriate styles and colours. By the mid-nineteenth century, many more customers aspired to the ideal of an aristocratic home, but felt they needed advice in achieving the right effect. The number of upholsterers ready with this advice increased accordingly. A German journalist, writing in 1800, described the typical upholsterer as someone who

as if worked by strings, tells one immediately what colours go together, how much each article costs, what one must choose in order to guard against the shape and style becoming old fashioned after some years, what changes must be made in a house, what sort of carpets to go in the dining room and what sort in the dressing room, what materials last longest; how much time he needs to furnish the whole house and so on and so on.

There is evidence that this oppressive advisory service was well used by the middle classes, in both England and America. Even the style conscious were prepared to trust a professional. In the 1850s, the art critic John Ruskin gave the London upholstery firm of Snell £2,000 and *carte blanche* to furnish his house. His wife Effie was probably not alone in her later complaint that Snell had done it as cheaply and vulgarly as possible and had pocketed half the money.

By the middle of the nineteenth century advisory work, and its inherent network of commission fees and recommendations, had become for many furniture manufacturers an important means of marketing their products. Increasingly the larger manufacturing firms, like Jackson & Graham in London, developed their own departments for interior decoration.

Furniture retailers – or house furnishers, as they called themselves – took on the role of decorators for the middle classes. The National Association of Retail Furnishers likened the work of the house furnisher to that of "the tailor, the couturier, or the maitre d'hotel," and claimed that "he must sell something more than 'goods'. He must make himself known as an artist whose rare natural endowments and long years of careful training have fitted him for exceptional service; whose taste, judgement and experience are worth paying for."

BED · ROOM · FURNITURE · ETC. · FROM · SPECIMEN · PAGE · IN "LIBERTY" · HANDBOOK. · PART III.

13. (*above*) BEDROOM FURNITURE ADVERTISED IN LIBERTY'S CATALOGUE, C.1900. *Leading city stores, with their lavish catalogues, large showrooms and enticing window displays helped to set furnishing fashions.*

14. (*left*) COLLINSON & LOCKE'S STAND AT THE PHILADELPHIA CENTENNIAL EXHIBITION, 1876. *Large firms like Collinson & Locke took stands at the major international exhibitions in order to gain prestige and overseas orders.*

15. (*opposite, above*) Henry Eyles, MAHOGANY CHAIR WITH A PORTRAIT OF PRINCE ALBERT, *1851. Produced for the Great Exhibition in 1851, this is a classic piece of exhibition furniture, made for show rather than use. The portrait, of the Exhibition's royal patron, is painted on a porcelain plaque inset into the back.*

16. (*opposite, below*) Bruce James Talbert, THE JUNO CABINET, *made by Jackson & Graham, 1878. Large cabinet-making firms such as Jackson & Graham employed well-known freelance commercial designers like Talbert to produce virtuoso exhibition pieces. This richly decorated cabinet won the firm a prize at the Paris Exhibition in 1878 and was sold to the Viceroy of Egypt.*

Furniture-Makers and Retailers

By the middle of the nineteenth century the Tottenham Court Road area of London's West End was established as the centre of the retail furniture trade, with department stores like Oetzmann's and Shoolbred's and specialist furnishing shops like Maple's and Heal's. Lavish décor and dazzling displays attracted a clientele from all over the country, as shopping developed as a leisure activity. Other leading West End stores were Liberty's, Hampton's, Waring & Gillow and Whiteley's. The development of hire-purchase trading and other sorts of credit facilities greatly enhanced demand. A growing number of retail outlets were established at the turn of the century which exploited various systems of paying "out of income", the most famous of which in London were the Hackney Furnishing Co. and the Deptford Furnishing Co., which later became Times Furnishing.

Many West End stores attracted publicity and press attention by announcing the introduction of innovations such as lifts, electricity or cash registers, or visits from celebrities such as Lily Langtry and Ellen Terry.

In 1865 Henry Mayhew noted the emphasis on the extravagant use of window-dressing in London shops. At first such practices were regarded as vulgar, and established firms preferred to rely on their reputation. In 1875 the *Furniture Gazette* reported on the different displays to be seen in London shops. Maple's and Shoolbred's were described as having "magnificent displays in their large well-arranged windows, resplendent carpets, non-curtain fabrics, and inlaid cabinet work, aiming more at the beautiful in the popular than in the severely high-art sense". Older, specialist firms like Gillow's or Jackson & Graham, would in contrast, make no display at all, "relying on their superior reputation alone" or show only one piece "distinguished for some rare excellence or colouring".

Methods of marketing became more sophisticated with the growth of the mass media in the late nineteenth century. Newly established women's magazines, trade journals and local newspapers increased opportunities for advertising. During the 1870s wholesalers and retailers produced lavishly illustrated catalogues to show vast ranges of stock. Catalogues often adopted the style and format of women's magazines and books on home-furnishing. Some employed the same writers. Retail catalogues were designed not simply to illustrate stock but also to make furnishing suggestions. Images of ideal homes were created to capture the imagination of the consumer. Some firms, such as Shoolbred's, established a reputation for artistic catalogues, good enough to "grace a drawing room table", which presented artists' impressions of interiors as well as drawings of individual pieces of furniture.

Exhibitions were an important promotional vehicle for the firms that could afford to use them. One of the first and perhaps the most famous was the Great Exhibition held in London in 1851; but others followed: New York in 1853; Paris in 1855; London again in 1862. The late nineteenth century has been described as "the age of exhibitions". While the majority of exhibitions, such as the Annual Furnishing Trades Exhibition and Market at Olympia established in 1896, were organized for manufacturers and wholesalers to attract retail customers, the most famous and spectacular were aimed specifically at the public. The tradition of big exhibitions continued into the twentieth century; the most famous in Britain being the Daily Mail Ideal Home Exhibition, first held in 1908. Despite the prestige attached to showing, and winning prizes at the international exhibitions, they involved significant outlay for little commercial return. Only firms producing work for the top end

17. (*left*) E. W. Godwin, DESIGN FOR THE MONKEY CABINET, *c.1876. The design, in one of Godwin's tiny sketchbooks, is for a small walnut cabinet with boxwood insets and monkey-shaped handles. Its simple, asymmetrical shape and square sectioned rails were features Godwin admired in Japanese design.*

18. (*below*) George Aitchison, DESIGN FOR WALL DECORATIONS AT 1 GROSVENOR CRESCENT, LONDON.

19. (*opposite*) DRAWING-ROOM IN THE QUEEN ANNE STYLE *from* T. Knight & Sons, Suggestions for House Decorations. *Books like Knight's were intended as much for the decorating trade as for the home-owner; the scheme shown here indicates precisely how the different mouldings are to be painted. The decorative paintwork panels and frieze dominate the room and would be difficult to combine with pictures.*

of the market tended to participate in these events.

It was customary for retailers to claim that they made the furniture they sold in their own workshops, sometimes stamping it so. The tradition can be traced back to the eighteenth century at least, when it was considered more prestigious to buy furniture from a craftsman-shopkeeper than from a dealer-shopkeeper. The public were prepared to pay more for a name which they believed was a guarantee of quality and for a product which carried suggestions of "honest" craftsmanship and nostalgia for a Golden Age.

The furniture trade was keen to promote the idea of complete furnishing schemes, since this was a way of boosting sales. The marketing of furniture in suites for the dining-room, drawing-room and bedroom encouraged the practice of furnishing whole rooms at once. The development of hire purchase and other systems for "buying out of income" facilitated this practice.

In order to satisfy the expression of individual taste, which became a key determinant in the selection of domestic furnishings, the furniture and furnishing trades supplied vast ranges of stock. Some wholesalers boasted several thousand lines to choose from. Variety in the furniture trade was created by an infinite diversification of design, supplied, at least in part, by a new breed of commercial designer, who had to be capable of working in several media. The botanist and design lecturer Christopher Dresser, for example, designed furniture, wallpaper and ceiling patterns, pottery, metalwork and glass. He also employed several assistants whose work went out under his name. Some of the best known designers, including Dresser, published their work in practical, illustrated books produced for the decorating and furnishing trades. Their designs were given wider publicity by being reproduced in, or pirated by, the trade press, and from the 1860s onwards more and more designers made their names in this way.

Nevertheless, few firms employed designers. Some large companies used them on a freelance basis, primarily to illustrate catalogues aimed at the retail market, and to develop new production lines and ideas which could then be pursued by the firm's regular employees. Other, smaller, firms would occasionally purchase designs from reputable designers like Bruce Talbert or C. F. A. Voysey. But in the majority of firms producing furniture for the mass-market, designs were made by the boss or manager, skilled craftsmen and women who could combine at least elementary draughtsmanship with a detailed knowledge of timber and construction. This furniture was not made from working drawings; it was more usual to work from photographs or pictures culled from a variety of sources, or by memorizing pieces in exhibitions or shop window displays. Copying was an accepted practice.

The structure of the furniture trade and the organization of the design process resulted in the production of a myriad of hybrid styles. This fuelled the production of a plethora of publications offering advice on furnishing and decorating.

Home-Furnishing Publications

From quite early in the nineteenth century, a range of advice books was available, written both for those new to the trades and for the interested amateur. Decorating could involve everything from the painting of external woodwork, to elaborate interior treatment and furniture painting. More and more home-owners had both time and the inclination to decorate and personalize their homes. *Smith's Art of Housepainting* (1821) was "intended for those gentlemen in the country, who live at a remote distance from any regular painter", and included "recipes and directions for servants or other people to use in maintaining decorations". It advised

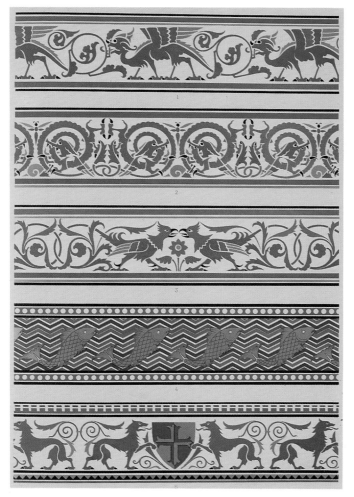

20. DECORATIVE FRIEZES *from W. & G. Audsley's book* Polychromatic Decoration, *1882. The Audsleys' book was one of a multitude of source books for the decorator published towards the end of the century.*

that some of the more complicated decorative techniques, like graining and marbling, were best learnt by watching a professional decorator, but otherwise encouraged "doing-it-yourself". Like Nathaniel Whittock's book, *The Decorative Painter's and Glazier's Guide* (1827), it was written in simple language and took an almost anti-professional stance; the preface to Whittock's book railed against trade secrecy, complaining that "the greater part of this information has been carefully kept even from those who eagerly desire to attain it". Whittock stated that most colours of paint could be bought ready mixed from "colourmen", and graining combs from established comb-makers, but the book also gave recipes for mixing paints and descriptions of how to make combs.

Charles Locke Eastlake's *Hints on Household Taste* (1868) was the first of many manuals produced in Britain that sought to promote an understanding of taste and artistry within the sphere of domestic design. It was followed by the equally popular *Art at Home* series, published by Macmillan in 1876, which gave room-by-room descriptions of the function and appearance of the major apartments in the house. Home writing reached a peak in the last two decades of the nineteenth century in the work of female correspondents such as

Mrs Panton in *Lady's World* and Mrs Haweis in *Ladies' Realm*. Although opinionated and even dogmatic in their writing, these women sought to lead their readers through the maze of contemporary styles on offer and to bring art and beauty within the reach of the middle-class home. Their advice was addressed to "that large borderland between the very rich who can hand over their houses to one or other of the high class decorators of the present day, and the very poor, who have neither taste nor ambition, and whose taste is not as conspicuous as it might be".

A key book on interior decoration in America was written by the novelist Edith Wharton with the architect Ogden Codman. *The Decoration of Houses* (1897) was her first publication on the subject, written, she claimed in her autobiography, to alleviate the boredom and frustration of an unsuccessful marriage. The "simple elegance" she recommended was based on seventeenth- and eighteenth-century European styles. Although she despised the sumptuousness of the Vanderbilt château on Fifth Avenue, the schemes she wrote about must have appeared to her readers to belong to a world of similarly fantastic wealth. The success of her books demonstrated the appeal of such grandeur to those who could never afford to live in that style.

21. COLOUR STUDIES *from the* Journal of Decorative Art, *1893. This journal was one of several magazines aimed at the decorating trade which regularly published design ideas.*

22. SMOKING-ROOM IN THE JOHN D. ROCKEFELLER HOUSE, NEW YORK CITY. *The increasing popularity of the Aesthetic Movement encouraged an interest in exotic styles. Moorish and Japanese styles were especially favoured and this room, decorated in 1865 by the New York firm Pottier & Stymus, and preserved in the Brooklyn Museum, is one of the most complete of its kind to survive.*

VICTORIAN VALUES

Mr and Mrs Veneering were bran-new people in a bran-new house in a bran-new quarter of London. Everything about the Veneerings was spick and span new. All their furniture was new, all their servants were new, their plate was new, their carriage was new, their harness was new, their horses were new, their pictures were new, they themselves were new, they were as newly married as was lawfully compatible with their having a bran-new baby, and if they had set up a great grandfather, he would have come home in matting from the Pantechnicon, without a scratch on him, French-polished to the crown of his head. For in the Veneering establishment, from the hall chairs with the new coat of arms, to the grand pianoforte with the new action, and up-stairs again to the new fire-escape, all things were in a state of high varnish and polish. And what was observable in the furniture, was observable in the Veneerings — the surface smelt a little too much of the workshop and was a trifle sticky.

(*Charles Dickens,* Our Mutual Friend, *1865*)

MOST OF this book deals with design and style in the home. But for the Victorian consumer, style in itself was only one factor in home furnishing. Other considerations were often far more significant: economy, comfort, convention, propriety and status. This chapter looks at the influence of some of these conventions on home decorating and furnishing in the first part of the nineteenth century.

During the early part of the nineteenth century, the idea of "home" took on a new significance for the urban middle classes. Many types of work which had previously been carried out on a small scale in the home were now removed into factories, offices and shops. Organization, supervision and control characterized these new large-scale capitalist workplaces. By contrast, the middle-class home became a place for eating, sleeping, caring for children, socializing and leisure: a haven from work. With this widening gap between work and home came a more marked division between the male and female spheres of activity. Increasingly, the middle-class man went out to earn a living, while the middle-class woman managed the home, probably employing at least one working-class woman to help with housework and childcare. Books and magazines about the home, from household guides to romantic fiction, reinforced the idea of home as a woman's place, as the proper (indeed the only) place where she could express her personality and as the embodiment of her womanly virtues. As one woman writer, Frances Power Cobbe, put it:

---

23. THE HALL AT LINLEY SAMBOURNE HOUSE, KENSINGTON. *The green walls, tiled floor, miniature conservatory on the landing and framed pictures of classical statuary give the hall a suitably serious atmosphere.*

The unhomeliness of homes of women in whom the feminine element is lacking is pitiable. The more womanly a woman is, the more she is sure to throw her personality over the home, and transform it, from a mere eating and sleeping place, or an upholsterer's showroom, into a sort of outermost garment of her soul; harmonised with all her nature as her robe and the flower in her hair are harmonised with her bodily beauty. The arrangement of her rooms, the light and shade, warmth and coolness, sweet odours, and soft or rich colours, are not like the devices of a well-trained servant or tradesman. They are expressions of the character of the woman. A woman whose home does not bear to her this relation of nest to bird, calyx to flower, shell to mollusk, is in one or another imperfect condition. She is either not really mistress of her home; or being so, she is herself deficient in the womanly power of thoroughly imposing her personality upon her belongings.

The division between male and female spheres was part of a complex process of differentiation and specialization in Victorian home life. Class, age and status were also crucial factors, highlighted in the arrangement and décor of homes. Certain rooms were associated with men and male activities, others with female. Children increasingly had separate areas, as did servants; upstairs/downstairs divisions became more marked. Public and private parts of the home were likewise separated out, with different areas for social and family activities. These differentiations, often extremely subtle, were acutely understood by Victorian middle-class consumers, and are evident in many aspects of design for the home.

Most Victorian workplaces tended to be designed with an emphasis on utility; machinery and plain, hard surfaces were felt to be appropriate to their function. Certain parts of the Victorian home — the kitchen, as the servants' workplace, for example — shared these features. But they were increasingly felt to be inappropriate

24. *A. J. Volck*, ENTERTAINING IN THE PARLOUR, *1862–3.*
Curvaceous Louis-style furniture remained popular for rooms used by
women until very late in the century.

in the home-as-haven, which was expected to be colour-ful, soft, plushy and personalized. The model of home adopted by the aspiring middle classes tended to be the aristocratic house, which epitomized leisure and com-fort. Highly ornamented furnishings, which repro-duced aristocratic styles and types affordably, enjoyed widespread popularity. The overmantel mirror pro-vides a good example of the downward dissemination of a furnishing type. Because of the high cost of manufac-turing sheets of glass and the tax imposed on them, large mirrors were, during the eighteenth century, owned only by the very wealthy. It became usual to have them framed like pictures, often in gilt frames, and to place them in a prominent location over the mantel-piece. The development of new plate glass manufactur-ing methods in the 1840s, combined with the repeal of duty in 1845, made mirrors much cheaper. Most middle-class households aspired to an overmantel mir-ror in at least one reception room, the size of the mirror acting as an indication of status. By the end of the century, "overmantels" incorporating mirrors were being made for working-class parlours.

Comfort and Warmth

James Arrowsmith, writing in 1854, praised the Grecian or modern style of upholstery, with its "round and soft stuffing" as opposed to the early nineteenth-century French "square and hard" style, "more calculated for the display of medallions and rich borders than ease and comfort". Soft furnishings of all kinds became, during the early Victorian period, an increasingly important part of interior decoration. Although Arrowsmith dis-tinguishes between Grecian and French styles, it was rare for upholstery to be described in these terms. Stylistic tags tended to be derived from the language of architecture and could only really be applied to solid furniture or patterns with recognizable architectural details. The *Upholsterer's Accelerator*, an early nineteenth-century manual for apprentice upholsterers, illustrates a variety of curtain and drapery treatments without refer-ring to styles at all; the different designs are referred to according to their overall shape: "a fan of pipes", "a swag raised at one side", "a geometrical valance". As the author rightly remarks, "New designs, however compli-cated, are only variations of the same parts in different proportions." For most of his customers, style was not the key selling point.

The real benefits of upholstery and soft furnishings lay in providing an appearance of colour, warmth and, above all, comfort. The development of spiral spring upholstery, patented in 1826, allowed for deeper and more springy stuffing than was possible before, and the demand for heavily upholstered furniture grew rapidly throughout the 1830s and 1840s. Buttoning, which emphasized the depth of stuffing, and therefore the extent of comfort, was introduced in the 1850s, when Viennese craftworkers are recorded in London.

Deep upholstery, which gave soft, rounded forms, was one means of expressing comfort and luxury, and of indicating surplus income. Newness and polish were important qualities too, as they reflected cleanliness, pride in the home and the presence of a maid. Other ways of expressing wealth included the extensive use of ornament and rich colour. Once again, mechanical

---

25. (*right*) PANEL OF BERLIN WOOLWORK, *mid-nineteenth-century. Berlin woolwork – a kind of embroidery in wools on canvas – was a popular home craft all over Europe from the early nineteenth century onwards. The patterns were printed so that they could easily be transferred to the canvas and made up into chair-backs, tea cosies or upholstery panels.*

26. (*below*) *Mary Ellen Best,* FOUR ROOMS IN YORK, *1830s. These four rooms were all painted by Mary Ellen Best soon after moving into her new home in York. The drawing-room (top left) and study (top right), where she painted herself at work, have both been decorated with boldly patterned papers. The drawing-room, with its formal arrangement of pictures, upholstered furniture and patterned carpet, is clearly the more formal of the two rooms. The scullery (bottom right) has built in dressers and discarded eighteenth-century chairs.*

means of mass-producing ornament, such as composition moulding and colour printing, allowed decorative products to enter more homes. Wallpaper was such a product, as the writer Charles Knight noted in 1858:

In those houses intended for the gentry and the middle classes, the use of paperhangings is now become universal, for dining and drawing rooms, and bedrooms, except sometimes the attics. In the kitchens, the old system of whitewashing or colouring in distemper is generally adopted, and we meet with it in the rustic cottage of the country and the artisan's or mechanic's tenement in the town. But frequently the walls of these humble dwellings are now hung with paper, thereby carrying decorative art (of however humble a character) further and further into and among the bulk of inhabitants throughout the country.

Many of the decorative products made for the mid-Victorian home had a strong element of fantasy in their decoration. "Fancy" and "novelty" were words frequently used by retailers; it was during the 1820s that "fancy work", the making of small decorative items such as

27. (*above*) HAND BLOCK-PRINTED FRIEZE PAPER *by William Woollams & Co., c.1870. A* trompe l'œil *or fancy wallpaper designed to look like a ruched net curtain.*

28. (*below*) DRAWING-ROOM FURNISHINGS FROM C. & R. LIGHT'S WHOLESALE CATALOGUE, *1881. Much drawing-room furniture was designed for 'occasional' use and part of its function was to be ornamental. Most of the heavier pieces here have castors to allow them to be moved and grouped, and are designed to stand away from the walls. Curves and buttoning denote comfort.*

29. *Robert Tait*, A CHELSEA INTERIOR, 1857. *The large double doors open to make one large apartment from two smaller rooms, carpeted and wallpapered as one.*

work-boxes and tea-caddies, first appeared in the London directories as a separate trade. Naturalistic or *trompe l'œil* effects in decoration, whether in carpets, on pictures or cups, provided another means of introducing fantasy into the middle-class home.

Economy – Knowing One's Place

The aristocracy and established middle classes resented this appropriation, albeit partial, of their life-styles. The long-lasting and largely unsuccessful attempts by the establishment to teach the new middle classes and the working classes their place through "design reform" and education are dealt with more fully in another chapter. Ideas of propriety, of what was appropriate to one's station in life, were expressed in other more pervasive ways. J. H. Walsh's book, *A Manual of Domestic Economy* (1857), warns the middle-class furniture buyer about being too ambitious:

The style of furniture which is to be chosen will influence the price very considerably inasmuch as upon it will depend in great measure the amount of ornamentation which is required, in order to carry out the whole with that degree of consistence and propriety which marks the well-ordered establishment. To those who have a long purse, expensive and highly ornamented furniture is a luxury befitting their means, but it should always be remembered that this outlay is not necessary to the comfort of a family. It would be useless to enlarge upon the different forms peculiar to the times of Louis Quatorze, the Renaissance, the Elizabethan Age, or the still older Gothic. These are all now equally prized by the different admirers of each, and all are almost equally costly and unsuited to the rigid economist, who will do well to keep as much as possible to straight lines, and the mouldings capable of being worked with a plane, considering that carvings and inlaid work require an expenditure of time and material which will compel a strong demand upon his pocket.

Many middle-class households, in Britain and America, valued durability over fashion. The increasing popularity of woollen velvets and plushes for upholstery and draperies, over the more expensive silks and the cheaper but more fragile cotton fabrics, is one indication of this careful and practical attitude. Walsh, while advocating economy, recommends furniture made from longer-lasting woods, "birch articles", he concludes, "are a very bad investment". He goes on to recommend buying second-hand furniture, then two-thirds the price of new. Clearly the vast majority of people furnished at least partly with old or hand-me-down furnishings and repaired things rather than always buying new. Thrift was supposed to temper aspiration; knowing one's place and living within one's means were cardinal virtues.

Propriety in House Layout

During the nineteenth century, the middle-class home grew more specialized and, despite the emphasis on the family unit, more fragmented. The miles of new terraced streets in towns and the suburban villas outside them expressed the status of their inhabitants but concealed new and more complex arrangements of rooms. House layouts varied enormously according to region, in both England and America, but certain general principles tended to apply.

At the top of the social scale it had always been customary for parts of the home to be semi-public; some houses, like Thomas Hope's The Deepdene, had published guidebooks. In America, the continuing import-

30. (*above*) *George Elgar Hicks,* CHANGING HOMES, *1862. The room divider has been drawn back to turn two rooms into one for the occasion, and the daylight allowed in; normally the shutters, blinds and curtains would have kept the rooms dark. The Louis-style chair with improbable arms and shell-shaped back is a showpiece.*

31. (*below*) *Samuel Rayner,* A BEDROOM, *c.1885. The blue, white and gold colour scheme, often recommended for Louis-style furnishings, is carried through from the wallpaper, fabrics and painted furniture to the porcelain on the wall shelf.*

32. *Mary Ellen Best,* OUR DINING ROOM AT YORK, *1838. The mahogany chairs are in the Greek or Modern style widely recommended for dining-rooms. There are spare chairs for extra guests. The deep red curtains lend warmth to an otherwise sombre décor.*

ance of home entertaining meant that reception rooms and family rooms could be located together on the main floor. But, especially in England, the emphasis on privacy in the home grew stronger as the century wore on. This was expressed in "picturesque" planning, where a house might have several different and separate wings and staircases for different classes of user; and individual rooms opening off corridors, rather than formal suites of rooms interconnecting, became more common.

This specialization occurred likewise in smaller homes. The differentiation between front and back became stronger, that is to say that the front part of the house was considered primarily for show, while the back was usually seen only by the family. The middle classes tended increasingly to socialize at home, and most homes had at least two "reception" rooms, a term which was in use by the 1870s, into which guests could be invited. An eight-roomed house might have a drawing-room, dining-room and breakfast room, a ten-roomed house might have a study as well, while a twenty-roomed house would be likely to have a boudoir or library in addition. The reception rooms were kept separate, as far as possible, both from service rooms like the kitchen

and from private family rooms like the bedrooms, and it was in the reception rooms that the greatest emphasis was placed on displays of wealth and taste.

These distinctions were imposed in new houses built for both middle- and working-class occupants. The West Hill Park estate in Halifax was built in the mid-1860s for four classes of tenant ranging from foremen and higher paid clerks to artisans and their families. They were given, according to the writer James Hole, flower gardens at the front as an "inducement to keep it tidy and neat", while the backs of the houses were completely hidden, "all unsightly but necessary operations being shut out from public eye". All but the smallest houses had a parlour, or front room, for "best", and Hole noted that those houses without a parlour had proved unpopular with their aspiring middle-class tenants.

Convention – Furniture for Different Rooms

Decorative treatments were devised for each room in the house. These related partly to historical convention and partly to current use, and had a bearing on colour schemes, choice of furnishings and room arrangement. As J. C. Loudon's *Encyclopaedia of Cottage, Farm and Villa Architecture* put it:

The colouring of rooms should be an echo of their uses. The colour of a library ought to be comparatively severe; that of a dining room grave; and that of a drawing room gay. Light colours are most suitable for bedrooms.

33. *Lili Cartwright*, THE HOUSEKEEPER'S ROOM AT AYNHOE, *December 1846. The housekeeper's room here has a certain status. Although the furnishings and paintings are likely to be the owners' cast-offs, the curtain makes it a private workroom and retreat.*

The preference for certain types of colour scheme meant that certain woods were preferred in each room. Trade catalogues and manuals give some idea of the range of furnishings available at different periods and of the relative importance of different types of room; kitchen furniture, for instance, hardly figures at all.

The Hall

The first room to be seen by visitors, the hall was a room of great importance. In larger houses, particularly country houses, a tendency developed from the 1820s to view the hall romantically as the heart of the home, as it had been in the medieval manor house. It was rare, though, for it to be used for banquets and social functions in anything like the medieval way. Often a high, two-storey room, it could be decorated with armour, antiques and curiosities, and portraits. It was a room for show, indicating the antiquity and nobility of the owner's family, rather than for practical use. Robert Kerr, writing in 1864, remarked that "antique furniture is particularly suitable here – more so than in any other part of the house". Later in the century, this type of hall became more of a living-room, smaller and more practical to heat and to manage.

The sense of grandeur which the hall was supposed to convey was just as important further down the social scale. The majority of working-class houses, especially in Britain, had no hall at all – the front door opened straight into the parlour – and even a narrow corridor hall was a prized feature of lower middle-class homes. In a small house, the hall allowed for a reception and circulation space removed from the front room. It usually led straight through on to the staircase and was often given similar decoration. The middle-class hall was a room of hard surfaces. Important guests arriving in the hall would be shown straight into a reception room; only servants and tradespeople might wait there. So whilst the hall had to be imposing, it did not need to be inviting. J. C. Loudon, writing in 1836, advised that "staircases should all be of a rather cool tone (providing) a link between exterior simplicity and interior richness". A dark, cool atmosphere was often created through the use of hard-wearing encaustic floor tiles, marbled or other vaguely classical wall treatments and dark woods; oak and mahogany were usually recommended. Hall chairs were almost never upholstered. Designed with hard, flat seats and straight backs they were kept against the wall. In addition they provided a deliberately un-

comfortable experience for those forced to sit on them, and an opportunity for display when not in use; their backs were sometimes decorated with real or imaginary armorials. The only other piece of furniture likely to be kept in the hall was a coat stand. Pictures and other decorations were often chosen carefully; stuffed animals or animal heads, and occasionally miniature conservatories or rock gardens were considered by the aspiring city dweller to be appropriate references to country life. The American Gervase Wheeler, in his book *Homes for the People* (1867) recommended brackets for flower vases, a thermometer or barometer and "a cabinet of dried grasses or other little museum curiosities".

The Dining-Room

One of the main reception rooms of the house, the nineteenth-century dining-room shared some of the solemnity of the hall. In the working-class home, dining took place in the kitchen; having a separate dining-room for social eating was an important distinction for the middle-class home. For practical reasons, however, the room was usually on the ground floor of the home, close to the kitchen. Loudon recommended that "the characteristic colouring of a dining room should be warm, rich and substantial". His advice was echoed by Frances Byerly Parkes, whose book, *Domestic Duties* (1829) was an American bestseller: "This style of colouring will be found to correspond best with the massive description of the furniture." Robert Kerr, writing over thirty years later, also suggested that the décor be "somewhat massive and simple", and that "the whole appearance of the room ought to be that of masculine importance". Although women used dining-rooms too, at formal meals it was traditional, in aristocratic homes, for the

34. *James Roberts*, THE DRAWING-ROOM AT BALMORAL, *1857. The bold tartan fabrics used to decorate Victoria and Albert's Scottish holiday home contrast oddly with the formality, symmetry and scale of the room layout, its unlived-in look.*

35. *Lili Cartwright*, THE DRAWING-ROOM AT AYNHOE, *November 1845. The huge vases on the table and in the corners of the room, the elaborate chimney garniture and the big oil paintings are clearly intended to convey an impression of traditional wealth and comfort. The lightweight chintz-covered chairs, in contrast, are modern and unostentatious.*

women to leave the room before the men, who would remain there to smoke and to continue drinking. The idea of the room as a male preserve persisted throughout the century, shaping the recommendations for colour schemes and styles.

Words used to describe the décor of the dining-room – warm, rich, substantial – could equally well be used of food, and the decoration and furnishings were meant to enhance the air of hospitality. As the room would normally be used in the evening, it had to look good by candle or oil light. James Arrowsmith, writing in 1854, recommended that for the dining-room:

Few ornaments are requisite, beyond the display on the sideboard, the walls coloured in distemper, or painted flat in oil of a warm colour, with gold or japanned mouldings; panelling in imitation of oak is also appropriate; the curtains claret or crimson cloth, trimmed with gold coloured orris lace, a brass rod with a plum fringed valance, or a valance alone are sufficiently genteel, observing that the valance is well wadded to intercept the light. A turkey carpet is most suitable, and from its durability, economical, but Axminster or Brussels in suitable colours are very good substitutes.

For furnishing the dining-room, by far the most popular style was Grecian or "modern", as it was often termed, and the most popular wood type mahogany. A dining-table, dining chairs and a sideboard or sideboard table were the essential pieces of furniture. Tables could be square, circular or rectangular, and were normally made to extend so that they could accommodate large dinner parties. Made with plain, polished tops the decorative elements were confined to simple classical mouldings on the legs and brass shoe castors, sometimes in the form of lion heads, on the feet. It was usual to cover the table itself with a heavy cloth. This was done in order to protect its polished surface; until the 1820s it was usual to remove the tablecloth for the dessert course. During the early Victorian period this way of eating became unfashionable; the cloth remained on the

table throughout the meal. The table top was therefore rarely seen by guests, but the dining-table remained an important, symbolic and well-protected piece of furniture in the middle-class household.

Chairs, normally in sets of six or twelve, were usually bought to match the table and were frequently leather-upholstered; leather would be less likely to absorb food and tobacco smells. In the early part of the century dining chairs tended to be made in the Grecian shape, with a heavy, projecting top rail usually carved with simple classical ornament, and back legs of sabre form. Later in the century, as the Grecian elements of the style became pared down, plain "balloon-shaped" backs became common. When not in use, some or all of the chairs could be kept against the walls in the traditional, formal manner. Sideboards, originally highly functional tables used for serving meals, became increasingly decorative pieces of cabinet furniture, with carved doors and higher, often carved or mirrored backs designed to frame displays of ornamental plate or china. Usually bought to match the dining suite, the sideboard was often fitted with a marble top, reflecting its early use as a servery.

The Library

In aristocratic and upper middle-class homes, the library was a separate room with its own furniture and in both England and America, it was regarded as a desirable feature of the middle-class home. Loudon claimed in 1838 that "in the present day no villa, or suburban residence, having more than two sitting rooms, can be considered complete without a library". In smaller homes, though, library and dining-room tended to be combined. The purpose of the library was not simply to house books. Robert Kerr described it in 1864 as "a sort of Morning room for gentlemen"; once again it was seen as a male preserve. The exclusion of women from formal education was in effect carried through into the layout and design of the homes they lived in. As in the dining-room, this meant decorating and furnishing the library in a lofty and serious manner. James Arrowsmith referred to it as "a room of much consequence, grave rather than gay" and advised that "the furnishing of it shall be rich and bold". He recommends crimson flock wallpaper, claret and gold hangings and bold classical cornices for richness and light in the evening; colour

36. *Erastus Salisbury Field*, THE SMITH FAMILY, c.*1865. Boldly patterned parlour carpets often figure in American group portraits of around this date.*

schemes close to those recommended for the dining-room.

Library furniture was usually dark and heavy, and the more serious, masculine styles – Gothic and Elizabethan – were favoured for it. Bookcases were frequently architectural in style, featuring gables and traceried glass fronts. Other furniture included steps, library tables and writing-desks for study, but there were normally a few leather-covered easy chairs in order that the man of the house could receive male friends, do business, drink or smoke in a comfortable club-type atmosphere. In America, Gervase Wheeler recommended that the library should act as a domestic museum, "the magnetic gathering place of a thousand tasteful trifles – relics, specimens, objects of art, curiosities, suggestive nothings – which serve to make talk independent of politics, dress, fashion and scandal".

The Drawing-Room

The drawing-room, in stark contrast, was considered a female space. Used for receiving guests and socializing, particularly before and after an evening meal, its name and function derived from the traditional withdrawing-room, to which women withdrew after dinner. It was the most important and prestigious room in the Victorian middle-class house, almost always at the front, and, in larger English houses, taking up most of the first floor. In smaller homes, it was situated at the front of the ground floor, often separated from the back reception room by folding partition doors, which allowed the room to be expanded on special occasions. Whatever its actual position, it was important that it be kept separate from the dining-room, or the male part of the house, and that the route between the drawing- and dining-room could be seen as processional.

The concept of the drawing-room as a room for women affected every aspect of its decoration and furnishing. Whereas dining-rooms and libraries had to reflect masculine virtues of solidity and seriousness, the ideal qualities of a drawing-room were thought (at least by men) to be "vivacity, gaiety, light and cheerfulness". Arrowsmith commented that "the arrangements require much taste and judgement, so that, in their disposal, the whole may be in perfect harmony. The walls", he advised, should be "panelled with watered silk, of pearl white, or light tints of pink, or lavender; the styles of the same ground as the panels, painted or embroidered in arabesque; every appropriate ornament, pilasters, &c, are to be procured, of the richest description". Pastels, white and gilding, combined with satinwood, walnut or rosewood furniture, were recommended as the basis for a feminine colour scheme.

Fantasy and curves were also allowable in the

drawing-room, and it was here that draperies and lavish upholstery were felt to belong. As the *Upholsterer's Accelerator* put it, "Draperies possess a fanciful richness, which adapts them particularly for Drawing Rooms". "Louis" was the ultimate drawing-room style – curvaceous, glamorous and expensive looking – and remained popular in both England and America throughout the century.

Most modest middle-class households would have chosen more economical Grecian/Modern style furnishings for the drawing-room. Even so, furnishing this room could be expensive. The range and variety of furniture types produced for the drawing-room was greater than for any other room in the house. It was here that the diversification and specialization of furniture was at its most extreme, and the range of novelty and fancy pieces available for this room continued to expand through the century. Thomas King's catalogue of 1839 listed the following items: chairs, easy chairs, Spanish chairs, commodes, card tables, couches, fire screens, glasses, loo tables, occasional tables, pier tables,

sofas, teapoys, work tables, fancy tables, flower stands, screens, music stools and chairs, secretaries and footstools. Fifty years later in 1881, the London wholesalers C. & R. Light listed baskets, cabinets, canterburys, chairs, chiffoniers, davenports, glasses, girandoles, ottomans, screens, settees, stands, suites, tables, trays and whatnots, each in several shapes and including a range of thirteen named styles.

Because it was the room on which the aspiring middle classes spent most time and money, it drew the most vicious criticism from the upper classes and those members of the design establishment who regarded their own taste as superior. *The Drawing Room*, a book of decorating advice by Mrs Orrinsmith, published in 1878, contained the following condemnation of the "parvenu" taste:

Who does not call to mind the ordinary lower middle class drawing room of the Victorian era? The very headquarters of the commonplace, with its strict symmetry of ornament and its pretentious uselessness. All things seem as if chosen on the principle of unfitness for any function; everything is in pairs that can possibly be paired. The cold, hard, unfeeling white mantelpiece, surmounted by the inevitable mirror, varying in size only with the means of the householder, totally irrespective of any relation to the shape or proportions of the apartment; the fireplace a marvellous exhibition of the power of iron and black lead to give discomfort to the eye. At the window hang curtains in the harshest folds, trimmed with

37. *Olivia de Ros*, THE DRESSING-ROOM AT HATFIELD HOUSE, *c.1820. In traditional country houses, each main bedroom had a dressing-room* en suite. *The general untidiness of the room, with the print of "Immortal Byron" tacked up on the wall, indicates that this was an informal, private space.*

Oh! that the Desert were my dwelling place!!!!!......   *Byron.*

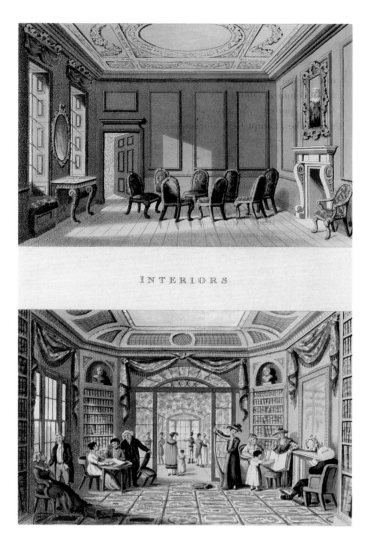

INTERIORS

38. (*left*) A CEDAR PARLOUR, AND A MODERN LIVING-ROOM, *illustrated in Humphry Repton's book* Fragments on the Theory of Landscape Gardening, *1816. Repton wrote a poem to go with these two illustrations showing changing life-styles and decorative schemes:* "No more the cedar parlour's formal gloom / With dulness chills, 'tis now the living room, / Where guests to whim, to task or fancy true / Scatter'd in groups, their different plans pursue. / Here books of poetry and books of prints / Furnish aspiring artists with new hints / Here, midst exotic plants, the curious maid / of Greek and Latin seems no more afraid."

39. (*below*) MODERN BEDROOM FURNISHINGS FROM C. & R. LIGHT'S WHOLESALE CATALOGUE, *1881. Light's catalogue, which was used by many London retail stores, featured every conceivable type of furniture. The rigidly symmetrical layout is done for clarity, not accuracy.*

40. (*opposite*) A. Mayor, A CITY BEDROOM, c.*1860. The pale colour scheme and lightweight furniture make the small room look spacious. The cracked silhouette and small ornaments indicate that the occupant was not wealthy.*

rattling fringes. On the carpet vegetables are driven to frenzy in their desire to be ornamental. On a circular table (of course with pillars and claws) are placed books – too often selected for the bindings alone – arranged like the spokes of a wheel, the nave being a vase of, probably, objectionable shape and material. Add a narrow ill-curved sofa, and spider-legged chairs made to be knocked over, dangerous as seats even for a slight acquaintance, doubly so for a stout friend – and all is consistently complete.

In larger homes, the drawing-room atmosphere might extend into an additional room known as the lady's boudoir. More private than the drawing-room, the boudoir was often decorated in a similar, though lighter and more informal style. Gervase Wheeler, in his book *Rural Homes, or Sketches of Houses suited to American Life* (1851) described it as "a little gem of a room – if octagonal, or oval, or quaintly cornered, so much the better – for the lady of the house; boudoir, book-room or work-room". James Arrowsmith, writing in 1854, recommended light blue satin paper on the walls to set off pictures in gold frames, remarking that "ladies generally display their taste in ornamenting it with drawings, and other articles, the productions of themselves, or friends".

The Parlour

In a social sense, the parlour ranked lower than the drawing-room. In the larger house with a drawing-room, the parlour was a second sitting-room, for use by the family and close friends. In smaller houses it was the drawing-room; the front room of a two up, two down terrace was increasingly kept for best. In either case, less emphasis was placed on display. The parlour chairs in Thomas King's 1839 furniture catalogue are the same general shape as the drawing-room chairs, but are far simpler, without ornate carving. Alternatively the dining-room might act as a parlour. It was recommended that they be decorated "in a medium style between that of a drawing room and a dining room" and C. & R. Light's catalogue of 1881 lists dining-room and parlour furniture together. By this date possible items of furniture for this combination room included the following: chiffoniers, corner cabinets, couches, dumb waiters, dinner wagons, sideboards, sofas, stands, suites and an immense variety of tables – loo, camp, coffee, consulting-room, cottage dining, extending, flower vase, pembroke and writing tables. In America, the furnishing of the parlour or country drawing-room followed much the same pattern; Andrew Jackson Downing's book, *The Architecture of Country Houses* (1850) recommended a sofa, a piano, some comfortably upholstered chairs, whatnots and small tables, and a large circular table around which the family could gather.

The Bedroom

In the eighteenth-century house, the bedroom was a relatively public space, used for relaxing and receiving guests. Though this fashion persisted in Europe, particularly in France, in Britain and America the bedroom became increasingly private. A feature of the fragmentation of the family within the home, it became desirable for the parents to have a bedroom separate from that of the children, and for brothers and sisters to be separated, on grounds of morality. As in other areas of life, the middle classes attempted to impose their values on the working classes; model dwellings built for artisans and labourers usually provided for two or three bedrooms. Live-in servants were effectively segregated from the middle-class family, confined either to the kitchen, a room off the kitchen, or an attic bedroom.

In terms of decoration, the bedrooms were differentiated according to the status of their occupants. Arrowsmith writes, "in the best apartments paper-hangings are generally selected chaste and handsome, with satin grounds, the figures in subdued colours, yet to harmonise with the hangings; the borders, at top and bottom of the rooms, of paper". He advised that hangings should normally be of patterned chintz or damask, though in less important bedrooms cheaper fabrics, like linen, cotton checks and stripes, and stuffs were more common. Mahogany was, according to J. H. Walsh, the most desirable wood for bedroom furnishings, although painted or japanned deal was acceptable, and very common. Health and hygiene were preoccupations in the furnishing of bedrooms; certain fabrics, such as moreen, were thought to harbour moths and vermin and became less popular as a result. The full tester bed also fell from favour; half testers and metal framed beds, which were easier to clean and allowed for better circulation of air, became more common even in the bedrooms of the better-off.

Thomas King's catalogue of bedroom furniture included bedpillars, French (canopied) bedsteads, washstands, dress tables, wardrobes and bedroom chairs, all

41. (*above*) Alice Squire, WOMAN IN AN ATTIC BEDROOM, c.*1860*. *The book, the writing desk and the woman's clothes suggest that she may be a governess boarding in the attic of the house where she works. This would explain the cracked ewer and old-fashioned, second-hand furniture.*

42. (*left*) Elizabeth Pearson Dalby, THE KITCHEN AT COMPTON BASSETT, WILTSHIRE, *1849. The kitchen, also the housekeeper's living-room, is simply decorated and furnished with whitewashed walls and plain chairs; even the blue and white crockery is utilitarian as well as colourful. The Staffordshire pottery figures and enamelled trays over the hearth are more decorative.*

with bobbin turned decoration and cane seats for economy and lightness.

In wealthier homes, the children's bedroom might serve as a nursery, normally located at the top of the house. Rooms designated for children soon acquired their own preferred decorative and furnishing schemes; instructive or figurative educational wallpapers were felt to be appropriate, as were wall surfaces which could be easily cleaned and repaired, and very simple trestle beds without hangings. When it came to servants' bedrooms, the divide and differentation were even more marked. Furnishings produced specifically for servants were cheap and deliberately plain, and it was usual for their rooms to be furnished with a mixture of second-hand furniture no longer required in other, more public parts of the house. Like the kitchen and scullery, these rooms were considered by middle-class householders to be working, utility rooms; ornament of any kind (except perhaps of an "improving" nature) would have been a frivolous and inappropriate distraction.

THE BATTLE OF THE STYLES

A bewildered gentleman may venture to suggest that he wants only a simple
comfortable house "in no style at all – except the comfortable style, if there be one".
The architect agrees; but they are all comfortable. "Sir, you are the paymaster, and
must therefore be pattern-master; you choose the style of your house just as you
choose the build of your hat; – you can have a Classical, columnar or
non-columnar, arcuated or trabeated, rural or civil or indeed palatial; you can
have Elizabethan in equal variety; Renaissance ditto; or, not to notice minor
modes, Mediaeval in any one of the many periods and many phases, – Old English,
French, German, Belgian, Italian and more.
(Robert Kerr, The Gentleman's House, *1864*)

THE CHOICE OF architectural and furnishing styles on offer to nineteenth-century consumers could be bewildering even to writers and analysts of the time. Most of the new upholstery and furnishing books attempted to dispel the confusion by including at least a chapter describing the features of various fashionable styles. In an age increasingly obsessed with classification and definition, it became usual to parcel up the past into neat, consecutive stylistic packages; Roman followed Greek, which followed Egyptian, each with its own distinct style. Non-European cultures – Indian, Turkish Persian, Chinese and Japanese – were also selected, classified and defined for the Western reader. Following the same approach as the eighteenth-century Grand Tour, archaeological sites and foreign countries were recorded and ransacked for Western travel books, encyclopaedias and museums, where styles were classified into chronological or geographical types. Trying to apply this approach to the present, and to one's own culture, posed problems, however. Two decorators, H. W. and A. Arrowsmith, who in 1840 wrote a book called *The House Decorator's and Painter's Guide*, concluded, "The present age is distinguished from all others in having no style which can properly be called its own".

Mass-production and the new mass market rapidly altered the economics of fashion. If a successful design could be endlessly mass-produced, then that design was potentially much more profitable for the manufacturer. At the same time, it was recognized that consumers would want to assert their individuality through their purchases; the customer wanted choice. The manufacturer, or more often the retailer, aimed to provide this choice at minimum origination cost, varying only design elements, or surface decoration, not shape.

The desire for a choice of products grew with the growing market. One commentator, writing in the *Journal of Design*, summed up the situation in 1849:

There is a morbid craving in the public mind for novelty as mere novelty, without regard to intrinsic goodness; and all manufacturers, in the present mischievous race for competition, are driven to pander to it. In the spasmodic effort to obtain novelty all kinds of absurdities are committed. The manufacturer cannot be content with harmonious blendings of colour, but is compelled to be most uncomplimentary in his colouring. One of the best cotton-printers told us that the creation of new patterns was an endless stream. The very instant his hundred new patterns were out he began to engrave others. His designers were working like mill-horses.

The consumer had to be able to distinguish the different designs in visual terms, but it helped if the designs could be identified also by name. This gave an opportunity for the styles to be linked to life-styles. The use of names linked with the past, particularly the aristocratic past, or with 'exotic' cultures was helpful in making the product desirable to an aspiring middle-class market.

Books about home furnishing advised that the style of interior decoration should match that of the exterior. But this was of course only possible for those who could afford either to design their own homes or to buy all their furniture new to match the house. Only the wealthy and the style-conscious had the means and the will to do this. For the new families of consumers, style in the art historical sense was less important than

43. *Thomas Hope*, THE STATUE GALLERY AT THE DEEPDENE, SURREY, *1825. Thomas Hope opened his Grecian-style house, The Deepdene, to the public, even publishing a guide book. But many still found it inaccessible. As one critical visitor remarked, "He has made a perfect hieroglyphic or enigma of most of his apartments, and produced something so childishly complicated and fantastic as to be impenetrable without a paraphrase and ridiculous when it is interpreted."*

44. (*opposite*) *Owen Jones*, EGYPTIAN ORNAMENT, *illustrated in* The Grammar of Ornament, *1856.*

45. (*above*) THE CHINESE ROOM AT MIDDLETON PARK, OXFORDSHIRE, *1840. A late and rare example of Chinese-style decoration. The imitation bamboo furniture, lacquer screen and cabinet are offset against Chinese wallpaper. The glass above the French windows has been painted or fitted with chinoiserie, or fantasy Chinese, scenes.*

comfort, appropriateness and rich effects. Creating a unified style throughout a home was not necessary or necessarily desirable. What mattered, now that ornament had become cheaper, was that style was no longer an aristocratic preserve.

The aristocracy reacted badly to these developments. It responded by laying greater stress on authenticity – old homes and antiques – and restraint. Even the word "new" developed very significant connotations. Mrs Arbuthnot, writing in 1826, described Eaton Hall, the Duke of Westminster's new Gothic-style home in Cheshire as "parvenu", and "the most gaudy concern I ever saw. It looks like the new bought and new built place of a rich manufacturer, the house decorated with a degree of gorgeousness that is quite fatiguing & takes away all appearance of real grandeur." Grand or gaudy, the choice was now greater than ever.

A Choice of Styles

A rash of books written during the nineteenth century attempted to reclassify and define historical styles. The earliest of these, such as William Wilkins's *Antiquities of Magna Graecia* (1807), were written in the eighteenth-century archaeological tradition and concentrated on classical sites, illustrating architectural and decorative details. Later books extended the area of study to include later periods. Rickman's *Attempt to Discriminate the Styles of English Architecture* (1817) was important in establishing new names for different periods of Gothic, while Owen Jones' *Plans, Elevations, Sections and Details of the Alhambra* (1836–45) applied an archaeological approach to Moorish ornament. Books like these laid the ground for a more authoritative and didactic approach to style and design.

The same desire to record and categorize was a feature of the ornamental encyclopaedias which appeared later in the century; from Owen Jones' *Grammar of Ornament* (1856) to Heinrich Dolmetsch's *Ornamentenschatz* (1887). The classifications and chapter headings each author chose varied according to personal taste and contemporary fashion, but all took a broadly similar line. The encyclopaedias were all chronologically ordered, analytical and comparative studies of ornamental details, they all concentrated on flat pattern, and they all set out to record and explain the ancient

46. THE DURBAR ROOM AT OSBORNE HOUSE, ISLE OF WIGHT. *The most extravagant Indian-style interior of the late nineteenth century, and a symbol of British imperial power, the Durbar Room was designed in 1890 by Lockyard Kipling, Professor of Architecture at Bombay, and Bai Rham Singh, an expert on Indian decoration. Early photographs show it crammed with furnishings, gifts and trophies from India.*

and the exotic through artefacts, which they used as illustrations. In gathering together a variety of decorative motifs and colour combinations, codifying them and presenting them as equal and interchangeable, the encyclopaedias provided rich source material for commercial designers to copy. Owen Jones recognized this, though he deplored it:

I have ventured to hope that I might aid in arresting the unfortunate tendency of our time to be content with copying, while the fashion lasts, the forms peculiar to any bygone age, without attempting to ascertain, generally completely ignoring, the peculiar circumstances which rendered an ornament beautiful, because it was appropriate. It is more than probable that the first result of sending forth to the world this collection will be seriously to increase this dangerous tendency, and that many will be content to borrow from the past those forms of beauty which have not already been used up ad nauseam.

Even a cursory look at these sources gives some idea of the range of styles available to be copied in any media. The *Grammar of Ornament* illustrated the following styles: the Ornament of Savage Tribes; Egyptian; Assy-

rian; Greek; Pompeian; Roman; Byzantine; Arabian; Turkish; Moresque; Persian; Indian; Hindoo; Chinese; Celtic; Mediaeval; Renaissance; Elizabethan and Italian. Later encyclopaedias were more Eurocentric, but more comprehensive chronologically; Dolmetsch's book included a large section on Renaissance, Baroque, Rococo and neo-classical ornamental detail.

Some idea of the relative popularity of these styles can be gained from the many contemporary treatises published for the builder, decorator or home furnisher. Usually written by someone in the trade, these books looked at historical styles, but always with a practical view to their exploitation in modern homes. Most were published in both Britain and America; all were used on both sides of the Atlantic. Frances Byerly Parkes' *Domestic Duties* (1825), Nathaniel Whittock's *Decorative Painter's and Glazier's Guide* (1827), J. C. Loudon's *Encyclopaedia of Cottage, Farm and Villa Architecture* (1833), H. W. and A. Arrowsmith's *House Decorator's and Painter's Guide* (1840), Thomas Webster and Frances Parkes' *Encyclopaedia of Domestic Economy* (1844) and Andrew Jackson Downing's *The Architecture of Country Houses* (1850) all deal with the application of style in the home. Whittock identifies six styles of interior decoration; Grecian, Roman, Gothic, Chinese, Egyptian and Arabesque. The Arrowsmiths, thirteen years later, give nine; Greek, Roman, Arabesque, Pompeian, Gothic, Cinque Cento, François Premier, Elizabethan and modern French. The decorator's stylistic repertoire was greater than that of the architect or furniture-maker. Almost all of the easily available source material was in printed form, and was therefore easier to copy as flat pattern than in three dimensions. In addition, the British and American climate and culture imposed more restrictions on the way housing and furniture was constructed. Loudon, Downing, and Webster and Parkes refer to only four basic furniture styles. Loudon listed: "the Grecian or Modern style, which is by far the most prevalent"; the Gothic or Perpendicular style, "which imitates the lines and angles of Tudor Gothic architecture"; the Elizabethan style, "which combines the Gothic with the Roman or Italian manner", and the style of the age of Louis XIV, or the florid Italian, "which is characterised by curved lines and excesses of curvilinear ornaments".

Chinese, Moorish and Indian Styles

These three groups of styles, "exotic" to Western eyes, and frequently confused by Western writers and designers, were rarely employed on Victorian furniture. They tended to appear far more frequently in association with specific products – lacquerwork, ceramics, cotton chintzes – made in imitation of Middle Eastern and oriental exports. Whittock described the Chinese style somewhat disparagingly as unsuitable for British homes, referring to the fanciful extravagance of Brighton Pavilion, completed for George IV in 1821 to the designs of the architect John Nash. The Pavilion had a "Hindu" exterior, with a skyline of onion-shaped domes, and a fanciful Chinese imperial-style interior,

full of fretted wood, carved dragon heads and painted Chinese figures, colourful and richly gilt. Richard Brown's book, *Domestic Architecture* (1841) illustrated a Persian Pavilion, a Chinese Residence, an Oriental Pavilion and a Morisco-Spanish Palatial Building, with confusing references to their decoration and furnishing. Owen Jones' *Grammar of Ornament* (1856) would have been more useful to most Victorian decorators. The Chinese section was short and dismissive – Jones called the Chinese "totally unimaginative" – but it included coloured illustrations of fret and diaper patterns, formalized plant ornaments, such as lotus, blossom and pomegranate. The author was later, incidentally, to repent, publishing a book on Chinese ornament. The Indian and "Hindoo" sections of the *Grammar* were lengthy by comparison, and again richly illustrated with diapers, geometricized plant forms such as the pinecone motif and brightly coloured flower patterns taken from carpets and textiles. Moorish ornament, Jones's particular interest, was the most comprehensively covered, with plates showing arabesque interlacement, arches, arabic script and complex abstract patterns.

At the Great Exhibition, held in London in 1851, "exotic" cultures, products and styles went on show to a Western audience and were much admired. Owen Jones, who had designed for the exhibition a special Alhambra Court in imitation of the Alhambra in Granada, noted that:

The presence of so much unity of design, so much skill and judgment in its application, with so much of elegance and refinement in the execution as was observable in all the works, not only of India, but of all the other Mohammedan contributing countries – Tunis, Egypt, and Turkey – excited a degree of attention from artists, manufacturers, and the public which has not been without its fruits.

But it was not until the 1862 exhibition, where the Japanese exhibited for the first time, that an "exotic" style was fully adopted for a Western mass market.

47. *W. H. Homann,* DESIGN FOR WALL DECORATIONS AT OSBORNE HOUSE, ISLE OF WIGHT, *late 1840s. The royal home at Osborne, designed by Prince Albert in his favourite Italian Renaissance style, had a range of lavish and idiosyncratic interiors. This design combines a classical framework of marbled dado and pilasters with Renaissance 'candelabrum' ornament and a large Louis-style overmantel.*

48. *(left)* DINING-ROOM IN THE BOSTON HOME OF JAMES M. BEEBE, *c.1885, photograph by T. E. Morrison. The enormous Renaissance-style sideboard, with its elaborate pediments, lion-head masks and heavy scroll brackets, is the focal point of the dining-room. The details are picked up on the chairs.*

49. *(below) John Diblee Crace*, DESIGN FOR A POMPEIAN-STYLE ROOM IN LONDON, *c.1860. The bold painted black and red colour scheme, the division of the wall surface and the delicate painted ornament are features of the Pompeian style.*

50. *(opposite) Thomas Hope*, BOUDOIR AT THE DEEPDENE, SURREY, *1818. Thomas Hope's boudoir is full of rich, classical ornament, much of it based on his studies of Greek and Egyptian motifs. The stridently coloured chimneypiece, overmantel and vast tented bed with swan pediment, and the sabre-legged chair are his reinterpretations of classical furnishings.*

Renaissance Styles

The nineteenth-century Renaissance Revival was among the most eclectic of all the revival styles, encompassing as it did Italian, German, French and Flemish Renaissance ornament. It consequently went by a number of names at different times. Whittock does not refer to it at all, while the Arrowsmiths distinguish between the Italian "Cinque Cento" and the French "François Premier". Italian Renaissance styles incorporated classical mouldings, Raphaelesque painted decoration very close to Pompeian in appearance, classical symbolism, nudes or semi-nudes. French, Flemish and German Renaissance styles featured heavy moulded or carved strapwork patterns, medallions and naturalistic ornament. Renaissance styles offered more possibilities than any others for rich textures, density and variety of ornament and contrasting materials.

Italianate villas were promoted for the British countryside in the early part of the century by architects such as John Nash and Humphry Repton, and the features of Italian Renaissance architecture were illustrated in Charles Parker's book *Villa Rustica* (1832–41) and Loudon's *Encyclopaedia* (1833). The Italian Renaissance palazzo also served as a model for Osborne House, summer residence of the British royal family on the Isle of Wight, which was completed in 1848. Osborne House was built by Thomas Cubitt, whose huge London firm was responsible for speculative house-building over vast

tracts of Victorian London. Houses in the district of Belgravia, which the firm developed from the 1820s, were decorated throughout with Italianate stucco cornices and ceiling roses and these became standard mouldings for Victorian town houses well into the 1870s. Albert, Prince Consort, helped to design Osborne and continued throughout his life to favour architects, artists and designers working in the Renaissance style. Through his influence, the sculptor and designer Alfred Stevens and Gottfried Semper, the German art theorist, both came to teach at the Government School of Design around the middle of the century, thereby influencing a generation of designers.

Stevens and Semper both designed in Renaissance styles for a wide range of commercial firms making ceramics, furniture and metalwork. After the Great Exhibition, at which the critics agreed that British products were noticeably poorly designed when compared to French and German goods, big British firms began employing Continental designers. Many of these designers were used to working in Renaissance revival styles. Semper designed an award-winning cabinet for the London firm Holland & Sons to take to the Paris Exhibition in 1855, while a rival firm, Jackson & Graham, showed a Renaissance cabinet designed by the French designer Eugène Prignot. Though Renaissance stucco mouldings could be found in most town houses, it was not until the 1860s that Renaissance-style furniture was produced in large quantities.

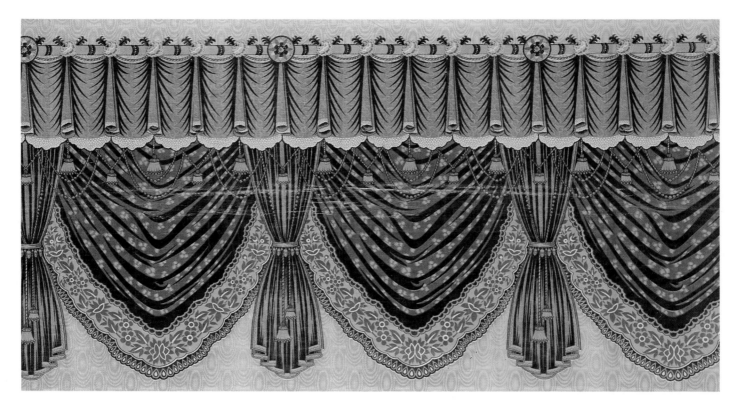

51. TROMPE L'ŒIL ROLLER-PRINTED COTTON VALANCE, *designed by James Burd of Mount Zion Works, Radcliff, 1825–40. The valance is in the Grecian style, with drapery swags, and simple regular pleating.*

Egyptian and Pompeian Styles

Egyptian ornament had been "discovered" by Western neo-classicists in the eighteenth century. Its popularity boomed in the very early nineteenth century due to Napoleon's North African campaigns and the subsequent publication of Vivant Denon's lavishly illustrated *Voyage dans la Basse et la Haute Egypte* (1802). Hieroglyphs, winged discs, caryatids, sphinxes, lotus and papyrus plants were among the motifs adopted by Western designers of furniture, ceramics and silver. Egyptian-style shapes were usually simple and geometrical, colours bold primaries. Frequently, Egyptian motifs were found on Greek-style furnishings; Thomas Hope's *Household Furniture and Decoration* (1807) illustrated severe, heavy, archaeological designs combining Egyptian and Greek elements. Although most later household furnishers and decorators borrowed ideas from Hope, the style was perhaps too academic to catch on with the Western middle-class market.

Roman and Pompeian styles were better known and therefore easier to market. Neo-classicism, a fascination with Greek and Roman classical antiquity, dominated upper middle-class taste for the last half of the eighteenth century. During the nineteenth century its popularity broadened to such an extent that classical motifs and decoration could be seen in almost every middle-class home, in the chimneypiece, the plasterwork and the mouldings of the sideboard. The stylistic terms "Roman" and "Pompeian" were used interchangeably when it came to painted decoration, because the wall paintings at Pompeii and Herculaneum were among the very few examples of Roman house painting known to the nineteenth-century decorator. The publications of Wilhelm Zahn (1829) and William Gell and J. P. Gandy's *Pompeiana* (1817–19, 1832) fuelled the popularity of Pompeian as a decorative style, and the London decorating firm of J. G. Crace revived the style in the 1860s with a range of Pompeian wall schemes. However, neither the Egyptian nor the Pompeian styles began to approach the popularity of the other classical style which dominated Victorian taste in Britain and America: the Grecian or Modern style.

The Grecian or Modern Style

Of the four dominant styles mentioned by Loudon in 1833, two – Grecian and Gothic – had been introduced as detailing in houses and on furnishings in the eighteenth century and were popular alternatives by the beginning of the nineteenth. Humphry Repton's book, *Observations on the Theory and Practice of Landscape Gardening* (1803) had dealt with the application of both styles to small family houses. For most of the nineteenth century, Grecian remained the more popular style. Architects like John Buonarotti Papworth and Decimus Burton designed streets, terraces, estates, sometimes whole towns entirely in the Grecian style; parts of Cheltenham in Gloucestershire and Fleetwood in Lancashire were laid out in this way during the 1830s. Books like T. H. Shepherd's *Metropolitan Improvements* (1827) assumed that Grecian was the only acceptable style. This was true also in America. Webster and Parkes' *Encyclopaedia* (1844) discussed other styles but clearly regarded Grecian as the standard. Downing's *Country Houses* (1850), though disdaining to illustrate any Grecian designs, commented that

The furniture most generally in use in private houses is some modification of the classical style. Modern Grecian furniture has the merit of being simple, easily made, and very moderate in cost. Its universality is partly owing to the latter circumstance, and partly to the fact that by far the largest number of dwellings are built in the same style, and therefore are most appropriately furnished with it.

Further evidence of the popularity of the Grecian style above the others comes from Loudon's contemporaries, the Arrowsmiths: the Greek style was "much more consonant to the social habits and intercourse of the great mass of the British public who require a cheerful and pleasing but not a gorgeous style of decoration". The same writers went on to complain about the inappropriateness of transposing classical motifs regardless of context (in a book which nevertheless traded in such transpositions):

In looking at the designs of the ancients, it is too common a practice to apply all the external ornaments of the Greeks and Romans to the interior of our own dwellings, without any regard being paid to their primitive uses, or any authority on which to found their present application; and thereby trying to make the interior of a modern drawing room resemble a temple.

The Grecian style of decoration could involve the use of a range of classical motifs; the palmette, the anthemion, the acanthus, dentil or key patterns. When applied to architecture or furniture, however, the style could equally be extremely plain, relying on proportions for effect. A Grecian chair, for instance, might follow the

lines of the klismos chair shape copied from Greek vase decoration, with sabre legs and a broad protruding back support, but have very little surface ornament. Grecian colour schemes tended, in the early nineteenth century, to be very restrained; white marble statuary and the black and terracotta of Greek painted vases provided the only sources for colour schemes. It was only later in the century that the realization that classical architecture and statuary had once been colourfully painted brought a new vitality to the Greek revival colour scheme. As the century progressed, Grecian-style furniture tended to become more florid and curvaceous in shape but generally retained minimal surface decoration, a factor which would have kept production costs down and ensured its continued popularity.

Most early nineteenth-century furniture trade catalogues and books feature Grecian furnishings more fully than any other style. *Household Furniture and Interior Decoration* (1807), by the wealthy traveller and collector Thomas Hope, illustrates a range of pieces based on his studies of Greek ornament on vase paintings. Hope's furniture and interiors were heavily archaeological and pure Greek-style furnishings were only really adopted by the wealthy avant-garde in Britain and on the American East Coast. George Bullock's large cabinet-making firm produced elaborate Grecian furniture with classical motifs in boulle-work and marquetry for wealthy clients like the Portuguese ambassador to London and Napoleon Bonaparte. Bullock managed to cash in both on the craze for the antique and on Napoleonic War patriotism. He called the marble from his Anglesey quarry "Mona", the Roman name for the island, and made a

52. *Alexander Jackson Davis*, THE GREEK REVIVAL PARLOUR IN THE JOHN COX STEVENS HOUSE, C.*1845. The columns, marble, cool colour scheme and restrained Greek-style furnishings combine to create a pure classical décor that few wanted or could afford.*

53. *Charles Hunt,* MY MACBETH, *1868. The elaborate gilt-framed overmantel mirror forms the focus of the room, reflecting the cool green Venetian blinds and curtains and the glass lustre ornament on the mantelpiece. The family's genre and landscape paintings are prominently displayed. The mahogany and horsehair chairs, in the Greek or Modern style, are solidly respectable.*

marketing virtue of the necessity to use British woods. As a contemporary admirer, Richard Brown, wrote of Bullock in 1822:

Most of his ornaments were selected from British plants, his woods were of English growth, which were admirably well polished. He has shewn that we need not roam to foreign climes for beautiful ornaments, but that we have abundance of plants and flowers equal to the Grecian, which if adopted, would be found as pleasing as the antique.

Designers closely involved with the trade intended to produce work which was less archaeological and more commercial. Bullock's firm made a vast quantity of plain furniture as well as prestige pieces for wealthy clients. *A Collection of Designs for Household Furniture and Interior Decoration* (1808), by George Smith, who also ran a cabinet-making firm, contains furnishings clearly influenced by Hope, but lighter and with a greater emphasis on comfort. Later furnishing catalogues likewise feature and illustrate large quantities of Greek-style furniture. The shapes were basically classical, but the ornament was normally restricted to a small amount of carving or moulding on a chair back rail or tripod table foot. Often the designs are not denoted by any stylistic tag at all, or

they are referred to as "modern". Thomas King's *The Modern Style of Cabinet Work* (1829) shows a range of very plain furnishings, with very little surface ornament at all. In the preface King explains that this is for reasons of economy: "a chaste contour and a simplicity of parts is attempted in all the objects, which, being in some degree confined in dimensions and form, present rather a difficulty in the adaption of Greek and Gothic ornaments". Whereas King always draws attention to the few Gothic-style pieces he has included, he does not bother to name or classify the Greek or Modern ones, which suggests that all his readers would have been familiar with the style. The use of the word "modern" to describe the pared down classical forms lasted until late in the century; the furniture wholesalers C. & R. Light used the term in their 1881 catalogue.

The Gothic Style

During the eighteenth century, the Gothic style in architecture and furnishings was fashionable amongst wealthy antiquarians and collectors: Horace Walpole and William Beckford were perhaps the most famous of these. By the early nineteenth century, however, Gothic was being recommended as a style suitable for much wider consumption. Repton felt that its picturesque and irregular qualities made it ideal as a style for small country villas, and illustrated some examples. But it was the detailing, rather than the massing, associated with Gothic which was adopted and adapted for use in the early nineteenth century. Because so little Gothic furn-

54. ST. MICHAEL'S GALLERY, FONTHILL ABBEY, *from John Rutter's* Delineations of Fonthill, *1823. Fonthill, designed by James Wyatt for the dilettante collector William Beckford, was a Gothic folly. Much of the detailing – the fan vaulting, the stained glass – was borrowed from church architecture.*

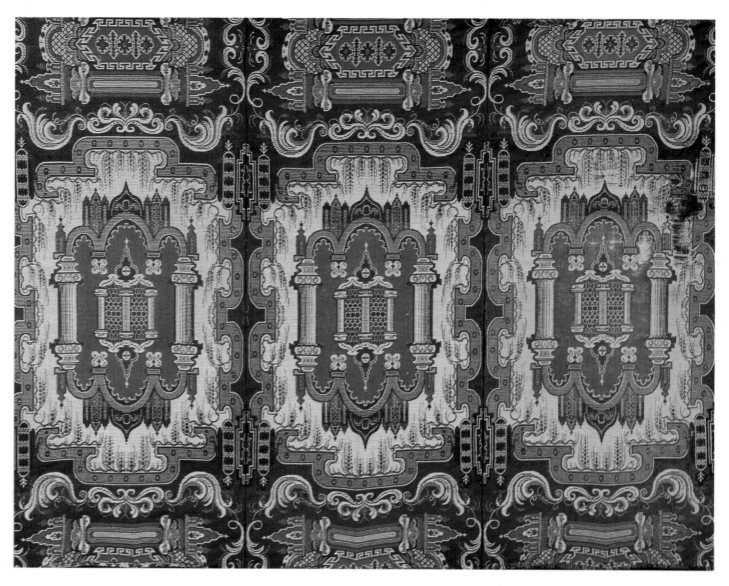

55. GOTHIC-PATTERNED KIDDERMINSTER CARPET, *1835–40. Most Gothic-style patterns of this date incorporated motifs from church architecture; pointed arches, ribs and tracery.*

The English have learnt better than to treat the Gothic with contempt; they have now discovered in it so much elegance and beauty that they are endeavouring to change the barbarous name, and with feeling partiality to themselves claim the invention for their own countrymen; it is therefore become here an established article of Antiquarian faith to believe that this architecture is of native growth, and accordingly it is denominated English architecture in all the publications of the Antiquarian Society.

The publication of Thomas Rickman's *Attempt to Discriminate the Styles of English Architecture* (1817) applied the archaeological approach to the study of Gothic, distinguished three phases of the style, and appropriated it as English. It was, however, taken up in America, partly through the publication of Andrew Jackson Downing's *The Architecture of Country Houses* (1850), which, following Loudon, recommended Gothic as appropriately picturesque for the rural villa and illustrated a number of Gothic interior schemes. In Britain, Gothic took on a greater significance as a national style. Before long it was adopted both by the Church and the State as symbolic of true Christianity and nationalism. It came to embody the ideals of the reform movement within the architectural and design establishments. But though many features of "reformed" furnishings filtered through into mass-produced commercial Gothic, in the furnishing pattern books and in many middle-class homes Gothic remained simply one option in the range

ishing survived, much of the inspiration for ornamental detail came from church architecture; stone and window tracery and figurative carving, pinnacles and gables. Usually on architecture and furniture these details were applied to a basically classical shape; a standard mahogany Grecian shaped chair might have a back carved like a rose window. As such, the style seems to have caught on quickly. George Smith's catalogue (1808) shows a range of furniture with Gothic motifs and from 1810 Ackermann's *Repository*, the fashionable magazine for the affluent middle classes, began to illustrate Gothic furniture and interiors, though with warnings against their inappropriate use: "No person of a genuine taste will introduce articles in this style into his apartments, unless there be a general correspondence in the appearance of the house."

The growing popularity of Gothic as an alternative to Grecian was fed by patriotism. All over Western Europe, Gothic was claimed as a national style. In 1807, the poet Robert Southey summed up the English enthusiasm for the style:

of styles on offer. Well before the end of the century it had been superseded as the national style.

Gothic furniture was at first expensive, due to the amount of hand carving usually required. Thomas King's catalogue of 1829 includes a Gothic bookcase with the comment that "generally Gothic is considered extremely expensive in execution; however, this design is arranged with the expectation of its being manufactured at a moderate price".

In flat pattern making and in architecture, where much of the decorative ornament could be cast or moulded, the expense was no greater than for other styles. The author and style-conscious antiquarian Sir Walter Scott wrote that "the gothic order of architecture is now so generally, and indeed indiscriminately used, that we are rather surprised if a country house of a tradesman retired from business does not exhibit lanceolated windows". Scott went out of his way to choose a different, individual and, as he saw it, more authentic style for his own highly influential house at Abbotsford in Scotland.

Antiquarianism and the Elizabethan Style

Loudon's third style, the Elizabethan, was not always easy to distinguish from Gothic in its various forms. As the Arrowsmiths, contemporary decorators, complained in their book, *The House Decorator's and Painter's Guide* (1840):

It is not unusual to see Gothic ornaments introduced and intermixed with those more properly appertaining to the Elizabethan period: a practice contrary to propriety and reason; and frequently in the same edifice, even in those laying claim to taste, we see the different styles of Gothic, from early Saxon to the more depraved Henry the Eighth's, mingled together, and forming an indescribable mass, alike discreditable to the possessor and designer.

The Arrowsmiths' book aimed to "remove the mistaken notion that our forefathers inhabited rooms in which colour and every other principle was superseded by the universal use of oak panelling". As decorators, they cannot have welcomed the new fashion for panelled rooms, but their concern for historical accuracy was fashionable. Loudon wrote in a similar way:

We may here observe that the pleasure derived from seeing or possessing curious ancient furniture, is of a kind quite distinct from that derived from seeing or possessing furniture in correct style, or in elegant form. The present taste for Elizabethan furniture is more that of an antiquary, or of a collector of curiosities, than that of a man of cultivated mind.

Antiquaries were becoming more common. The new archaeological approach to Gothic, and the determination to prove its British roots, were elements of a growing fascination with the British past. This fascination is evident in media ranging from the illustrated topographical books of John Britton and Henry Shaw to the popular romantic medieval novels of Walter Scott. In design terms, this movement became associated not with the Gothic style, but with the Elizabethan. For one thing, it was becoming clear that there were few surviving domestic precedents for the new Gothic furnishings. A later historical period offered more possibilities. The term "Elizabethan" was in any case loosely applied to

furnishings of the sixteenth, seventeenth and early eighteenth centuries, which allowed for plenty of scope. More importantly, Gothic was becoming too popular; the style-conscious felt the need to dissociate themselves from it. Buying real antiques was one way of doing this. Elizabethan was the new aristocratic style.

A kind of antiquarian in-crowd formed and flourished in the early part of the century. Collectors and patrons, furniture manufacturers, dealers, designers and writers and publishers supported one another, knew one another and worked together on various projects. The building and furnishing of Walter Scott's own house at Abbotsford provides a well-documented example. Abbotsford, a Scottish farmhouse refurbished from 1818 to look "somewhat like an old English hall", was one of the earliest and most influential antiquarian homes. An avid collector of curiosities – especially Scottish curiosities – Scott designed his home to house his bits of stonework and woodwork, armour and old furniture. Many of his antiques were bought through his friends the London dealers John Swaby and Daniel Terry, who were also selling to patrons like Lord Byron. New furniture in the Elizabethan style was commissioned from George Bullock's firm, which also dealt in antiques. Some pieces, like the library reading-desk, were made up out of fragments of earlier woodwork. The armoury ceiling pattern was based on medieval carvings at nearby Melrose Abbey. The designs for the new furniture were by Bullock's associate Richard Bridgens, who later published them as part of his book

56. GOTHIC-PATTERNED GLAZED COTTON, c.*1840*.

57. *David Roberts*, THE HALL AT ABBOTSFORD *(detail), 1834. One of the most romantic of all antiquarian interiors, Abbotsford was created and furnished by the novelist Sir Walter Scott. He amassed a collection of ancient armour and worked with designers and dealers to create from a small Scottish farmhouse a medieval baronial hall.*

Furniture with Candelabra and Interior Decoration (1825–6).

As the demand for antiques and Elizabethan-style furnishings grew, so the network of publishers, furniture-makers and dealers grew too. Bridgens' pieces were mostly designed to order for wealthy customers. Adapting the Elizabethan style for a contemporary mass market was far more problematic. Thomas Hunt's book *Exemplars of Tudor Architecture adapted to Modern Habitations* (1830) drew attention to the dearth of surviving documented examples of Elizabethan furniture. All his examples come from a few houses – Penshurst, Cotehele, Haddon, Conishead Priory – and few were suitable, he felt, for adaptation to the commercial market.

Henry Shaw's illustrated *Specimens of Ancient Furniture* (1836), was aimed at the collector and connoisseur rather than the trade, though it was used by both. The introduction, by the collector and antiquarian Sir Samuel Rush Meyrick, began by stating that "modern furniture is too poor". He continued, "a feeling has now arisen for the ancient decorative style, which it is hoped the present work will materially assist, for however beautiful the elegant simplicity of Grecian forms, they are not of themselves sufficient to produce that effect that should be given to the interior of an English house". The book went on to illustrate a number of pieces of

Elizabethan and antique furniture, some from country house collections, others by courtesy of London antique dealers. Several are obviously composite, made up out of fragments from different pieces.

New Elizabethan-style furniture could be purchased to blend with antiques. Loudon, writing in 1833, remarked that the popularity of Elizabethan pieces "distinguished by rude and grotesque carvings" was on the increase. He illustrated only a few examples of them, however, claiming that, "it is seldom necessary to manufacture objects in this manner, farther than by putting together ancient fragments which may be purchased at the sale of old buildings". Often made either of oak, or ebony and ivory, Elizabethan furniture could incorporate carved strapwork, bobbin-turned or spiral-turned decoration. Other more fragile and ephemeral elements of Elizabethan furnishing likewise had to be made new. Popular pieces included cane-seated chairs and elaborately carved buffets with cup and cover supports, both types actually based on seventeenth- rather than sixteenth-century furnishings. Complementary fabrics included velvets, damasks and, from the early 1800s onwards, Berlin woolwork which could be embroidered to look like tapestry. Topographical scenes incorporating ruins featured on decorative china and prints, to complete the antiquarian effect.

Antique furniture dealers, or "brokers", had existed in the eighteenth century, but their numbers grew rapidly in the first part of the nineteenth. Loudon attributed the growth in the trade partly to the French Revolution and to "the recent changes in the fortunes of many of the English nobility". This meant that:

Much of the furniture of these styles formerly almost exclusively used by the great, has been exposed to sale, and consequently has attracted the attention of gentlemen of less opulence. Hence it is that we now have upholsterers in London who collect, both in foreign countries and in England, whatever they can find of curious and ancient furniture, including fragments of the fittings up of rooms, altars and religious houses, and adapt them for modern uses.

58. *Henry Shaw,* COLOURED ENGRAVING OF COUCH FROM PENSHURST PLACE, KENT, *1836. This couch, from Shaw and Meyrick's book,* Specimens of Ancient Furniture, *is captioned "Date the time of Queen Elizabeth". Many of the details – the legs, the shell ornament – look eighteenth- rather than sixteenth-century, and the colourful upholstery was probably later still.*

59. *John Scarlett Davis,* THE LIBRARY AT TOTTENHAM, c.*1835. An antiquarian interior, incorporating old and new furniture. Some of the furniture – the small chairs, the side table, the cabinets of curiosities at the end of the room – are Old French in style, while the four chairs in the corners would have been acquired as Elizabethan.*

The line between reproduction, restoration and faking in these upholstery shops became more blurred; casting and imitative wood carving skills were much in demand.

The antiquarian craze was particularly strong in England. Prince Puckler-Muskau, who visited a number of country houses on a visit to England in the late 1820s reported that:

In the apartments there was a quantity of old furniture, preserved with great care to prevent its falling to pieces, in its frail condition. This fashion is now general in England. Things which we should throw-away as old-fashioned and worm-eaten, here fetch high prices, and new ones are often made after the old patterns. In venerable mansions, when not destructive of convenience, they have a very good effect.

In contrast, the style lacked historical significance for most Americans. Downing recommended it particularly for collectors and for European immigrants, to remind them of the homes they had left.

In Britain, antiques were not just required for venerable mansions. Increasingly, the aspiring middle classes looked for antiques for their homes. Demand began to outstrip supply. The provenance of antiques was not always important; they must often have been passed off as something other than what they were. In any case many collectors were less interested in stylistic authenticity than in having something old and curious. Under these circumstances, the antique trade could flourish.

"Old French" or "Tous les Louis"

The last of Loudon's four styles he referred to as "Louis XIV". His contemporaries also called it "Louis XV" or just "Old French". Like the Elizabethan style, its popularity had to do with changing social patterns in Europe. One writer commenting on the popularity of "Elizabethan" style furnishings remarked that in 1831:

Already there is a great and constant demand for carved cabinets, scrolled chairs, tapestried hangings, and figured velvet cushions; and France and Germany are ransacked for these articles in order to restore to our ancient manor houses and Tudor mansions their appropriate internal fashion of attire.

The trade boomed during the early 1830s. Loudon commented in 1836 that:

During the past year, and for two or three years preceding, it has become fashionable to import, for fitting up English mansions, the furniture, chimney pieces, wainscoting, and carved wooden ornaments of dismantled French châteaux; and particularly to employ them in houses built in the Elizabethan manner.

Much of this discarded château furniture was only about a century old, having been made during the reigns of Lousi XIV and Louis XV. It nevertheless qualified as antique, and was sufficiently popular for several antique dealers to specialize in it; Loudon mentions Nixon & Son of Great Portland Street, London.

The Old French style had its source books. The mid-eighteenth-century pattern books of Thomas Chippendale, Matthias Locke and Thomas Johnson were all reprinted in the mid-nineteenth, and were later combined in a collected edition produced by John Weale, *Old French and English Ornaments* (1858).

60. FLORAL STRIPE LOUIS-STYLE WALLPAPER, *block-printed, with a burnished ground. c.1860.*

As with the other styles, much of the furniture had to be made new, to match or supplement the old, or to achieve modern shapes, colour schemes and standards of comfort. Bulging curves, scrolls, shell and rockwork ornament characterized much of the new furniture produced in this style. Paint and gilding were frequently used. Thomas King's catalogues of the 1830s contained Old French designs to be carried out in wood, and noted that costs could be kept down by gilding the furniture. If the furniture was to be gilt, carving would only be required "in the boldest scrolls, or in the massive foliage". Moulded composition ornament could be used

61. *(above)* SUGGESTED SCHEME FOR A ROOM *by Gillow & Co.,*
1819. The chairs and tables designed for the room are basically
Grecian in shape, but with curves and scrolls added. The cabinet and
plant stands are more evidently in the Old French style. The cabinet
and its stand may be antiques.

62. *(right)* WALLPAPER PANEL WITH A SEASCAPE, *1825–50.*

for all the other mouldings and finer details. This
economy was already familiar to picture-frame makers,
who also dealt in gilt wood.

As the century progressed, new production methods
had brought prices down. Loudon noted in 1833 that
production costs had recently fallen, due to the reces-
sion and the fall in the price of manual labour. New
furnishing materials like papier mâché, which could be
moulded and painted, allowed for more curvaceous
shapes and more adventurous colours. In America, the
New York furniture-maker John Henry Belter developed a type of moulded plywood furniture which
could likewise be bent into scrolls and curves. Papier
mâché and Belter furniture were both developed for
mass-production, and by the 1850s and 1860s the products were widely available, bringing the exuberance of
Old French furnishing to a wide market. At the Great
Exhibition of 1851, the New York Exhibition of 1853
and the Paris Exhibition of 1855, a significant proportion of British and Continental exhibits – cabinets,
carpets, ceramics – were in the Louis styles. By the 1860s
many furniture firms made little else; vast quantities of
Louis furniture were mass-produced in the Grand

Rapids firms of Michigan.

When Loudon described the Louis style as one that
was "unsuitable to persons in moderate circumstances",
he was not just talking about the price. The pieces produced in the Old French style could appear far richer
and more elaborate than the eighteenth-century furnishings on which they were based. As with Elizabethan-
style furnishings, the overall impression of antiquity
and wealth was more important than historical accuracy;
the new furnishings could be referred to as Louis XIV
or Louis XV, while incorporating motifs randomly from
either or both periods. Old French furnishings were
designed to be ostentatious, and it was this to which
Loudon really objected.

The view that the style lacked propriety, particularly
when adopted by the aspiring middle classes, was one
which was to be taken up fervently by the design reform
movement. Of all the styles available to Victorian consumers, Old French was the most exuberant, the most
fanciful and the most self-consciously aristocratic.
Worse still, as far as the reformers were concerned, it
was popular, foreign and had feminine associations. It
was to be an obvious target for the establishment.

THE REFORMED HOME

We manufacture everything except men; we blanch cotton, and strengthen steel,
and refine sugar, and shape pottery; but to brighten, to strengthen, to refine, or to
form a single living spirit, never enters into our estimate of advantages.
(*John Ruskin*, The Stones of Venice, *1853*)

IT WAS DURING the nineteenth century that design became a political issue. With the boom in manufacturing industry in Britain, America and parts of Europe, and the growth of new markets, came the realization that economic growth would increasingly depend on trade and successful competition in producing manufactured goods. The rapid recovery of the French economy following the Napoleonic Wars established France as a major manufacturing nation and a source of concern to her competitors, notably Britain. From the 1830s, and especially in Britain, the way products were designed and marketed consequently became matters of special government interest. There grew up an official design establishment, producing official reports and setting up schools, trade exhibitions and museums. These activities were meant to improve standards of design appreciation amongst both the makers and the users of products.

The main impulse behind this design reform movement was therefore economic, but other factors contributed to it. Patriotism was a powerful force, with several countries seeking to establish something which could be classified as a national style. Morality and religious revivalism developed useful stylistic associations. In England, where the design reform movement began, the Gothic style, though Continental in origin, came to be thought of as quintessentially English, and, through its associations with surviving church buildings, morally correct. The fact that it was seen as a masculine style gave it additional weight and authority. Perhaps most importantly, it had several committed, articulate and powerful champions to promote it through the design establishment. As a result of this, the design reform movement became linked with the Gothic style and with certain ideas connected to it. The impact of the reform movement on the furnishing of the ordinary home may have been minimal, but its influence on the architectural and design professions, and on some of their clients, was both deep and lasting.

The first official appearance of the design reform movement came in 1836, with the publication of a government Select Committee Report. The aim of the Report was to "inquire into the best means of extending a knowledge of the arts and of the principles of design among the people (especially the manufacturing population) of the Country". It took evidence from a wide range of architects, designers, manufacturers, makers and decorators. These witnesses were carefully selected, and much of their testimony supported certain predetermined ideas.

The thrust of the Committee's Report was as follows. Standards of design and drawing were far higher on the Continent, particularly in France, than in England. This was attributed to government support of art education in those countries, in the form of free schools of design, and free access to museums, libraries and exhibitions. In England, by contrast, the Committee concluded that "from the highest branches of poetical design down to the lowest connexion between design and manufacturers, the Arts have received little encouragement in this country".

63. *Axel Haig*, THE WINTER SMOKING-ROOM AT CARDIFF CASTLE, *1870. Cardiff Castle was designed by William Burges for his erudite, wealthy and eccentric patron the Marquis of Bute. The wall decorations, which represented the signs of the zodiac, the seasons and days of the week, combined fantasy with symbolism. When this picture was shown at the Royal Academy in 1870, the Marquis wrote to his fiancée to reassure her: "Pray don't imagine, my dear, that the house is all done up as if we are living in the reign of Henry III."*

64. *(above) A. W. N. Pugin,* **WALLPAPER FOR THE HOUSES OF PARLIAMENT,** *by Samuel Scott for J. G. Crace, 1847. As with all Pugin's designs, ornament was significant; the crowned rose, portcullis and initials VR for Victoria Regina symbolize the authority of Crown and Parliament.*

Much of the discussion concerned foreign competition. As one witness, the architect J.B. Papworth, put it, "art dwells with manufacture more in France than in England". Instead of buying new British furniture, he argued, "we get a great deal of that very old matter of furniture from abroad, which arrives in shop-loads, much to the disadvantage of our designers and our workmen".

The taste of the consumer was also blamed for low design standards. Samuel Wiley, of the papier-mâché manufacturing firm Jennens & Bettridge, complained, "the public taste is bad; I could sell them the worst things, the most unmeaning, in preference to the most splendid designs and the best executions". Another witness, the retailer J. C. Robertson, described the difficulties of the designer having to "'work to the head' or fancy of the customer", though he managed to turn the blame back on to foreign competitors, in particular the widespread import of "wretched prints and stucco images" from Italy, as having contributed to a drop in standards of English taste.

65. *(below) A. W. N. Pugin,* **CONTRASTED CLASSICAL AND GOTHIC GATEWAYS,** *1836. The illustrations to Pugin's book,* Contrasts, *were designed to show graphic contrasts between the mediaeval and modern society as expressed in architecture. For Pugin, the modern classical style was mean, cheap and fundamentally immoral. Gothic architecture, particularly that of the pre-Reformation period, was the only true and honest style. Paupers and a man with a placard advertising cheap knowledge pass the classical gateway, sandwiched between shops, while the mediaeval gateway frames a procession of devout scholars.*

KINGS COLLEGE STRAND

CHRIST'S COLLEGE OXFORD

CONTRASTED COLLEGE GATEWAYS

The Committee's recommendations included the setting up of government-funded practical Schools of Design along French and German lines. It encouraged the institution of free public museums where "casts and paintings, copies of the Arabesques of Raphael, the designs at Pompeii, specimens from the era of the revival of the Arts, everything, in short, which exhibits in combination the efforts of the artist and the workman" could be displayed. Other recommendations included the removal of the taxes on glass and wallpaper, which the Committee felt prevented the take-up of stained glass, wallpaper and engravings as cheap forms of home decoration. Most of these suggestions were put into practice: the first school of design opened in London in 1837, with branches in Manchester, Birmingham, Sheffield, York and Newcastle by 1843; the Public Libraries and Museums Act of 1845 paved the way for free local institutions; and the 1840s saw the repeal of the taxes. The progress of design reform, however, was not so straightforward.

Style Wars

The testimony of another witness, the London decorator George Morant, is interesting for the information it contains on attitudes to particular styles. Morant noted the popularity of the "Louis Quatorze" style and commented that "I think it is a captivating style of art to the

66. *(above) A. W. N. Pugin,* THE DINING-ROOM AT ABNEY HALL, CHESHIRE, *late nineteenth century. The decorative scheme at Abney illustrates Pugin's stylistic dogma. The furniture is solid wood, and designed to emphasize its structure. All ornament is geometric and non-naturalistic, and where possible, significant.*

67. *(below) A. W. N. Pugin,* ARMOIRE MADE FOR J. G. CRACE'S STAND IN THE MEDIAEVAL COURT AT THE GREAT EXHIBITION, *1851. The intricate tracery patterns and carved details were based on Pugin's studies of fifteenth-century woodwork. In line with his belief that all ornament should be appropriate, the shields on the cresting bear Crace's monogram, with floral motifs and symbols representing architecture.*

68. *(above)* FIRESCREEN WITH A WOOLWORK PANEL OF SIR
WALTER SCOTT, C.*1840. Pugin's published design for this firescreen
shows a heraldic motif on the panel. It is doubtful whether he would
have approved of such a figurative and naturalistic picture, but as
designer he could not control its production, still less its use or
adaptation within the home.*

69. *(right) Owen Jones*, WALLPAPER DESIGN, C.*1870.*

uneducated in art, from its requiring a great deal of
gold and gilding, and which therefore generally produces a magnificent effect, though sometimes the forms
may be very disagreeable. It is very seldom you see it in a
pure state, as what it was formerly at Versailles. It is of
that particular style that they can turn it and twist it
about as they like; it is only copying and copying." Both
Morant and the Committee clearly felt that the Louis
style was inappropriate for the British consumer, and
deplored the lack of purity and correctness of the
revived style. The Committee asked Morant whether he
felt Greek or Gothic would be more appropriate to
British culture and architecture. Morant favoured the
Greek style.

On the question of style, Morant was in agreement
with J. C. Loudon, whose book, *An Encyclopaedia of
Cottage, Farm and Villa Architecture*, had first come out in
1833. Loudon explained that his book contained few
examples of designs in the Louis Quatorze style "be-

cause we think that a style distinguished more by its
gorgeous gilding and elaborate carving than by anything else, unsuitable to the present advancing state of
public taste". Loudon likewise felt that the Grecian or
Modern style was the most appropriate one for
nineteenth-century Britain. But, in the same year, 1836,
another book was published which was to challenge and
change the established view. The debate about style –
Grecian or Gothic – was to take on a new, moral
dimension.

A Moral Style

A Modern Greek town is quite insupportable. I am sitting in a
Grecian coffee room in the Grecian Hotel with a Grecian
mahogany table close to a Grecian marble chimneypiece,
surmounted by a Grecian scroll pier glass, and to increase my
horror the waiter has brought in breakfast on a Grecian sort of
tray stamped with the infernal Greek scroll.

So wrote A. W. N. Pugin, of Fleetwood in Lancashire, a
town laid out by the classical architect Decimus Burton.
Augustus Welby Northmore Pugin was the son of the
French draughtsman and designer A. C. Pugin, who
worked mainly in the Gothic style. Trained by his father,
the younger Pugin showed early promise and won his
first major commission, designing Gothic furniture for
Windsor Castle, in 1827 at the age of 15. He was later to
condemn these early designs, which like most contemporary Gothic furniture featured medieval decoration on
basic classical shapes, as a "complete burlesque" of
Gothic, but he had already demonstrated his outstand-
ing skill as a draughtsman. By the time he was 20, Pugin
had designed for the royal silversmiths, had worked as a

70. *Louis Haghe*, THE MEDIAEVAL COURT AT THE GREAT
EXHIBITION, *1851. The Mediaeval Court, a showcase for the design
reform movement, contained furnishings intended to educate the public
in good taste.*

stage designer at Covent Garden and had set up his own decorating firm producing Gothic and Elizabethan furnishings. He had also become a keen collector and antiquarian, importing old furniture and antiques from the Continent and building up a vast personal library of architectural books. In 1835 he published his first book, *Gothic Furniture in the Style of the 15th Century*, and won his most important design commission, for the Gothic detailing and interior designs of the New Palace of Westminster, London's Houses of Parliament.

The competition for the design of the New Palace – the old one had burnt down in 1834 – marked a watershed in the official attitude to style. Gothic and Elizabethan – not Greek – were specified as the only suitable styles for the new building, which had to be a symbol of national identity. For Pugin, the New Palace was to become a life's work, and one in which he was able to implement in practical terms many of his most deeply held beliefs. In 1835 he converted to Roman Catholicism, and his next book, *Contrasts: or a Parallel between the Architecture of the 15th and 19th Centuries*, published the following year, presented his personal creed.

For Pugin, the Gothic style had become synonymous

with the Catholic, or pre-Reformation style; it was therefore the only style with true moral and theological weight. His life became a campaign for the Gothic, and in all his subsequent writings and practical work he promoted what he believed to be its key features. Pugin's attitude to Gothic was markedly more all-embracing and more spiritual than that of his contemporaries and consequently his designs were very different. They represented much more than just another range of motifs. Many of his ideas were derived from a close study of Gothic buildings and such furniture and pictures as survived, and his approach was almost archaeological. He used architectural fragments and antiques as inspiration and as teaching material and believed in returning to primary sources. Gothic, he believed, was an "honest" style. This meant that a piece of Gothic furniture should not conceal its structure or the means by which it was made. He was fond of features which emphasized construction, like pegged joints in table legs or iron hinges placed on the outside of cabinet doors. He deplored veneers and marquetry, which made cheap furniture look expensive. He favoured simple geometrical flat patterns – fleurs-de-lis or quatrefoils – over anything remotely naturalistic; fabrics and wallpapers had to look two-dimensional. Simplicity and propriety were two other Gothic virtues. All ornamentation had to be appropriate, significant and purposeful, otherwise it was immoral. Plain surfaces were to be encouraged. Where ornament was required it should be hand crafted and not machine worked; Pugin

71. *(above)* HOLLYHOCK CHINTZ ILLUSTRATING "FALSE PRINCIPLES", *1850. This chintz, with its naturalistic floral pattern, was one of the items chosen from the Great Exhibition to demonstrate what Henry Cole called "false principles" of design.*

72. *(right)* WALLPAPER SHOWING THE CRYSTAL PALACE AND SERPENTINE, *by Heywood, Higginbottom & Smith, 1853–5. This wallpaper, with its figurative scenes and* trompe l'œil *framing devices, is a textbook example of "false principles".*

strove for a medieval craft ideal where beauty lay in individuality. Medieval forms of decoration – stained glass, inlay, hand-carving, wrought metal, encaustic tile inlay, embroidery, hand block printing – were of course preferable to more modern and therefore degenerate techniques.

Pugin's work at the Palace of Westminster demonstrates many of his beliefs. He believed that every design detail was worthy of attention, and produced drawings for everything from thrones and stained glass to clerks' desks and umbrella stands. Every design element had its place in a hierarchy according to its function. Its decoration reflected its status and use; all motifs and patterns symbolized some aspect of the building's meaning.

Pugin did not live to see the Palace completed, but the impact of this building, of his many other commissions and, most importantly, of his writings was immediate, immense and widespread. His belief in the supremacy of Gothic, and his ideas on design affected a whole generation of architects and designers in Britain and abroad, even though few of them shared his faith.

Henry Cole and the Great Exhibition

One of the most influential of all Pugin's admirers was the civil servant Henry Cole. Cole became a key figure of the new British design establishment which grew out of the 1836 Select Committee Report. The aim of those involved was to promote design education and initiate reform. A diverse group of people, which included officials, enthusiasts, designers and enlightened manufacturers, was associated with this movement, which was to culminate in the Great Exhibition held in London's Hyde Park in 1851.

An able administrator, Cole had studied art and was interested in antiques. In 1846 he joined the Society of Arts, and immediately won a prize with a design for a simple, sparsely decorated tea service. As Cole explained, he was not against decoration, but was trying to "obtain as much beauty and ornament as is commensurate with cheapness". Encouraged by his success, he conceived the idea of setting up a company to produce artistic products. The company, Felix Summerly's Art Manufactures, aimed to improve public taste and to revive what Cole perceived as "the good old practice of connecting the best Art with familiar objects in daily use". The idea was an experiment to get artists to design everyday products, in the belief that these products would be intrinsically more beautiful than anything

73. *William Holman Hunt*, THE AWAKENING CONSCIENCE, *1853–4. Hunt intended the lavishly gilt mirror, the veneered furniture, polished, new and ornate, to symbolize the decadence and immorality of the woman's surroundings.*

designed commercially. The firm went into business in 1847, commissioning designs, mostly for tableware, from artists Cole knew, among them Daniel Maclise and Richard Redgrave, a botanical lecturer at the government School of Design.

Grafting the idea of the medieval artist–craftsman on to the reality of a mid-nineteenth-century commercial world was an ambitious experiment and not a particularly successful one; Cole abandoned the firm a year later. The aim had been to draw art and production together, as the Select Committee had recommended. But the artists involved were not used to designing for production, and had little contact with the manufacturers. So although they were careful to design ornament that was appropriate to the function of the piece – a bread knife with the handle carved as a sheaf of corn, a waterjug painted with waterlilies – the results sometimes appeared awkward and ill-proportioned.

In 1849, Cole began to publish the *Journal of Design and Manufactures* (1849–52), in which he and his friends could set forth their ideas on design reform. Adopting some of Pugin's teachings, the *Journal* campaigned against excessive and inappropriate ornament. Writers like the architect and ornamentalist Owen Jones contributed their own, often highly dogmatic, theories. Jones, always interested in colour, had begun to formulate theories on its use in decoration. He insisted that primary colours were preferable, and that in every "great" culture – the Egyptian, the Arab – design was based around primary colours; secondary and tertiary colours were decadent. He developed similarly rigid principles about ornament. Of these, eventually published in full in his *Grammar of Ornament* in 1856, several, including the precept that "all ornament should be based upon a geometrical construction", were to be highly significant for later designers.

At the same time, Cole was organizing annual exhibitions of art manufactures at the Society of Arts, a body set up almost a century earlier to promote "the Arts, Sciences and Manufactures". These exhibitions, held from 1847 to 1850, were intended to teach people about good taste. The first catalogue began:

It is an universal complaint among manufacturers that the taste for good art does not exist in sufficient extent to reward them for the cost of producing superior works; that the public prefer the vulgar, the gaudy, the ugly even, to the beautiful and perfect: that a subject with bright colours and costly gilding is preferred to one of chaster design, symmetrical form and subdued elegance.

A desire to raise standards of design and taste was the stated aim of the Society of Arts exhibitions. The president of the Society was Prince Albert, a dedicated supporter and influential patron of the arts, who for some years had been keen to establish a major industrial

74. *Augustus Egg,* PAST AND PRESENT NO 1, *early 1850s. The rich red wallpaper with Gothic fleur-de-lis pattern and matching tablecloth and simple decorative scheme are of the type favoured by the design reform movement. But the delicate painted papier-mâché chair, where the children are building their house of cards, would have been regarded by design moralists as cheap, gaudy and sham.*

A Cottage Sitting-room exhibited by Kendal Milne & Co at the Manchester Art Museum for Wm Morris & Co

The Bedroom Furniture

Arranged by Wm Morris & W A S Benson

75. *(above)* A COTTAGE SITTING-ROOM AT THE HORSFALL MUSEUM, MANCHESTER, *illustrated in the* British Architect, *1884. This room was part of a display intended to teach artisans in Manchester how to furnish their homes tastefully and thereby improve their life-styles. William Morris participated in the experiment, helping to supply and select suitable furnishings. As on other occasions, the reformers imposed their own aspirations on others and misjudged the economics of the enterprise; most of the things displayed were far too expensive for artisans to buy.*

76. *(opposite)* THE MORNING-ROOM AT EATON HALL, CHESHIRE, *1887. Alfred Waterhouse, the architect chosen by the Duke of Westminster to remodel his enormous Cheshire home, regularly worked in the Gothic style. The stencilled decoration, the use of the fresco on the chimney wall and many of the decorative details contrast sharply with the owner's French eighteenth-century furniture.*

exhibition in Britain. Both France and Germany had a tradition of design exhibitions and it was the success of the 1849 Paris exhibition which prompted Prince Albert to draw up a plan for a Great Exhibition of the Industry of All Nations. Cole, now experienced in organizing exhibitions, became the key promoter, helped by numerous friends and acquaintances. These included Pugin, Jones, the architect and critic Matthew Digby Wyatt, and the painters William Dyce and Richard Redgrave, who taught at the government Schools of Design. Thus almost every major figure in the design reform establishment was closely involved with the design, planning, management, judging or assessment of the Great Exhibition.

Both the building, nicknamed the Crystal Palace, and the exhibition have come to symbolize the confidence and ostentation of mid-Victorian Britain as an imperial power. The Palace, a giant prefabricated glass house, decorated inside (by Jones) in stark primary colours, was a spectacular technological achievement. The exhibition contained a vast array of raw materials, machinery and products from all over the world. It was a huge success, paving the way for over fifty years of spectacular trade fairs. But the organizers found, ironically, much to confirm their dissatisfaction with contemporary products; "the absence of any fixed principle in ornamental design is most apparent" wrote the critics, "the taste of the producers is uneducated".

So that the exhibition might be a lasting lesson to the uneducated, the superintendents, led by Cole, acquired from it a range of items to serve as good and bad examples of design. Initially put on show in Marlborough House, London, these were to form the core of the collections of the new South Kensington Museum, later the Victoria and Albert. Approved products included traditional Near Eastern and Indian objects,

favoured as being untainted by technological processes. Also selected were items designed by Pugin which had featured in the exhibition's special Mediaeval Court. In this way true medieval principles and the reformed Gothic style became official good taste.

In contrast, products with naturalistic or exuberant ornament, and furnishings in Louis or other elaborate decorative styles were singled out as warnings in a special section illustrating "false or wrong principles". Cole, Jones and the other reformers were optimistic that good design and taste were matters simply of explanation and education. Many of their contemporaries were more realistic. Charles Dickens, though Cole's friend, satirized him in his novel *Hard Times* as the utilitarian Inspector Gradgrind, lecturing schoolchildren on the principles of good taste:

You are to be in all things regulated and governed by Fact. You must discard the word Fancy altogether. You don't walk upon flowers in fact; you cannot be allowed to walk upon flowers in carpets. You don't find that foreign birds and butterflies come and perch upon your crockery. You must use combinations and modifications (in primary colours) of mathematical figures which are susceptible of proof and demonstration. This is a new discovery. This is fact. This is taste.

Similarly satirical reactions to Cole's principles appeared in 1852 in an article by Henry Morley. In 'A Houseful of Horrors', an imaginary Mr Crumpet, recently returned from the Marlborough House exhibition of False Principles, complained to his friend Mr Frippy:

My snug parlour maddens me . . . the matter is this: I have acquired some correct principles of Taste. I am perpetually grieved by rooms, papered as this is, in which we are now sitting. Though the room is small, the paper has a large pattern, boldly defined in stripes of lilacs, lilies and moss roses very nicely drawn. There is no fitness in the paper as a background to a parlour, or as a background to anything; the direct imitation of flowers is also impertinent. Fancy scrolls and ideas suggesting flowers, that is to say, ornaments designed with a present sense of the beauty of natural forms, balanced with geometrical correctness, and with an exact regard to the proportions of the colours, are the proper things. The flowers on your wall being imitated from nature are full of shadows, and those at which you are now looking contradict in an absurd way, Mr Frippy, the real position of the windows.

Frippy replies:

My dear Crumpet, you have picked up some wholesome views, but you have swallowed them too eagerly and choked yourself.

We say in this country that there's no accounting for tastes, and it will be many years before mere abstract principles of choice in ornament can become familiar.

Neither critical satire nor public lack of interest deterred the reformers from their mission. Though few in number, they were now well established and powerful. Cole went on to oversee the establishment of the South Kensington Museums, to supervise the reform of the government Schools of Design under a new Department of Practical Art, and to administer several more major trade exhibitions. Jones published, in 1856, his mammoth and didactic *Grammar of Ornament*, and continued to design, write and publish prolifically. Pugin died young, and disillusioned, in 1852, complaining that he had "passed his life in thinking of fine things, studying fine things, designing fine things and realizing very poor ones". But his influence on the architects, designers and critics of his generation had been profound, and there were others to take up the cause.

The Nature of Gothic

The writer and artist John Ruskin shared Pugin's passionate belief in the supremacy of the Gothic style. A Christian and a socialist, Ruskin's commitment to Gothic was a political as well as a religious crusade. He believed firmly in the medieval craft ideal and in individual

77. J. P. Seddon, TILE DESIGN, c.1870. Seddon was a prolific designer as well as architect. His numerous tile designs frequently feature conventionalized plant forms in a few bold colours.

creativity. He loathed the idea of mass-production and factory working and saw industrial capitalism as the oppression of working people. In his most influential book, *The Stones of Venice*, published in 1853, he wrote:

Look around this English room of yours, about which you have been proud so often, because the work of it was so good and strong, and the ornaments of it so finished. Examine again all those accurate mouldings, and perfect polishings, and unerring adjustments of the seasoned wood and tempered steel. Many a time you have exulted over them, and thought how great England was, because her slightest work was done so thoroughly. Alas! if read rightly, these perfectnesses are signs of a slavery in our England a thousand times more bitter than that of the scourged African, or helot Greek.

On design, Ruskin stated, "I believe the right question to ask, respecting all ornament, is simply this: was it done with enjoyment – was the carver happy while he was about it?" A keen geologist and watercolourist, Ruskin believed deeply in the beauty of nature, which he felt should form the basis of all ornament, whether naturalistic, conventional or abstract. It was this feeling for nature, and his belief in observation and honesty in art, that drew him to support the work of the newly formed and much maligned Pre-Raphaelite Brotherhood of artists. William Holman Hunt's painting, *The Awakening Conscience*, researched with the Pre-Raphaelites' attention to detail, and painted in a North London '*maison de convenance*', Ruskin analysed in the following appreciative letter to *The Times* newspaper in 1854:

There is not a single object in that room – common, modern, vulgar (in the vulgar sense, as it may be), but it becomes tragical, if rightly read. That furniture so carefully painted, even to the last vein of the rosewood – is there nothing to be learnt from that terrible lustre of it, from its fatal newness; nothing there that has the old thoughts of home upon it, or that is ever to become part of a home? Those embossed books, vain and useless, – they are also new, marked with no happy wearing of beloved leaves; the torn and dying bird upon the floor, the gilded tapestry, with the fowls of the air feeding on the ripened corn; the picture above the fireplace, with its single drooping figure – the woman taken in adultery.

So Ruskin joined the ranks of the design reformers. His commitment to the importance of art in everyday life led to his teaching drawing and design at the East London Working Men's College, and to his (unsuccessful) attempts to found an ideal medieval rural community, the Guild of St George, in industrial Sheffield, where he also set up a free museum. He corresponded widely with other social reformers working in the new industrial cities; Manchester, the East End of London, Chicago and Boston. Ruskinian ideals matched quite closely Shaker principles of equality, honest craftsmanship and spiritual purity, which by the 1860s had become quite fashionable on the American East Coast. Many of Ruskin's correspondents and followers shared his mission to bring beauty and nature into the homes of the industrial worker, though they interpreted it in various ways. In Manchester in 1884, Morris & Co. helped to furnish an artisan's ideal home as part of an instructive public museum display. The widespread formation of guilds and societies founded on what came to be called Arts and Crafts principles is dealt with in a later chapter.

The Next Generation

The concept of design reform, and the belief in Gothic as the one true style were both well entrenched in architectural and design cricles by 1855. Because of the small number of practices, and the way they were run, architectural offices were a powerful medium for the transmission of ideas; one generation of architects trained the next. Other important forums for discussion included the Mediaeval Society and the Hogarth Club in London. Reformist ideas were interpreted differently by the young architects of the mid-century, according to their individual circumstances. Those who were privileged to work only for a few wealthy and like-minded patrons, or for the Church, could afford to stick to their principles and continued to design in Gothic styles well into the 1870s. But those, like the commercial designers, who depended upon a much broader and more changeable market, were forced to be more flexible.

In the first category came architect/designers like William Butterfield, George Edmund Street, John Pollard Seddon and William Burges. Both Street and Butterfield were closely involved in a group called the Ecclesiological Society, set up originally in 1836 to promote the Anglican liturgy and Gothic architecture in church-building. The Ecclesiologists favoured an earlier, and therefore "purer", pared down style of Gothic, preferring that of the fourteenth century to Pugin's fifteenth-century revival styles. The wave of church-building which took place from the 1840s provided an opportunity for the Society to implement its ideas, and throughout most of their working lives, Butterfield and Street were able to concentrate on building or restoring churches, parsonages and other religious buildings and designing church furnishings. Seddon likewise trained and practised mostly as an architect, but because his family had a large cabinet-making business, he also became a prolific designer of furniture, tiles and pottery, always working in a Ruskinian Gothic style.

William Burges' devotion to Gothic as a style had less to do with religious conviction. A follower of Pugin – he had been given a copy of *Contrasts* for his fourteenth birthday – Burges trained and worked as an architect. He was lucky in coming from a privileged and wealthy family, and in finding sympathetic and even wealthier patrons; his main patron, the Marquis of Bute, was the richest man in Britain. Like Pugin, Burges was a collector, an antiquarian, and a medievalist, but he lacked Pugin's seriousness and conviction. His designs for interiors were richly colourful; those at Cardiff Castle (1869) and Castell Coch (1875), both for the Marquis of Bute, were theatrical Gothic fantasies. His furniture and furnishings were massive, wildly ornamental, often bejewelled, and full of symbolism and elaborate jokes. He brought, as Pugin had, an archaeological approach to the design of Gothic furniture. The so-called Yatman cabinet, which he designed in 1858, was a wooden, gable-topped writing-desk, richly painted with mythological and historical scenes, the shape of which was based on surviving French medieval cupboards.

Burges' Yatman cabinet was one of the exhibits at the highly influential International Exhibition held in Lon-

don in 1862. This, the first major successor to the 1851 exhibition, and likewise largely organized by Cole, again included a Mediaeval Court. In the Court were Burges' cabinet, a number of Ecclesiological Society products, and painted Gothic furniture designed by two younger architects who had both trained with Street, Richard Norman Shaw and Philip Webb. Webb's furniture was shown on the Morris & Co. stand, along with pieces designed for the firm by Seddon. All this furniture was reformed Gothic in style, though most of it was designed to recall the earliest phase of Gothic, that of the thirteenth century. The furniture was generally heavy, with square sectioned uprights, gables, simple chamfering and tracery, but was richly decorated with painting and geometrical inlay. It was derided by the media as fantastically impractical, but admired by avant-garde desig-

---

78. *William Burges*, WASHSTAND FOR THE GUEST CHAMBER OF HIS HOUSE IN MELBURY ROAD, LONDON, *1880. The long strap hinges, the pierced lower doors, the whole concept of furniture painted in this way were ideas Burges drew from mediaeval paintings and manuscript illustrations, but the jewel-like quality of his furniture and the use of many contrasting materials and techniques – marble, bronze, mirror, gilding – were products of his own inventiveness.*

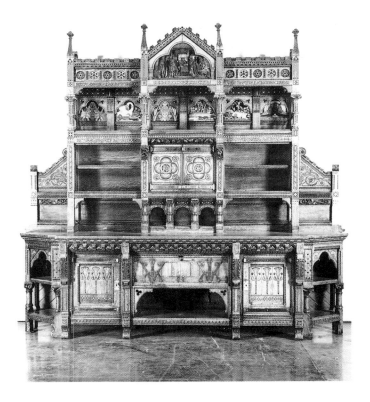

er. It included some of his own designs for furniture and wallpaper, along with illustrations of designs he admired, both historical and contemporary. In the same year, Talbert, who had left architecture to design for cabinet-making and metalworking firms, published an influential book, *Gothic Forms Applied to Furniture, Metalwork and Decoration for Domestic Purposes*. This was aimed at the furniture-making trade rather than the consumer, and contained thirty pages of his own designs for Gothic furniture. The emphasis of each book was different, but they both contained a similar message about the need for truth to materials, honesty of construction, and the rightness of Gothic. Many of these underlying precepts derived from Pugin: superfluous ornament was ugly, and true beauty in design resulted from an object's fitness for its purpose.

But whereas Pugin and his more purist followers rejected machine-made products, this furniture was designed for mass-production. Marquetry veneers were used instead of solid wood inlays, nickel-plated steel instead of brass, mass-produced tiles or enamels instead of hand-painted wooden panels. Carved detail was usually restricted to simple chamfering or notches, and diagonally-set boards were often used instead of ordinary

79. *(opposite) Charles Locke Eastlake,* OAK CABINET WITH PAINTED PANELS, *c.1867. Though perhaps the most influential writer on design reform, Eastlake designed little himself. The pieces that can be attributed to him are generally very solid and sparse; one contemporary described them as being "in construction too much like a packing case".*

80. *(above) Bruce J. Talbert,* SIDEBOARD *made by Holland & Sons, 1866. This piece, designed by Talbert for Holland's stand at the Paris Exhibition in 1867, contains many classic Reformed Gothic features; decorative hinges, diagonal boarding, stump columns, geometrical roundels, conventionalized plant forms, significant ornament — here the animals denote food and eating — and inscriptions.*

ners. Likewise much admired were the products displayed on the Japanese stand, which to Western eyes had a pre-industrial purity and richness; Burges described the Japanese Court as "the real mediaeval court of the exhibition".

Design Reform and Mass-Production

Both the Mediaeval and the Japanese Courts had a significant impact on the commercial design and manufacturing world. Some of the architect/designers who had exhibited there, most notably Shaw, soon turned from reformed Gothic to other, more flexible design styles. But a new generation of writers and commercial designers were adapting reformed components and motifs to suit the mass market. The most famous and probably the most influential were Charles Locke Eastlake and Bruce James Talbert. Both men had trained as architects and knew some of the leading design reformers. Eastlake turned to journalism early in his career and in 1868 published a book based on a series of articles he had written four years earlier. The book, *Hints on Household Taste in Furniture, Upholstery and Other Details*, was a powerful attempt to popularize the Gothic style he admired, and was written for the middle-class consum-

81. *Christopher Dresser,* DESIGN FOR A FRIEZE IN THE NEW STYLE FOR AN UPPER WALL, *1874–6. Christopher Dresser, a prolific commercial designer and botanist, produced some of the most adventurous, often almost abstract, designs of the late nineteenth century. He had the words "Truth, Beauty, Power" painted on his study door and saw his designs as emanating from these ideas.*

panels. The resulting furniture was heavy, geometrically patterned and in many cases richly colourful. It was not universally admired; one contemporary designer, J. Moyr Smith, described Eastlake's furniture as being "in construction too much like a packing case". But by 1870 it was widely fashionable. Some of the larger and more adventurous firms employed designers – the London firms of Holland's and Gillow's employed Talbert, for instance – others simply copied designs from books or journals.

American Modern Gothic

It was through Eastlake that design reform theories became widely disseminated in America. Pugin's works were known to the writer Andrew Jackson Downing, who promoted Gothic as a correct style for much of rural America, through his book *The Architecture of Country Houses* (1850). His contemporary, the architect Alexander Jackson Davis also pioneered the use of Gothic in America; Lyndhurst (1838) and Kenwood (1842) were important Gothic houses in the New York area that he built and furnished in the Gothic style. However, Gothic could not have the same nationalistic connotations in America as it had in Britain, despite the large numbers of new villas with Gothic detailing – gable ends, pointed windows – built right across the United States.

In contrast with much of the more purist writing on design reform, Eastlake's book, *Hints*, had a practicality which appealed to designers, decorators and house-holders in America. The book had by 1879 been through six American editions, and its author's name was synonymous with the new Gothic style. Talbert's work, too, was widely known in the States; *Gothic Forms* was published there in 1873, and plates from it were used, unattributed or described as "Eastlake", in Harriet Prescott Spofforth's influential book, *Art Decoration Applied to Furniture*, published in 1878. Clarence Cook's *The House Beautiful* (1878) likewise advocated principles of propriety, honesty, simplicity and hygiene derived from Eastlake. The "Modern Gothic" style, as it became known, reached a peak of popularity in the States around the time of the Philadelphia Centennial Exposition in 1876, where a plethora of products from many nations and periods were on show to the American public. Interest in art and design boomed as a result of the exhibition, and a range of magazines, books, clubs and further exhibitions appeared in the following years. Trade in products and better travel opportunities for designers, craftsmen, patrons and consumers likewise helped the exchange of ideas. American firms like Daniel Pabst in Philadelphia, Kimbel & Cabus of New York and Mitchell & Rammelsburg of Cincinnati adopted reformed Gothic precepts and adapted them for the American market.

Often "Eastlake" furniture bore little resemblance to its originator's designs or precepts. The term came to mean furniture made of oak, walnut or ebonized wood, decorated with spindles, chamfering and incised geometrical decoration. Eastlake himself remained a committed reformer, and this dismayed him; as he stated in 1878:

I find American tradesmen continually advertising what they are pleased to call "Eastlake" furniture, with the production of which I have had nothing whatever to do, and for the taste of which I should be very sorry to be considered responsible.

Design reform principles were to influence generations of architects and designers from William Morris through Frank Lloyd Wright and the Bauhaus to the Modern Movement. But in their antagonism to machine production on the one hand and to opulence and frivolity on the other, they were doomed to limited appeal. True principles for the few were, for the majority, just another short-lived fashion.

82. *(opposite, above) Andrew Jackson Downing,* INTERIOR IN A SIMPLE GOTHIC STYLE, c.*1850. The American writer Downing read and admired Pugin's works. In his book,* The Architecture of Country Houses, *he helped to promote Gothic as a proper style for rural America. Pugin would probably have regarded the architectural and constructional detailing of the furniture shown here as superficially, not truly, Gothic.*

83. *(opposite, below)* THE LIBRARY OF JOHN A. BURNHAM, BOSTON, MASS., *1876. The massive, hooded chimneybreast, the gabled bookcases and simple curtain without a valance were all features of the Reformed Gothic interior as advocated by Eastlake.*

MORRIS & CO.

*The great advantage and charm of the Morrisonian method is that it lends itself to either simplicity or splendour. You might almost be as plain as Thoreau, with a rush bottomed chair, a piece of matting, and oaken trestle table; or you might have gold and lustre (the choice ware of William de Morgan) gleaming from the sideboard, and jewelled light in the windows, and walls hung with arras tapestry.
(Walter Crane,* The English Revival in Decorative Art; William Morris to Whistler, *1911)*

THE FOUNDING OF Morris & Co., the London firm of decorators established by William Morris in 1861, has long been thought to mark a turning point in the history of nineteenth-century decoration and design. As early as 1883 a writer in the *Spectator* declared: " 'Morris' has become a household word for all who wish their material surroundings to be beautiful yet appropriate for homely use," and noting the extent of the firm's influence, he went on to remark, "all the better kinds of designs in the shops are, as far as they are good, cribs from Morris, just altered sufficiently to prevent unpleasantness." By 1896, the year of Morris's death, the company had become synonymous with artistry and innovation in design, and was credited with having, almost single-handedly, reformed public taste and revolutionized the appearance of the domestic interior.

Much of this acclaim was due to the reputation of Morris himself. Author, poet, designer and socialist, Morris was a figure of gargantuan stature in the decorative arts and his talents were as varied as they were famed. As a designer he was responsible for a vast quantity of work that ranged from textiles and wallpapers to ceramics and stained glass, while as a manufacturer his uncompromising insistence upon quality and craftsmanship led to the revitalization of many techniques of production that had all but disappeared. His influence as a theorist was no less important.

84. *William Morris,* STRAWBERRY THIEF, *printed textile, 1883. Morris's first design for printed textiles was made in 1873. The freshness of his patterns, employing simple, naturalistic motifs, represented a welcome release from the strict formality and heraldic motifs favoured by the neo-Gothic school, and within a decade the printed chintzes had become one of the most well-known and successful of the products made by the firm.*

Morris began lecturing on the decorative arts in the late 1870s and by the end of his life he was widely regarded as one of the most articulate and forceful of contemporary spokesmen on taste and design. It was he, for example, who popularized the notion that decoration was not a minor art, of secondary importance to painting and sculpture, but part of the great unity of art. This view, derived from Ruskin, was to become the cornerstone of Arts and Crafts philosophy and Morris's championship of what he ironically termed "The Lesser Arts" did much to raise their status and to prepare the way for the next generation of artist-craftsmen who followed in his wake. Similarly, it was Morris who first focused public attention upon the need for art and beauty in every walk of life. Many other writers and designers came to hold this view but no one, prior to Morris, had proclaimed it as forcefully, and his belief that beauty was as necessary to man's survival as food, shelter and a living wage was the motivating force behind all his efforts in manufacture and design.

Initially, Morris's interest in decoration was inspired by his dismay at the degeneracy and shoddiness of commercially manufactured goods, and many of his criticisms of mid-century design echo those of other theorists such as Pugin, Redgrave and Cole. Pugin's invective against the philistinism and inhumanity of nineteenth-century industrial society, along with his advocacy of Gothic art were to prove particularly influential. Increasingly, though, aesthetic considerations were overlaid by political concerns, and with his growing commitment to socialism in the 1870s and 1880s, Morris came to regard art as a major force in the improvement of society and in bettering the lot of the working man. His aim became "an Art made by the people, for the people, as a happiness to the maker and the user", and

85. THE DINING-ROOM AT 7 HAMMERSMITH TERRACE, LONDON. *A close friend and colleague of Morris, Emery Walker, the owner of this house, also shared many of his tastes, and the use of light, rush-seated furniture, naturalistic patterns and rich colours comes closest to Morris's ideal of having "nothing . . . that you do not know to be useful or believe to be beautiful". The wallpaper is Willow and the fabrics are Chrysanthemum and Evenlode.*

in the example of the medieval craft guild he identified the model of a free and egalitarian society where men were united both in the collective organization of their lives and in the enjoyment derived from their work. In this way, he introduced a social and political dimension to the teachings of the Gothic Revival, and his vision of a society where all men would work, take pleasure in their labour, and share their delight in its results, was of paramount importance for late nineteenth- and early twentieth-century designers such as W. R. Lethaby and Walter Crane.

Ultimately, though, the notion of "Art for All" was to prove an impossible ideal. Those very qualities of craftsmanship and individuality that were so highly prized by the artists associated with the firm made their products too expensive for working people to afford, and it is one of the ironies of history that Morris & Co. decorations survive today only in large, stately homes. Also, with much of the firm's later furniture being little more than pastiches of eighteenth-century styles, the innovatory status of their designs has increasingly been called into question. Nevertheless, Morris's mission "to revive a sense of beauty in home life" and "to restore the dignity of art to household decoration" had a profound effect upon middle-class attitudes to interior design, and the "Morris look", with its striking combination of simple furnishings, luxuriant patterns and rich colours, established a new style for fashionable decoration that spread far beyond England to Europe and America.

Red House and the Founding of the Firm

Morris & Co. was first registered as Morris, Marshall, Faulkner & Co. As well as Morris, the original partners were the artists Dante Gabriel Rossetti, Ford Madox Brown and Edward Burne-Jones, the architect Philip Webb, the surveyor Peter Paul Marshall, and Charles Faulkner, a mathematician and Oxford don. Each of the partners contributed a share capital of £1 and the firm began trading with a loan of £100 borrowed from Morris's mother on 11 April 1861.

Looking back in 1883, Morris recalled the circumstances leading up to this event: "I got a friend to build me a house very medieval in spirit in which I lived for five years, and set myself to decorating it. We found, I and my friend . . . that all the minor arts were in a state of complete degradation . . . and accordingly in 1861 with the conceited courage of a young man, I set myself to reforming all that, and started a sort of firm for producing decorative articles." The house to which he refers was the Red House, and the friend, its architect, was Philip Webb. Both were to influence Morris in his choice of career and the Red House, in particular, played a decisive role in determining the scope and character of the firm in its early years. Its history is therefore worth examining in some detail.

The Red House was built for Morris on the occasion of his marriage to Jane Burden. Some years prior to this event, in 1853, he had gone up to Oxford to study theology. There he met Burne-Jones, a fellow-student at Exeter College, who unlike Morris was not wealthy but the son of a Birmingham frame-maker. There too, Morris and Burne-Jones first read Ruskin. Much of

86. A COLLECTION OF EARLY MORRIS FURNISHINGS, *1860s. Much of the firm's early furniture was inspired by simple Gothic forms and was decorated with figurative paintings. The examples illustrated here include a wardrobe painted by Burne-Jones with illustrations of Chaucer's* Prioress's Tale, *and a cabinet decorated by Morris with scenes from the life of St George. The settle and the refectory table were designed by Webb and were originally made for the Red House. The chairs are variants of the highly popular Sussex range and the Pomegranate wallpaper and Lily carpet were both designed by Morris.*

their time had been spent devouring the works of Carlyle, Malory and Sir Walter Scott, and through them they had developed a deeply felt sympathy for the Middle Ages that was to last throughout their lives. It was Ruskin, however, who opened their eyes to the importance of nature as the foundation of Gothic art, and in the impassioned descriptions of medieval craftsmen contained in *The Stones of Venice* (1853), he showed them how "art was the expression of man's pleasure in labour" and instilled in them the conviction that artists should learn craft skills and master techniques of production as well as paint pictures and produce designs.

Fired with enthusiasm for these ideas and becoming increasingly disenchanted with the prospect of a religious life, the two abandoned their original intention of entering the Church and left the university, Morris to become an architect and Burne-Jones to paint. Morris entered the offices of the Gothic Revival architect, George Edmund Street, where Philip Webb was already employed as chief clerk. Shortly afterwards he was introduced to Rossetti, who persuaded him to take up painting full-time. In 1857, the three worked with other artists on the project to decorate the walls of the Oxford Union Debating Hall and it was there that Morris first made the acquaintance of Jane Burden, a local girl who modelled for many of the figures in the murals. The two were married in the spring of 1859 and in the late

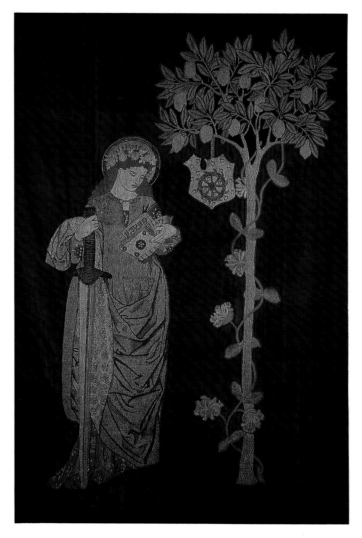

87. *William Morris*, ST CATHERINE, *embroidery, c. 1860. One of twelve embroidered panels devised for the dining-room at the Red House. The subject was inspired by Chaucer's* Legend of Good Women.

summer of 1860 they moved into the Red House, near Bexleyheath, in Kent.

The exterior of the Red House is now recognized as a direct descendant of the town and country rectories that Webb had been working on under Street and its vernacular style has long since ceased to be regarded as revolutionary. The interior, by contrast, was much more unusual and contained plain brick fireplaces, rough wooden floors and an open timber roof where construction was frankly revealed. The decorations designed by Morris and his friends were even more eccentric. They included pictorial friezes, painted hangings and bands of "wild foliage pattern" painted on the ceiling and walls and, according to the painter William Bell Scott, who visited the house in the 1860s, "the adornment had a novel, not to say startling, character, but if one had been told it was the South Sea Island style of thing one could have believed such to be the case, so bizarre was the execution". The most significant features, however, certainly as far as the later history of the firm was concerned, were the furnishings and embroidered hangings used in several of the principal rooms.

The furniture was almost all especially made for the house. Morris had tried to buy furniture from commer-

cial manufacturers but, disliking the excessive carving and ornament characteristic of much contemporary work, he commissioned friends to design the more important pieces for him instead. Much was produced by Webb, whose work included table glass and copper candlesticks as well as traditionally styled bedroom cabinets and oak tables and chairs. Other pieces were adorned with paintings executed by Rossetti and Burne-Jones. These included the massive settle-cum-cupboard in the hall, which was painted with scenes from the *Niebelungenlied*, and the large wardrobe given to Morris as a wedding present by Burne-Jones, decorated with characters from Chaucer's *Prioress's Tale*.

The Red House was not Morris's first experience of furniture design. Several years earlier he had been similarly unable to find commercially produced work to his taste when he moved into rooms that he shared with Burne-Jones at 17 Red Lion Square in Holborn. On this occasion he had gone to Tommy Baker, a local cabinet-maker, with simple designs of his own and Webb's devising. Henry Price, one of the joiners employed there, recorded the visit in his diary:

A gentleman who in after years became a noted socialist, and poet as was, an Art Furnisher, called at our shop and got the guvnor to take some orders for some very old-fashioned furniture in the medieval style . . . A large cabinet about 7 feet high and as long, a seat forming a bunk, with arms each end carved to represent fishes. There were some tables and high-back chairs like what I have seen in Abbeys and Cathedrals. A large oak table on tressells.

The seat to which Price refers was the massive settle later installed in the drawing-room at the Red House, whose shutters were painted by Rossetti with scenes from the life of Dante. Also decorated by Rossetti were the "high-back chairs" which he likened to "those that Barbarossa might have sat in", whose backs were painted with figures of Sir Galahad and Gwendolin.

The extent to which this furniture differed from commercial work was quite considerable, and the simplicity and plainless of its forms contrasted sharply with the fashion for carving and elaborate inlay popularized by French styles of design. Moreover, while the inspiration was clearly medieval, in keeping with progressive tastes, the pieces produced for the Red House owed more to the example of Pre-Raphaelitism than to the work of architects associated with the Gothic Revival. Morris and his friends had read journals such as *The Builder* and *The Ecclesiologist* during their Oxford years; they were well-versed in the arguments and aesthetics associated with design reform. But throughout his life Morris remained largely uninterested in the claims of commerce and industry and during this early period his sympathies were allied more to contemporary developments in painting than correct principles of design. Rossetti's influence was particularly significant.

Rossetti had become fascinated with the romance and literature of the Middle Ages, and for much of the 1850s he was engaged upon a series of so-called "Froissartian" watercolours depicting chivalric and Arthurian themes. Many of the same subjects recur in the paintings on the furniture of this date, and the design of some of the more unusual pieces is clearly related to the highly idiosyncratic canopied seats and beds that appear in his paintings. The other members of the firm were all familiar with Rossetti's work – Morris even owned a couple of his watercolours – and it is therefore likely that it was these highly personal imaginings, rather than the more conventional work produced by other medievalists such as Pugin and G. Scott, that inspired the furniture at the Red House and Red Lion Square.

The embroidered hangings had a more obviously historical source and their use at the Red House was a deliberate attempt to imitate the decorations in a medieval interior. Two schemes were devised: one for the principal bedroom and another for the dining-room. Of the two, the scheme for the dining-room was much the more original and consisted of a set of hangings containing twelve female figures, separated by trees, and stitched down on a cloth decorated with foliage and other ornament. The panels were sewn by Jane Burden, whom Georgiana Burne-Jones described as "an exquisite needlewoman", with occasional help from her sister Elizabeth, and the work was carried on over a period of several years.

Morris's interest in embroidery began during his

apprenticeship with Street, when he had his first opportunity to study historic samples during a visit to the Low Countries that the two made in 1856, and he subsequently taught himself traditional techniques of stitching and laying down of threads at Red Lion Square. Later it became one of the most prestigious and well-known areas of the firm's work, and during the 1870s the company received a number of commissions for elaborate decorative friezes, including the one produced for Sir Isaac Lowthian Bell at Rounton Grange, Northallerton, North Yorkshire.

Morris & Co. worked on the interiors of this house for several years and their decorations included a Morris & Co. Hammersmith carpet and woven wool and silk hangings for the drawing-room as well as several items of furniture that were later upholstered in J. H. Dearle's Compton chintz of 1896. The embroidered frieze was hung in the dining-room and consisted of five panels based on Chaucer's *Romaunt of the Rose*; the figures were designed by Burne-Jones, and Morris provided the background elements. Morris & Co. were at their best, and their most typical, however, with the large foliate panels designed as portières and wall-hangings in the second half of the 1870s, and it was with examples such as the Artichoke hanging, produced in 1877 for Smeaton Manor, Yorkshire, rather than with the large pictorial compositions, that the firm's work became most sought-after and well-known.

The success of the embroidery department was due partly to the appeal of Morris's designs and partly also to the growing enthusiasm for Art Needlework that

88. THE DINING-ROOM AT ROUNTON GRANGE, NORTHALLERTON, YORKSHIRE, *late 1870s. Morris & Co. provided a number of decorations for this house but their most striking contribution was the design for an embroidered frieze used in the dining-room. The figures were drawn by Burne-Jones and the background by Morris. The embroidery itself was executed by Margaret Bell and her daughters, Florence and Ada Phoebe, and took several years.*

89. THE BEDROOM AT KELMSCOTT MANOR, OXFORDSHIRE. *Morris took over the lease of Kelmscott Manor, a late sixteenth-century building of Cotswold stone, in 1871, and the family used it as a country retreat until May's death in 1939. Comparatively few alterations were made to the interior but the master bedroom has subsequently been decorated throughout with Morris & Co. designs. The wallpaper is the Willow pattern and the curtains are a version of the design for Vine. The four-poster bed is original and is hung with a set of embroideries designed and executed by May with assistance from Lily Yeats.*

emerged in the latter half of the nineteenth century. Many of the company's patrons were skilled needle-women with a keen interest in artistic work, and Morris himself did much to strengthen the influence of the Art Needlework movement. He was one of the first designers to be associated with the prestigious Royal School of Needlework, founded in 1872, and his emphasis on traditional stitching, fine materials and formalized designs did much to break the grip of the mechanically worked canvas embroidery that was favoured in the 1840s and 1850s.

In 1885 the management of the firm's embroidery section was handed over to Morris's daughter May, who helped produce the magnificent set of bed-hangings used in Morris's bedroom at Kelmscott Manor, Oxfordshire. Also during this period, the company began selling patterns for smaller items, such as cushions, cloths and firescreens. These were produced as kits.

The design was printed on to cloth and was supplied with specially dyed silks and wools which enabled the customer to execute the work at home. So popular did these smaller, cheaper items prove to be that they soon came to subsidize the production and sale of larger panels, and by the end of the nineteenth century no fashionable interior was complete without at least one example of a Morris & Co. embroidered cushion or screen.

Many of the same decorations and furnishings that were used at the Red House later appeared in Burne-Jones's home, The Grange, and the interiors there, represent an interesting parallel to those at Bex-leyheath. A watercolour view of the dining-room by T. M. Rooke includes an oak table identical to that designed by Webb for Morris's hall, while the painted sideboard beyond was decorated by Burne-Jones during the period that he was living at Red Lion Square. The door-curtain was adapted from the embroidered hangings used in the Red House dining-room and the chair is a version of the range developed by the firm *c.*1865. Despite these similarities, though, the Red House was neither particularly influential nor well-known outside the small circle of artists associated with the firm. A medieval interior *par excellence*, its appearance was too idiosyncratic to exercise wide appeal and the work produced there should be viewed more as a reflection of the personal interests and affinities of those concerned than as a systematic attempt to reform public taste.

Nevertheless, the house acted as an important catalyst in the founding of the firm. It fomented the group's interest in decoration and design, and provided an important testing-ground for their emergent skills and ideas. It also demonstrated that artists had as much to offer as commercial designers in the production of domestic goods; and in the practical experience that it gave of furnishing and decorating work, it provided the vital impetus needed for the establishment of the firm.

Stained Glass

The activities at the Red House established a bias towards hand-crafted goods and the firm began trading from craft workshops at 8 Red Lion Square. There they developed a co-operative method of working that contrasted sharply with the specialized practices endorsed by commercial manufacturers. Tasks were shared out fairly evenly and the partners collaborated in the design and production of mural decoration, carving, stained glass, metalwork, jewellery, tiles, furniture and embroidery "besides every article necessary for domestic use". The tiles, in particular, illustrate this collective approach, and Webb, Faulkner and Burne-Jones as well as Morris himself, each took turns in painting the designs which were then fired in a kiln installed in the basement of the Holborn premises. Later, much of this work was taken over by William de Morgan, whose Chelsea workshops were supplying the majority of

90. (*above*) *Thomas Matthew Rooke*, THE DINING-ROOM AT THE GRANGE, *1898. Edward and Georgiana Burne-Jones moved to The Grange in North End Road, Fulham, in 1867 and many of their furnishings and decorations are similar to those used at the Red House. The oak dining-table is identical to that designed for Morris's hall and the portière was adapted from the hangings in the dining-room at Bexleyheath. Other Morris-style furnishings include the Sussex chairs, the Ladies and Animals sideboard painted by Burne-Jones in 1860, and the panels of Morris Minstrel Figures stained glass.*

91. (*below*) *Edward Burne-Jones*, "SLEEPING BEAUTY" PANEL, *1864. Commissioned by the painter Birket Foster for a fireplace in his house, The Hill, near Witley, Surrey. The pictorial tiles were by Burne-Jones and the Swan pattern surround was by Philip Webb.*

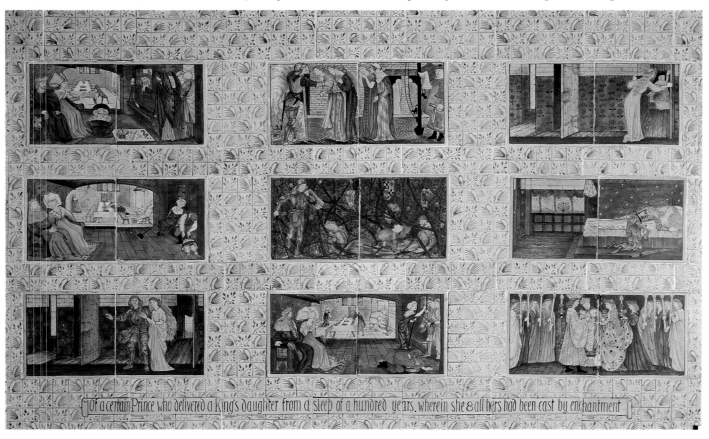

92. *Ford Madox Brown*, THE DEATH OF SIR TRISTRAM, *1862.*
Brilliantly coloured and radically simple in design, stained glass was
the most lucrative and successful of the products first manufactured by
the firm. This example was one of thirteen panels, illustrating the story
of Tristram and Isoud, commissioned for the decoration of the entrance
hall at Harden Grange, West Yorkshire.

93. (*opposite*) THE GREEN DINING-ROOM AT THE SOUTH
KENSINGTON MUSEUM, *1867. The most important of the firm's early*
commissions, the decorations for this interior were largely devised by
Philip Webb, who provided the moulded foliage pattern and the frieze
of running hares. The green colour of the panelling was particularly
influential and E. W. Godwin was one of many Aesthetic architects
and designers whose ideas for painted woodwork were derived from this
scheme.

Morris & Co.'s tiles from 1872, but prior to this date, a number of quaint pictorial panels, like the Sleeping Beauty decoration, designed in 1862 for Birket Foster's house, The Hill, were produced at Red Lion Square.

Initially, however, much of the firm's work was produced not for the domestic market but for the Church, and consisted mainly of stained glass. With hindsight it is easy to see why this should have been the case. The mid-nineteenth century had witnessed an enormous growth in church building. Between 1840 and 1876, the Anglicans alone erected 1,727 new churches in England and Wales and rebuilt or extensively restored a further 7,144. Many of these were built in the Gothic style which was particularly well-suited to elaborate embellishment and this, coupled with the growing influence of the High Church Movement, with its emphasis on liturgy and ritual, led to a greatly increased demand for church furnishings and decorations. In addition, several of the artists associated with the firm had already had considerable experience of designing for stained glass: Rossetti had been working for Powell & Sons of Whitefriars since the 1850s, and in 1856/7 he introduced Ford Madox Brown and Burne-Jones, who designed for them until 1861. This combination of factors – rapid market growth and knowledge of the medium – made it perhaps inevitable that the firm should specialize in this field, and stained glass remained an important area of its work until the late 1860s.

The earliest commissions came from architect friends, such as G. F. Bodley, and the firm provided windows for his churches of St Michael and All Angels, Brighton (1861), St Martin's, Scarborough (1861–2), All Saints, Selsey (1862), and All Saints, Cambridge (1866). During the late 1860s, however, these ecclesiastical commissions began to be supplemented with orders for secular work, and by the end of the decade the firm was supplying more windows for houses than for churches.

Many Victorians were fascinated by glass, the price of which fell throughout the century with the lowering of excise duties and as manufacturing techniques improved. The attractions of stained glass, moreover, were considerable. Firstly, it let in light while retaining an element of privacy and secondly, the designs could be as elaborate as cost, if not good taste, would allow. It became especially favoured in red-brick Queen Anne homes, and by the end of the century examples of stained or transfer-printed glass could be found in almost every English and American artistic interior worthy of the name.

Morris & Co.'s contribution to this fashion consisted of both small decorative panels and large window schemes. The Long Gallery at the Red House had

contained leaded windows decorated with lively bird and flower designs by Philip Webb, and Morris himself was responsible for the minstrel figures used in the windows of the dining-room at The Grange. These figures were sometimes given wings and hung in churches, but small decorative roundels like the Penelope panel, purchased by the South Kensington Museum in 1864, were produced exclusively for domestic use. Among the more elaborate schemes was a series of windows made in 1862 for the Yorkshire home of the Bradford industrialist Walter Dunlop, called Harden Grange.

This commission comprised thirteen panels illustrating the story of Tristram and Isoud, and the designs represented a collaborative effort on the part of Rossetti, Brown, Morris and Burne-Jones. Stylistically, they owed much to the influence of the historian, Charles Winston, whose authoritative book *Ancient Glass* had advocated a return to medieval methods of manufacture and design. Up until the 1850s, the dominant fashion had been for complex, illusionistic subjects, incorporating painterly devices such as gradations of tone, perspective and depth. Winston, however, advised what he termed the mosaic system of glass painting, where the figures were boldly defined by the leading and where the design was built up from large areas of pure colour with the minimum of stippling and shading. Morris, who was responsible for the selection of quarries and the fixing of lead lines, also emphasized the importance of

94. (*above*) *Ford Madox Brown*, SUITE OF BEDROOM FURNITURE IN STAINED DEAL, *1861–2. Like much of Brown's "artisan" furniture, this suite was stained green, a practice that was widely copied in Art furnishings of the 1870s and later. Taylor, however, complained of its impracticality, observing, "A glass of hot brandy and water, if slightly upset, produces an ugly ring on an ordinary French polished mahogany table . . . On our stained furniture, these marks become much more offensive – the stain comes off, re-polish or not, the mark remains."*

95. (*opposite*) *Morris & Co.*, BUFFET IN MAHOGANY AND SATINWOOD, *c.1899. Much late Morris & Co. furniture reflects the popularity of revivalist styles during the last decades of the century and was produced in fashionable woods such as rosewood and mahogany. Both the shape and finish of this example were inspired by Sheraton originals but the Art Nouveau-style pewter hinges, handles and ornament provide a more contemporary note.*

preserving the contrast between the "absolute blackness of outline and the translucency of colour", and, building on Winston's work, he described "the basic components of good glass painting . . . as well-balanced and shapely figures, pure and simple drawing, and a minimum of light and shade".

Clarity of design and brilliance of colour were therefore the keynotes of the firm's work, and even in the 1870s, when their glass became more obviously pictorial, it never completely lost the qualities of simplicity and conventionalization that had earlier distinguished it from other commercial work.

Morris & Co. Furniture

Stained glass was one of the main exhibits at the 1862 Mediaeval Court where Morris & Co. made its first public appearance: the other was furniture, and the exhibition provides an interesting record of how the painted chests and cabinets, of the kind used at the Red House, were originally received.

Painted furniture was not an entirely new phenomenon in 1862, and the Mediaeval Court also included other examples by the architects William Burges and William Butterfield. Burges's Yatman cabinet (1858), drew much attention and was highly acclaimed. However, whereas Burges' pieces were sophisticated architectural fantasies of which the painted stories were an integral part, Morris & Co.'s designs consisted of basic rectangular shapes that simply provided an easel for Pre-Raphaelite paintings. The subjects of the decorations bore no relation to the function of the objects for which they were made, and the furniture itself was crude and unevenly constructed. Critical reactions were predictably, therefore, quite mixed, and many observers objected to the deliberate archaisms evident in much of the firm's work. The *Building News* was especially scathing and declared the exhibits to be:

The most thoroughly medieval of any in the Court, they are consequently the most useless . . . their hangings, their music-stand, their sofa, their chests, would all suit a family which might suddenly be awakened after a sleep of four centuries, and which was content to pay enormous prices suitably to furnish a barn . . . they are no more adapted to the wants of living men than medieval armour would be to modern warfare, middle-aged cookery to civic feasts, or Norman oaths to an English lady's drawing room. They would all be very well as curiosities in a museum, but they are fit for nothing else.

Fortunately for Morris, more sympathetic views prevailed and the company was awarded two gold medals, and in the region of £130 worth of goods was sold.

Despite this "success", painted furniture proved to be a passing phase in Morris & Co.'s development, and ironically, with the dismantling of the Mediaeval Court, the intensely medieval phase of its work also drew to a close. There was a lingering demand for decorated cabinets and hand-made goods but, for the most part, the furniture of the mid-1860s and later followed a simpler and more economical style of design.

This trend is exemplified in the range of turned wood and rush-seated Sussex chairs, developed *c*.1865, which epitomize the "simple, honest furnishings" with which the firm is now most closely associated. The prototype for this range was the country version of a "Sheraton Fancy chair", discovered by Warrington Taylor in the workshop of a Sussex carpenter. Taylor, who was the firm's business manager from 1865 to 1870, had wanted Morris to produce "chairs you can pull about with one hand", and the light and delicate construction of the Sussex range contributed much to its appeal. Sir Robert Edis, author of the influential *Decoration and Furniture of the Town House*, praised the armchair as "comfortable for use, pleasant to look at and cheap in price" and declared

96. *Philip Webb*, ADJUSTABLE CHAIR IN EBONIZED WOOD, c.*1867.*
*Like the Sussex range, the design for this chair was adapted from a
prototype discovered by Warrington Taylor in the workshop of "an old
carpenter at Hurst Monceau". It was widely acclaimed as a major
breakthrough in "design for use" but in fact, Webb has simply taken the
idea of the traditional neo-Georgian easy chair with inclined seats and
added bobbin-turned stretchers.*

it to be "fitted for almost any room". At least four
versions of the original design were made – two designed by Webb, one by Rossetti and one by Madox
Brown – and, selling for between 10 *s.* and 30 *s.* each,
they remained in almost constant production until the
company went into liquidation in 1940.

Ford Madox Brown was a key figure in the production of more of this simple wooden furniture. The
oldest and most experienced of the artists working for
the firm, he had been designing furniture since the
mid-1850s. His earliest pieces were made by Charles
Seddon & Co. and Hueffer, his biographer, recalled:
"his designs forecast those that the 'Firm' afterwards
gave to the world. Adaptation to need, solidity, a kind of
homely beauty and above all absolute dissociation from
all false display, veneering and the like; these things
Madox Brown had in his mind." His designs for Morris
& Co. included eight different chairs, four tables, a
piano and several bookcases and couches – all
carpenter-, as opposed to cabinet-made, and mostly
decorated with green stain, an innovation that proved
somewhat impractical in articles intended for domestic
use. Morris & Co. also produced several pieces that
Brown designed for his own use, including a bedroom
suite comprising wash-stand, dressing-table, bed and
towel rail. The design of these furnishings, in particular,
came closest to Morris's ideal of "good citizen's furniture, solid and well-made in workmanship" with "nothing about it that is not easily defensible, no monstrosi-
ties or extravagances, not even of beauty lest we weary
of it", and an example of the bedroom suite was used in
one of the bedrooms at Kelmscott Manor, Oxfordshire.

Brown himself described his furniture as suitable for
workmen. A socialist like Morris, he declared "what was

good enough for artisans was fit for his own use", and in
an attempt, perhaps, to underline this point, he later
produced similar items for a "model artisan's dwelling"
shown at the Manchester Jubilee Exhibition of 1887.
Precisely how popular these pieces were with workmen,
however, is open to debate. There is no evidence to
suggest either that artisans could afford to purchase
Brown's work or, indeed, that it appealed to their tastes.
Thus, like much of the firm's joiner-made furniture, his
designs proved far more influential within Arts and
Crafts interiors of the early twentieth century than in
workmen's homes, and his wash-stand of 1886 directly
inspired Ambrose Heal's innovative range of "Simple
Bedroom Furniture" of 1899.

With the dissolution of the original partnership and
the reorganization of Morris, Marshall, Faulkner & Co.
as Morris & Co. in 1875, Brown parted company with
Morris. The two quarelled over the remuneration that
Brown should receive for his shareholding, and he
never again worked directly with the firm. Philip Webb's
association, by contrast, was much more long-lasting and
in addition to assisting with the manufacture of tiles and
stained glass, he contributed pictorial elements to some
of the firm's wallpapers and textiles, and produced
designs for the early metalwork, jewellery and table-
glass. Webb also supervised many of the company's
larger interior schemes, including the prestigious orders
received in 1866/7 for the decoration of the Armoury
and Tapestry rooms at St James's Palace and the Green
dining-room at the South Kensington Museum, which
represented their only commissions for public work. His
most significant contribution, however, lay in his designs
for furniture, which were not only extremely varied, but
also much acclaimed.

Webb's early furniture falls into two distinct categories: sturdy tables and chests made from traditional
materials such as oak, and richly decorated sideboards
and cabinets executed in stained or ebonized woods.
The first owed much to the massive thirteenth-century
Gothic style popularized by medievalists such as William
Butterfield, and, having worked for many years as an
architect, Webb was always more closely in touch with
contemporary trends in neo-Gothic design than other
members of the firm. The second represented the more
costly side of the firm's work. In the same lecture where
he had first mentioned "good citizens' furniture", Morris also described "what I call state furniture, by which I
mean sideboards, cabinets and the like which we have
quite as much for Beauty's sake as for use", and he
continued, "we need not spare ornament on these, but
may make them as elegant and as elaborate as we can by
carving, inlaying, or painting, these are the blossoms of
the art of furniture". Within this category can be included the ebonized and painted settles produced by
Webb between 1861 and 1865, examples of which were
used at Kelmscott House, Hammersmith and Old Swan
House, Chelsea. The basic form of this design derived
from the canopied furniture, usually beds, chairs and
thrones, that appears in the illustrations of fourteenth-
and fifteenth-century manuscripts which Morris had
undoubtedly drawn to Webb's attention during the late
1850s. Webb elaborated these quaint historic prototypes

and, with the addition of gilded and embossed leather panels, made them more elegant and appropriate to contemporary tastes. Morris's admiration for these ornate and sumptuously decorated pieces may seem somewhat inconsistent with his interest in furniture that was simply made and functional in style. However, he always considered Webb's sideboards and settles to be not so much objects of utility as works of art, and this distinction explains his willingness to stock examples that, in comparison with the Sussex range, were both costly and of limited appeal.

Webb's other furniture, produced during the 1870s, was more practical and economical. It comprised a number of undecorated mahogany tables, cabinets and chairs whose elegant, attenuated forms illustrate a progression to a lighter and more refined style of design. These proved far more commercial than the massive settles and painted cabinets of the previous decade and many appear in late Morris & Co. interiors, such as Great Tangley Manor in Surrey, and Standen in Sussex.

During the 1880s, Webb became increasingly occupied with architectural commissions, and the design of Morris & Co.'s furniture was largely taken over by his assistant, the American-born designer, George Jack,

97. *William Morris*, EVENLODE, *printed textile, 1883. One of many textiles produced using the indigo-discharge method of printing. As well as indigo, which produced shades of blue, the other dyes employed were madder and weld, providing additional shades of yellow, green, red, brown, orange and purple.*

with additional help from Mervyn Macartney and the metalworker W. A. S. Benson. About the same time (1887), the firm acquired the workshops of Holland and Sons in Pimlico, and much of their work following this move was cabinet-made in fashionable materials such as rosewood and mahogany, and featured elaborate marquetry ornament and inlay. Jack and Macartney favoured revivalist styles, and although certain of their pieces adapted eighteenth-century forms in a novel and contemporary manner, the majority were straightforward reworkings of Chippendale and Sheraton designs. The work produced by W. A. S. Benson was more original, but by the early 1900s the company was advertising "some of the best forms of the Chippendale and Queen Anne period, especially in regard to carved drawing room and dining room chairs". Shortly afterwards it began stocking antiques.

To some extent this change of direction was determined by the vogue for neo-Georgian furniture that came to dominate interiors of the 1890s and after, and it should not necessarily be regarded as a retrogressive trend. Hermann Muthesius, for example, considered the firm's main contribution to nineteenth-century furniture as being to bring Chippendale and Sheraton "back into fashion", and to many observers the revivalist pieces were amongst the most attractive and finely made of their designs. To modern eyes, however, the furniture of the late nineteenth and early twentieth centuries, much of it barely distinguishable from that of other commercial firms, represents a disappointing development, and in comparison with the more original contributions of Webb and Brown, the later work of Morris & Co. appears conservative and conventional.

Textiles and Wallpapers

The decade 1865–75 saw the dramatic transformation of the firm from a small amateur association of independent artists and architects to a large professionally organized business employing upwards of fifty staff. The emphasis on craft activities disappeared and by the late 1870s, the company, now under Morris's sole control, had expanded into workshops at Queen's Square and Ormond Yard. It was also producing a wide range of commercially manufactured goods that were sold through its retail showrooms, opened in 1877 and situated in London's fashionable Oxford Street.

The first of these new products was wallpaper, which was sold by the firm from 1864. Initially, Morris had tried to print his patterns himself using zinc-etched plates and transparent colours but the results proved unsatisfactory, and the work was handed over to the manufacturers, Jeffrey & Co. of Islington, who block-printed all the firm's subsequent designs. Wallpapers were followed by chintzes in 1875, and in 1876 Morris began designing patterns for silk brocades. The first of these were woven on power-looms by M. C. Macrea of Halifax, but in 1877 a hand-operated Jacquard loom was installed at Ormond Yard. Monsieur Bazin, a silk-weaver from Lyon, was employed to help set up the loom, and with additional assistance from a retired Spitalfields weaver, the production of furnishing silks

98. *William Morris,* TRELLIS, *Wallpaper, 1864. Lecturing on pattern in 1881 Morris declared: "any decoration is futile . . . when it does not remind you of something beyond itself." His own designs were often inspired by nature and the idea for Trellis was suggested by the rose-trellis in the garden at the Red House. Philip Webb designed the birds and the wallpaper was used in the morning-room corridor at Standen.*

---

was ready for commencement at the end of 1878. The company's weaving operations were always fairly limited, though, and the heavier damasks and woollen cloths continued to be woven by outside firms.

It is one of the most common misconceptions about Morris that he was implacably opposed to machine production of any kind. Nothing could have been further from the truth, and when he first became interested in weaving he lamented the lack of capital which prevented him from buying his own power-loom. What he did object to, however, was the effect that machines had on working men's lives, the conditions in nineteenth-century factories and the poor results that inevitably ensued with cheaper mass-produced designs. But, where methods of machine production differed little from those of hand-produced work, and where no obvious deterioration in quality was involved, he was happy to employ modern manufacturing techniques and did so on several occasions in the production of textiles and carpets.

Stylistically, Morris & Co.'s wallpapers and textiles were extremely diverse, but the dominant note in both was one of controlled, yet luxuriant naturalism. Large formalized floral and foliate motifs combined with bold, meandering stems in patterns that were brightly coloured and realistically drawn. The realism of the designs, in particular, contrasted sharply with the severely conventionalized style employed by designers such as Owen Jones, but colour also played an important role in

distinguishing the company's patterns from other contemporary work. Morris's dislike of what he termed the "crude, inharmonious and over-bright" tones popularized in the mid-century through the use of chemical aniline dyes, led him to experiment with natural vegetable dyes. In 1881, these experiments culminated in the revival of the obsolete art of indigo-discharge printing, which was carried out at the firm's new Merton Abbey works, situated near Wimbledon on the River Wandle. This technique involved bleaching out the design from cloth previously submerged in a vat of indigo, then repeating the process for other colours as they were required. It was laborious and time-consuming but produced much deeper and less fugitive hues, and the distinctive palette of rich reds, blues and greens that emerged was as different from the dull tertiary tones admired by Aesthetes as it was from the harsh, garish colours that had been favoured earlier.

It is not merely the appearance of Morris & Co.'s work that concerns us here, however, but also the application of the designs, and Morris was unusual in having extremely decided and innovative views on this subject. Chintzes, for example, were to be used for curtaining, loose covers and upholstery and he advocated combining several different patterns in the same room. In this way, they would provide the high-points of contrasting colour that he claimed were essential in a harmonious decorative scheme, and Morris's inclusion of these fabrics in almost all his major interiors led to their becoming as important as woven textiles and they were never again classified as for summer use only.

The choice of wallpapers was to be determined by the character and function of the room. Thus, "if there is a reason for keeping the wall quiet," Morris suggested "choose a pattern that works well all over without pronounced lines, such as Diapers, Mallows, Venetians, Poppys, Scrolls, Jasmine etc.," and "if you venture on a more decided patterning . . . you ought always to go for positive patterns . . . the Daisy, Trellis, Vine, Chrysanthemum, . . . Acanthus or such." The exacting nature of these recommendations is somewhat surprising, for despite the fact that Morris designed over fifty patterns for wallpapers, and a further forty-nine were eventually produced by the firm, he always regarded them as something of a "makeshift" decoration, appropriate only when more luxurious materials could not be found. For his own home he preferred the richer effects of woollen hangings such as Bird, which was designed in 1876 for the walls of his drawing-room at Kelmscott House in Hammersmith, and in 1883 his advice to American clients at the Boston Fair was to use "heavy cloths . . . hung from the skirting to within two feet of the ceiling. The cloth hooked to the top rails, and . . . slightly plaited — only just enough modulation of the surface being allowed to just break the pattern here and there". This system of decoration was both attractive and practical, but few of Morris's customers followed his advice and the majority preferred to use silk damasks stretched across battens that were attached to the walls. Morris did not invent this style of decoration, which had originated in the eighteenth century, but his use of it in interiors such as Rounton Grange and Holland Park did much to revive its popularity, and from the 1880s silk wallhangings became a luxurious addition in many Aesthetic homes.

The first designs for carpets appeared in 1875 and were machine-woven by outside firms such as the Royal Wilton Carpet Works and the Heckmondwike Manufacturing Co., Yorkshire. Morris's reservations about the limitations of this technique were overcome by his awareness of the need to produce inexpensive floor-coverings of artistic design. He had earlier demonstrated his commitment to this idea with a design for linoleum, a cheap and hygienic type of floor-covering that was used extensively during the second half of the nineteenth century, and selling for around 5 s. a square yard the machine-woven carpets were well within the reach of a middle-class clientele. Their appearance differed from those of other manufacturers in two important respects. Firstly, they were made in large rectangles or squares with wide borders, and were loose-fitting rather than fitted to the skirting. Secondly, their patterns were uncompromisingly two-dimensional. Morris had a particular dislike of the cabbage-rose and scrollwork designs popularized in the mid-century and, like other reformers of domestic design, he argued that the illusionism of these motifs was both inappropriate and visually disturbing on a flat and solid surface like a floor. His own patterns, therefore, employed a range of small formalized and unshaded leaf forms, and in examples such as the Wilton carpet used in the sitting-room at Standen, the decorative nature of the design is enhanced by the use of emphatic regular repeats.

In the winter of 1879 Morris began experimenting with small hand-knotted rugs, and shortly afterwards looms for weaving larger designs were erected in the coach-house at Kelmscott House. A circular issued by the firm in the 1880s declared them "as an attempt to make England independent of the East for carpets which may claim to be considered as works of art", and their designs are far more flamboyant than those of the machine-woven work.

Oriental rugs had become increasingly popular in the 1860s and 1870s. Charles Eastlake had praised their harmonious colouring and stylized irregularity in his *Hints on Household Taste*, and he advised his readers to "choose the humblest type of Turkey carpet or the cheapest hearthrug from Scinde and be sure they will afford you more lasting eye-pleasure than any English imitation". However, many of the rugs being imported into Europe in the mid-century were of an inferior quality, utilizing garish colours and crudely executed designs, and Morris's interest was in historic carpets rather than modern work. He had begun purchasing oriental rugs in the early 1860s and the floors at the Red House were apparently strewn with coverings of this kind. By the 1870s he had built up a substantial collection of Middle Eastern designs and he was widely considered to be an expert in this field. He was frequently called upon to advise upon the acquisition of antique carpets by the South Kensington Museum, and many of the designs for Hammersmith rugs reflect the influence of the examples that he had studied there. The palmette border on the large Old Swan House

99. (*below*) *William Morris*, "BULLERSWOOD" CARPET, *1889. Woven for the drawing-room of the Sanderson family's home Bullerswood, near Chislehurst, Kent, this was the last of Morris's designs for hand-knotted Hammersmith carpets. It measures 24 feet 3 inches × 12 feet 10 inches and was the most expensive that the firm produced.*

carpet, for instance, was copied directly from a Persian original, while the large medallions found in examples such as the McCulloch carpet, designed in 1900 by John Henry Dearle for 184 Queen's Gate, clearly derive from Middle Eastern prototypes.

With the production of floor-coverings, textiles and wallpapers, Morris & Co were able to provide a complete range of goods for the decoration and embellishment of the home and it is arguably with these, rather than with its more costly furniture and glass, that the firm made its most significant and lasting impact on nineteenth-century taste. They were used in large numbers by the more fashion-conscious members of the affluent middle class, and, much admired by exponents of modern design, Morris patterns were collected by museums and connoisseurs abroad. Textiles, for exam-

ple, were stocked by Samuel Bing's Maison de l'Art Nouveau in Paris, and were sold by Cowtan & Tout Inc. of Madison Avenue, New York, who were the firm's main retail agents in the United States. Other agents located in Berlin (Hirchwald), Frankfurt (Walther), Melbourne and Philadelphia (Woodville & Co.) also helped to publicize the Morris style, and by the early 1900s the firm's name had become internationally renowned for originality and artistry in design. However, it was with their wallpapers that the company reached its largest market. Selling for between 4 *s.* and 16 *s.* a roll, their prices compared favourably with those of other hand-printed work, and as early as the 1860s critics had praised them as "not only luxurious in effect, but of high artistic excellence". Their use of naturalistic motifs in patterns that were nevertheless formalized and "correct" appealed particularly to progressive intellectual tastes and the *Daily Telegraph* described them as a great favourite with university dons, "whose wives religiously clothed their walls in Norham Gardens and Bradmore Road [Oxford] with Morrisonian designs of clustering pomegranates". Their popularity within Aesthetic circles was even more pronounced, and the profusion of Morris & Co. wallpapers to be seen in Norman Shaw's artistic colony at Bedford Park was deemed by Moncure Conway to be "so serious that a branch of the Blooms-

100. (*above*) THE GREAT PARLOUR AT WIGHTWICK MANOR, STAFFORDSHIRE. *The interiors of this half-timbered neo-Tudor house were designed in a rich but comfortable manorial style and included much fine carved panelling. John Henry Dearle's woven textile, Diagonal Trail, covered the walls, and examples of the firm's chintzes were used on the seating.*

101. (*opposite*) THE MORNING-ROOM AT STANDEN, SUSSEX. *Built by Webb between 1892 and 1894 for the solicitor James Beale, Standen is the most complete of any surviving Morris & Co. interior and illustrates how the firm's furnishings and decorations were intended to be used. The morning-room shows Morris's innovative practice of draping printed cottons – in this case the Daffodil chintz – from the picture-rail to the skirting. The table is by Webb and the seats are upholstered in the Strawberry Thief.*

bury establishment will probably soon become necessary in the vicinity".

Today, many of the patterns are still in production and time has not dimmed the freshness and individuality of the designs. They prove equally effective in urban terraces as in rustic or suburban homes, and for most historians of taste they have become synonymous not simply with the best of Morris's work, but also with all that is most appealing and distinctive about Victorian design.

Morris & Co. Interiors

Morris's approach to house furnishing was summarized in his much-quoted dictum, "have nothing in your house that you do not know to be useful or believe to be beautiful", and his guiding principle when furnishing a room was to consider utility and function along with comfort and taste. He had a particular horror of the clutter and ostentation characteristic of many affluent Victorian interiors and his lectures include frequent attacks on the acquisitiveness of the rich. "I have never been in a rich man's home which would not have looked better for having a bonfire made outside of nine-tenths of all it held", he wrote in 1882, and he warned that "by the accumulation of useless things not only are beautiful things kept out, but the very sense of beauty is perpetually dulled and ground away". Furnishings, therefore, were to be kept to the minimum dictated by the client's needs, and with typical understatement he defined these

as a cupboard for books, a table sturdy enough to work at, a few comfortable chairs, a couch to lie on and a fireplace to keep warm.

To some extent his own homes reflect this functional approach. Kelmscott Manor, the seventeenth-century house that he rented with Rossetti from 1871, contained relatively little furniture and, with the exception of the fine seventeenth-century tapestries that he acquired with the house, the majority of the contents were either second-hand, or fairly commonplace antiques. Similarly, Kelmscott House, Morris's London home, was decorated in his favourite "homely" medieval style and included a few choice examples of the firm's art furniture but none of the knick-knacks and extraneous ornaments so beloved of contemporary taste. By Modernist standards, the drawing-room appears anything but sparse, but in comparison to interiors described by one authority as "a multitude of small tables, chairs, palm-stands and other articles, so disposed as to leave but narrow lanes through which one must thread one's way gingerly and warily", it was a model of artfully contrived restraint.

Few of the company's patrons warmed to these notions of restraint and, to be fair, Morris did not often attempt to impose his own strong preferences on their tastes. The majority of those employing the services of the decorating department were rich and cultivated and desired interiors that would reflect their status, sensibilities and wealth. For them, the appeal of the firm's work lay not in its potential simplicity but in the opulence and uniqueness of its more extravagant goods. Ironically,

102. (*above*) THE DINING-ROOM AT 1 PALACE GREEN, *1892.*
Decorated for George Howard, 9th Earl of Carlisle, between 1872
and 1876. The frieze, illustrating the story of Cupid and Psyche, was
designed by Burne-Jones, the painted foliage and ornament on the
panelling was devised by Morris and the fireplace was designed by
Philip Webb.

103. (*opposite*) THE DRAWING-ROOM AT KELMSCOTT HOUSE,
HAMMERSMITH, C.*1900. Morris's London home contained many*
items of furniture and fabrics made by the firm and this room includes
the Prioress's Tale wardrobe and Webb's settle from the Red House,
Morris chairs and the Birds woven textile on the wall. Helena Maria
Sickert described it as "a most harmonious and peaceful house . . . most
exquisitely kept . . . the beautiful blue tapestry hangings all around the
big living room . . . looked as if they had just been hung up . . . the
atmosphere was deliciously homely."

therefore, the typical Morris & Co. interior was characterized not by simple Sussex furniture and cheap cotton prints but by a profusion of rich texture and colourful pattern achieved through the use of expensive painted decoration and costly hand-made fabrics, furnishings and rugs. The following paragraphs review a few of the more famous examples of the firm's work and begin with the first of the company's large domestic commissions, begun in 1872, in Palace Green.

No. 1 Palace Green was built by Philip Webb and was the London home of George Howard, later 9th Earl of Carlisle. Howard, who was a talented artist and connoisseur, had already met Morris prior to 1872, but it was probably at Webb's suggestion that the firm was called in and their work on the interiors spanned a period of about ten years. They provided many of the textiles – the St James' silk, for example, was hung on the drawing-room walls – and several items of furniture including a piano decorated in gesso by Kate Faulkner, which was given pride of place on the landing of the main staircase. Their most notable contribution, however, was the decoration of the dining-room, which contained a large pictorial frieze designed by Burne-Jones and painted foliage and ornament, planned by Morris, on the ceiling and walls. This team effort was one of

several collaborations between Morris and Jones and was often repeated in the production of tapestries and embroideries as well as in other decorative schemes.

The subject for the frieze was based upon Morris's epic poem, "The Earthly Paradise". Burne-Jones had produced a set of illustrations for this work in 1865 but he experienced some difficulty in translating the small-scale compositions for the engravings into large oils and reworked the paintings over a number of years. Exasperated with the delay, Howard finally lost patience with Jones, and in 1875 he called in Walter Crane to complete the scheme. Judging from contemporary photographs, the result was highly successful, and Morris's painted decoration – picked out in gold and red on a vivid peacock blue ground – was especially worthy of note. It echoes the style of work employed in similar projects, such as Peterhouse Combination Rooms, Cambridge, and the bold acanthus leaf motif recurs in many of his wallpaper and textile designs of the same period. Critical estimations of the firm's work were therefore high and a writer in the *Studio* of 1899 enthused:

It would seem a rash statement to affirm of the decoration of any single apartment that it was absolutely the best example of the style it obeyed. Yet if ever it was safe to speak thus unreservedly, it might be concerning the beautiful dining

room at the Earl of Carlisle's house Palace Green, representing as it does the united efforts of Burne-Jones, William Morris and Philip Webb.

The Howards were more circumspect. Rosalind Howard always regarded the house as somewhat impractical for domestic use describing it as "built for parties", with space that should have been used for the sitting-room "sacrificed to a fine arrival staircase. Not very sensible." Nevertheless, the family employed the company again at Castle Howard, Yorkshire, and at Naworth Castle, Cumberland, both of which contain examples of Morris wallpaper and carpet designs.

The work carried out between 1880 and 1888 at 1 Holland Park for the Greek merchant Alexander Ionides was much more extensive, and the house was widely regarded as a showcase for the company's designs. It included Morris & Co. tapestries, wallpapers and painted patterns as well as woven textiles, embroideries and carpets, and the total cost of the decorations and furnishings came to a staggering £2,361! The study, for example, contained a version of the Forest tapestry designed by Morris and Webb in 1887, while a contemporary photograph of the antiquities room illustrates Morris's Carbrook carpet of 1883, the Flower Garden and Oak woven silks, a Morris

embroidered tablecloth and foliage decoration on the ceiling. The opulent mixture of rich textiles, antique furniture and *objets d'art* exemplified affluent Aesthetic taste of the mid-1880s and in 1892, Gleeson White, who described the house as "Epoch-Making", declared that "it represents the first flower of the 'movement' in aesthetic furnishing which has now developed".

Similarly artistic schemes were devised for the interiors at Old Swan House, built by Norman Shaw for Wickham Flower, MP. Flower, like Ionides, was a discerning and knowledgeable patron. He collected blue and white porcelain and bought Pre-Raphaelite art, and his choice of Morris & Co. as decorators was further proof of their popularity within Aesthetic circles during the last quarter of the century. The company was employed from 1881 and their work illustrates the same fondness for a rich accumulation of pattern as was evident at Holland Park. This is especially apparent in the drawing-room, where two vast Hammersmith carpets cover the floor, a flowered silk drapes the walls and additional painted pattern is used on the ceiling and in the window reveals. However, whereas at Holland Park, wallpapers and textiles were combined with careful control to produce a coherent and, on the whole, homogeneous scheme, the juxtaposition of bold con-

104. (*opposite*) THE ANTIQUITIES ROOM AT 1 HOLLAND PARK, *1880s. The total cost of Morris & Co.'s work on this house came to over £2,361 prompting Lewis Foreman Day to remark: "It is far from fullfilling Mr. Morris's ideal of 'Art for the People by the People', and it is a strange inconsistency of fate that he . . . should be so largely engaged in art which is essentially, and must always be, for the very few who have the taste to appreciate it and the purse to pay for it."*

trasting designs at Old Swan House was somewhat overpowering, and the interiors display a tendency towards over-decoration that was evident in other commissions, such as Stanmore Hall.

Stanmore Hall in Middlesex was the last of the interiors executed during Morris's lifetime. It was owned by the industrialist William Knox D'Arcy, who was immensely rich. He had made a fortune from gold-mining in Australia, and on returning to England in 1888 he formed the Anglo-Persian Oil Company, better known today as British Petroleum. Stanmore was clearly intended to reflect its owner's wealth and no expense was spared in making it the epitome of luxury and a showcase for fashionable design. It was built by J. M. Derick in 1847, but in 1889 D'Arcy commissioned the Ipswich architect, Brightwen Binyon, to update and remodel the interiors. Morris & Co. were called in to provide all the decorations.

This was the largest of the firm's commissions, incorporating textiles, woodwork, and painted pattern as well as metalwork and mosaic. It was also the best-known of their interiors; yet Stanmore is a fascinating example of Morris & Co. working without Morris.

During the late 1880s Morris became increasingly preoccupied with political work and much of his time was spent lecturing and travelling to promote the socialist cause. He was also clearly much out of sympathy with the "improvements" that Binyon had made, and he described Stanmore as "such a wretched uncomfortable place! a sham gothic house of fifty years ago now being added to by a young architect of the commercial type — men who are very bad". This, coupled with his obvious dislike of D'Arcy himself, meant that his involvement in the project was marginal and the supervision of the

105. (*below*) THE DRAWING-ROOM AT OLD SWAN HOUSE, CHELSEA, *1880s. Morris's liking for large designs, and a mixture of materials and motifs is exemplified in the combination of highly patterned carpets, textiles and painted decoration that appears in this room. The walls are covered with the St James silk and Utrecht Velvet was used for the upholstery. The piano was decorated in gesso by Kate Faulkner.*

firm's work was largely handled by his assistant, John Henry Dearle.

Dearle had originally been taken on by Morris in 1878 to work in the newly opened shop in Oxford Street. Shortly after, he was transferred to the glass-painters' shop and in 1879, "influenced by the evident intelligence and brightness of the boy", Morris chose him as the first of the company's tapestry-weaving apprentices. Dearle proved remarkably adept at this work and within two years he was training other apprentices and contributing elements to the designs. About 1885 he was made manager of the Merton Abbey Works and on Morris's death he became art director of the firm. His work included innumerable designs for textiles and wallpaper, and although many have since been described as simply imitative of Morris's work, certain of the carpets and woven fabrics, in particular, show his talents to have been both versatile and original. At Stanmore, he was responsible for the distinctive Persian Brocatelle silk used on the walls of the drawing-room, the Golden Bough silk and linen, and a machine-woven carpet called Stanmore. He also planned the decorations in the hall, where every surface from the ceiling to the floor was ablaze with brilliant colour and boldly ornamented pattern designed in his preferred Anglo-Eastern style. Stanmore was not, however, the work of Dearle alone

106. (*above*) THE DRAWING-ROOM AT STANMORE HALL, MIDDLESEX, *1891. A late and particularly ostentatious example of their work, the interiors at Stanmore Hall reflect the taste of the patron rather than those of the firm. The decorations were supervised by Dearle who designed the Persian brocatelle fabric, the carpets and the painted decoration in the drawing-room.*

107. (*opposite*) THE HALL AT STANMORE HALL, MIDDLESEX, *1891. The riot of pattern in the ceiling, walls and floor, is to some extent offset by the simple elegance of W. R. Lethaby's limestone chimneypiece and massive eight-legged hall table. Nevertheless, features like the leopard-skin rug, majolica ewers and French marquetry chair do much to detract from the coherence of the scheme.*

and, with contributions from several other designers associated with the firm, the result was an eclectic and somewhat confusing mixture of styles. W. R. Lethaby, for example, was responsible for the more modern elements within the scheme. He provided five new stone fireplaces and the massive eight-legged table in the hall, whose design looks forward to the simplicity of Arts and Crafts furniture. George Jack's work was more in accord with the opulence of D'Arcy's taste. He designed the Georgian dining-table and chairs and the ornate coffer-shaped writing cabinet, richly inlaid with decoration of rosewood, ebony and holly, that appears in photographs of the drawing-room. The high-point of the decorations, though, was the set of medievally inspired Holy Grail Arras tapestries which hung in the dining-room and were woven by the firm between 1890 and 1894.

For Morris, the production of Arras tapestries represented the fulfilment of a youthful dream. As early as 1854 he had proclaimed his admiration for medieval examples that he had seen hanging in the cathedrals of Amiens and Beauvais, and the embroideries produced for the dining-room at the Red House were an attempt to imitate the appearance, if not the manufacture, of these designs. During the 1850s he also visited the Gobelins tapestry works in France, and in the 1870s he came to know of the work produced by the Royal

Windsor Tapestry Works in England. Both firms, however, were found wanting in terms of the quality of their designs, and in 1877 he began to experiment with compositions of his own. As with all the manufacturing processes with which he was involved, Morris's knowledge of the tapestry medium was gained through a mixture of practical experiment and the study of historical texts. The technique that he employed was that of high warp weaving, where the warp threads are arranged vertically. This method was used in the production of sixteenth- and seventeenth-century tapestries but had long fallen into disuse, and using a loom set up in his bedroom at Kelmscott House, Morris taught himself the basic principles of weaving with the aid of an eighteenth-century French manual. His first panel was a small design nicknamed Cabbage and Vine, but with the move to Merton Abbey he was able to set up large-scale looms along with vats for dyeing wools. The Stanmore tapestries represent the culmination of his efforts in the field. They depict a series of episodes in the Quest for the Holy Grail and their frieze-like format and use of rich *millefleur* ornament echoes the style of the early Flemish examples that he so admired. Comprising six pictorial hangings and additional verdure designs, they were both the largest and the most technically ambitious of the hangings made by the firm.

108. (*above*) *Morris & Co.*, THE KNIGHTS OF THE ROUND TABLE SUMMONED TO THE QUEST BY A STRANGE DAMSEL, *1890–4. One of six Holy Grail tapestries designed for the dining-room at Stanmore Hall. Morris selected the subjects and planned the overall scheme but the designs for the figures were executed by Burne-Jones and the designs for the background and accompanying verdure panels were provided by Dearle.*

In many ways the production of tapestries can also be seen as representing the climax of Morris's career, since they drew together the many different strands evident in his work. These can be summarized as: a love of medieval art, an interest in reviving traditional craft skills, a commitment to producing decorations that were both beautiful and usable, and a desire to improve and educate public taste. In addition they underline the exclusivity of the firm's most artistic work. The production of tapestry was time-consuming and thus expensive and one of Morris & Co.'s early twentieth-century trade cards estimates the price of The Passing of Venus tapestry, whose dimensions were comparable to the largest hanging in the Holy Grail series, as being in the region of £1,700. They were clearly, therefore, beyond the means of all but the company's richest clients.

In 1882, Morris wrote, "on the whole one must suppose that beauty is a marketable quality and the better the work is all round both as a work of art and in its technique the more likely it is to find favour with the public". By 1896 the optimism inherent in these remarks had waned, and Morris died a disillusioned and disappointed man. The mere production of works of beauty had not inevitably led to improvements in taste and by the end of his life he had come to regard the widespread enjoyment of art as impossible within a capitalist society. Also, he increasingly perceived his own efforts as wasted in "ministering to the swinish luxury of the rich". This assessment of his achievements is unjustly severe. It is true that Morris did not revitalize interior decoration from its roots, but his influence upon the late nineteenth-century artistic home was unsurpassed. Moreover, with their wallpapers and textiles the company not only produced a range of genuinely affordable artistic goods but also helped to reform the appearance and quality of many of the machine-made goods that Morris professed to despise.

109. (*opposite*) *Morris & Co.* LITHOGRAPH OF AN INTERIOR, *c.1900. During the twentieth century much of the work produced by Morris & Co. appeared increasingly conservative but in the years immediately following Morris's death certain of the furnishings maintained their reputation for contemporaneity. The dining table illustrated here is a case in point and was designed by W. A. S. Benson; the chairs, however, are more conventional and derive from Georgian prototypes.*

THE AESTHETIC MOVEMENT

*A newly-created atmosphere of home beauty now exists which is absolutely a
revelation and a source of such positive and intense happiness that it cannot be
ignored by any human being with a capacity beyond that of a mere rustic
clod-hopper and untutored savage.*
(Journal of Decorative Art, *1886)*

URING THE 1870s critics became increasingly aware
of evidence for what they termed "Art within the
Home". At first this trend was noticeable only in the
houses of a wealthy and design-conscious few who
commissioned painted decorations and custom-made
furnishings for the embellishment of their homes. By
the 1880s, however, it had become much more widespread, and with the advent of commercially produced
"Art Manufactures", which included Art wallpapers, Art
furniture and Art fabrics, "Art" became a commodity
available to a far broader range of homes. Coinciding
with this development went a heightening of public
interest in all aspects of interior design, and furniture
and decoration became subjects much discussed in contemporary journals and magazines. So intense and
pervasive did this interest become that a concern with
the appearance of the interior was almost universal
within fashionable circles and by the end of the century
writers like the one above were pleased to note that the
"Home Beautiful", as it was called, had become a
compelling ideal to which many people of taste and
education aspired.

The origins of the "Art at Home" movement lay in the
wave of Aestheticism that swept through Europe and
America during the third quarter of the nineteenth-
century, whose influence left few areas of the fine and
decorative arts untouched. In England, Aestheticism

emerged firstly in the fine arts and arose initially as a
reaction to the sentimentality and fake historicism of
mid-Victorian narrative and neo-classical art. Its adherents rejected the notion that art should have a social,
moral or even political purpose and in its place they
propounded the view that beauty was as much the
product of the formal qualities of painting as of its
content or ideas. Whistler's famous libel action against
Ruskin in 1878 was an impassioned defence of this view
and it became a *cause célèbre* for the Aesthetic Movement
as a whole.

Within the decorative arts Aestheticism was both
more nebulous and more broad-based. In its most
undiluted form it represented an attempt on the part of
a small group of artists and architects to check the
excessive ornamentation and rampant eclecticism of
contemporary styles. In this sense, the Aesthetic Movement can be seen as a continuation of the spirit of
reform that was evident in the mid-century, but whereas
the Gothic Revival had fostered "correct principles" and
an admiration of medieval forms, the most committed
exponents of Aestheticism drew upon many periods and
emphasized purity of form, elegance of line and the
application of art to all aspects of decoration and design.

In practice, however, Aestheticism was always more
an attitude of mind than a set of precepts or styles, and
as the Movement gained momentum the term "Aesthetic" was applied almost indiscriminately to anything that
was fashionable or new. Aesthetic furniture, Aesthetic
book illustration and Aesthetic dress were but a few
examples of the ways in which the term was used and
one enterprising retailer even advertised "Aesthetic
Mixed Seeds for Cage Birds"! Nevertheless, for those
more devoted disciples of the Movement, who congre-
gated in fashionable areas of London, such as "passion-

---

110. *Kate Hayllar,* SUNFLOWERS AND HOLLYHOCKS, *1889. Shops
such as Liberty's specialized in the sale of imported Japanese goods,
and with comparatively little effort many interiors could be given an
attractively Aesthetic touch through the introduction of accessories such
as Japanese vases and screens. Here, they are combined with a
neo-Jacobean table and Sheraton-style chair and the setting is the
artist's family home near Wallingford in Berkshire.*

ate" Brompton and artistic Bedford Park, Aestheticism meant nothing less than the cultivation of beauty in every area of life. For them, beauty could reside both in objects of daily use and in works of art, and according to contemporaries much of their time was spent rhapsodizing equally over the artistic qualities of Botticelli and their teapots. Their idols were Rossetti, Burne-Jones and Oscar Wilde, and their rallying cry was "Art for Art's Sake".

Wilde, in particular, made the pursuit of beauty into a veritable crusade and was the most conspicuous apostle of the Aesthetic Movement. He was also its most successful publicist. Having read Walter Pater and studied under Ruskin at Oxford, he came down to London in 1878 and dazzled fashionable society with his eloquent expositions of the new artistic ideas. Like Whistler, he denied that "in its primary aspects painting has any more spiritual message for us than a blue tile from the walls of Damascus or a Hitzen vase. It is a beautifully-coloured surface, nothing more, and affects us by no suggestion stolen from philosophy; no pathos pilfered from literature; no feeling filched from a poet; but by its own incommunicable artistic message", and in his famous remark that one of his greatest difficulties was in living up to his blue and white china, he encapsulated much of the mood and character of the Aesthetic Movement. His influence was considerable. He brought the Aesthetic gospel to America in his much publicized lecture tour of 1882–3, and with his long hair, poetic dress and affected speech, he spawned a generation of earnest and poetic young men for whom art was life

seen through a temperament, and whose reactions to any object of beauty were both exaggeratedly ecstatic and inordinately complex.

Many of the more extreme tendencies of the Aesthetic Movement were widely scorned by the more conservative elements within society and the antics of Wilde and his followers were frequently mocked and satirized in the theatre and in the popular press. *Punch*, for example, ran a series of cartoons representing the fictional family, the Cimabue Browns, which brilliantly parodied the more eccentric enthusiasms and attitudes of this group, while Gilbert and Sullivan's satirical "Aesthetic" opera *Patience* opened to packed houses on both sides of the Atlantic. Despite this mockery, however, Aestheticism was not a trivial or inconsequential concern, and its influence upon the domestic interior was profound, if somewhat short-lived. In its most precise manifestations it offered an alternative mode of decoration to the dominant Gothic or classical styles and fostered a taste for more subtle colours, dark woods and lighter, more angular forms. In more general terms it also effected a radical change in attitudes to interior design. The Aesthetes made art chic and fashionable in a way that it had never been before and their preoccupation with the beautification of the home swept away the last vestiges of uninterest in decoration that had pertained in the previous decades. Finally, in the work of its main exponents – E. W. Godwin, A. L. Liberty, Whistler and Walter Crane – the Movement made an important contribution to the development of modern styles.

This chapter examines the dominant characteristics of the Movement within artistic and commercial design and focuses particularly upon the influence of Japanese art during the 1860s and 1870s.

The Discovery of Japan

Stylistically, Aestheticism was quite diverse, and as its popularity grew it came to embrace a considerable range of disparate styles and forms. In its earliest phase, however, the Movement was dominated by the vogue for Japanese art, which was the most important of the external influences on European and American design during the second half of the nineteenth century. The Aesthetes fetishized blue and white china and swooned over oriental prints, and Westernized versions of Japanese colours, decoration and forms were adopted within almost every area of the decorative arts. Indeed, for a short period during the 1860s and 1870s, Japonisme, as the fashion has been termed, and Aestheticism were virtually synonymous.

The story of how Japanese art first arrived in Europe is well known, and the account of how a number of cheap Hokusai woodcuts were first "discovered" in Paris in 1857 as the packing for oriental china has now become apochryphal. These prints were much admired by artists, and when Madame de Soye's shop, La Porte Chinoise, opened selling ginger jars, blue and white vases and other oriental curios in the following year, it became a favourite meeting place for painters and writers associated with the Parisian avant-garde. The introduction of Japonisme into England was both a more prosaic and a more long-drawn-out affair.

The first complete English exhibition of Japanese art was held at the Old Watercolour Society in Pall Mall in 1854. Prior to that time the culture and customs of the country were almost completely unknown in the West. For over two hundred years Japan had enforced a policy of exclusion, restricting trade to occasional dealings with the Chinese and Dutch, prohibiting foreign access to her ports, and even limiting the building of ships to vessels so small that Japanese seamen could not navigate the open seas. In short, Japan did all she could to isolate herself from the West.

---

114. (*opposite*) THE INTERIOR OF DE VERE GARDENS, KENSINGTON, *1887. By the 1880s, oriental ornaments and accessories had become increasingly fashionable within affluent London drawing-rooms. This interior reflects a particularly enthusiastic appreciation of Japanese designs and probably belonged to a collector. It includes a quantity of Far Eastern artefacts and curios, Japanese matting, open bamboo-work, and lanterns, as well as an elaborate oriental-style painted ceiling.*

115. (*below*) E. W. Godwin, DESIGN FOR A WALL DECORATION AT DROMORE CASTLE, EIRE, C.*1868. The decorations for Dromore Castle represent the earliest example of Japanese influence in Godwin's work and include motifs derived from Japanese prints interspersed with panels of Morris's Trellis wallpaper. This particular design was never executed owing to the incurable dampness of the walls, a fact that prompted Godwin to advise: "When offered a commission in Ireland, refuse it!"*

During the 1840s, however, a series of political and economic crises precipitated a period of social unrest and, weakened by internal struggles, the ruling Tokugawas were no longer able to fend off the expansionist ambitions of the West. In 1853, the American Commodore Perry sailed with a "friendly" force of six men-of-war, armed with 580 officers and men, determined to establish a military and economic foothold in Japan. The first commercial treaties with Britain and America were signed in 1858, and by 1859 a small number of European merchants had settled in Japan. Shortly afterwards, the full-scale commercial colonization of the country began.

Nevertheless, The opening up of Japan's borders did not immediately signal the beginnings of an interest in her culture. Items from the 1854 display were purchased for the Science and Art Departments at the new South Kensington Museum on the recommendations of Redgrave and Cole, but the exhibition as a whole provoked little comment, and there was no suggestion in the contemporary press that it was an event of any great significance. Similarly, although "oriental" roller-printed cottons were being marketed by Daniel Lee of Manchester in 1858, their work represented one of only a very few isolated instances of Japanese-style design and it was not until 1862, when Sir Rutherford Alcock, the first British Minister in Japan, showed a selection of his collection of lacquer, bronze and porcelain at the International Exhibition, that critical attention in England became sharply focused on the art of the Far East. Alcock's display made an enormous impression upon artists and *cognoscenti* of the day, and the origins of the influence of Japanese design on native taste can be

E.491-1963

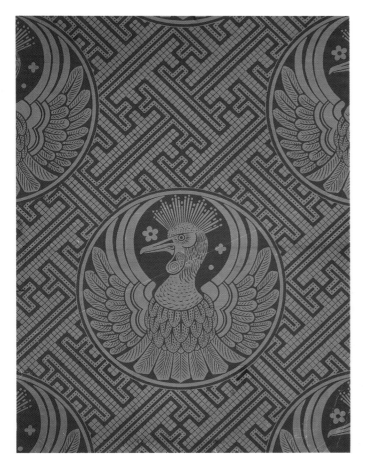

traced almost exclusively to this event. Moreover, what began as a minority interest involving a comparatively small group of painters, architects and connoisseurs, rapidly assumed the proportions of an epidemic until in 1874 *The Cabinet Maker* proclaimed "Fashion has declared for Japanese art", and four years later another authoritative publication observed "there has been such a rage for Japanese design of late that we are tolerably well acquainted with it. From the highest to the lowest, from the Worcester Royal Porcelain Works to Parisian children's fans we have had imitations of Japanese style."

The reasons for this enthusiasm were linked to two distinct, yet related trends within English design. Firstly, Alcock's display occurred at a time when many artists and architects were searching for new forms with which to revitalize design. By the 1860s Gothic had become widely accepted as the officially sanctioned style of the design establishment; but within more progressive circles it was increasingly felt to have run its course, and, in the hands of commercial manufacturers, it was thought to be in danger of becoming as debased as any of the other currently available historical styles. Japanese art, by contrast, appeared not only enticingly exotic but also refreshingly unfamiliar, and its light colours and asymmetrical, yet graceful and elegant forms represented the perfect antidote to the heaviness and overwrought elaboration that characterized both commercial and reformed design.

Secondly, the arrival of Japanese art in England also coincided with a desire on the part of other designers to escape from the complexities and divisions of Victorian society and to return to the simplicity and harmony of a pre-capitalist, pre-industrial age. Originally, this view, as

has been shown in previous chapters, had led to a nostalgia and sympathy with the medieval world. Increasingly, though, it was to inform an appreciation of Japanese art and design. Thus, William Burges, who was one of the first English collectors of oriental prints, made several connections between medieval and oriental art. For him, Japanese art was the product of a primitive, feudal society not dissimilar to that of the Middle Ages, and as such it embodied the same virtues of innocence, and honesty of expression that he so admired in Gothic art. Its forms were therefore to be studied and praised and his review of the 1862 Exhibition, published in the *Building News*, included the comments:

To any student of our reviving arts of the thirteenth century, an hour or even a day or two spent in the Japanese department will by no means be lost time, for these hitherto unknown barbarians appear not only to know all that the middle ages knew but in some respects are beyond them and us as well.

Burges' somewhat superficial linking of two separate and distinctly different decorative styles was clearly based more upon his romanticized notions about the conditions within Japanese society than upon a clear understanding of its art. Nevertheless, such views did much to enhance the appeal of oriental design within informed circles and lent its forms a certain respectability and artistic pedigree.

Where Burges led others followed, and the artists Whistler, Rossetti, Burne-Jones and Frederic Leighton were amongst the many enthusiasts who purchased items from Alcock's collection when it was disposed of after the closure of the exhibition. Rossetti and Whistler, in particular, were strongly attracted by the exoticism of

116. (*opposite, left*) *E. W. Godwin*, PEACOCK, *block-printed wallpaper, 1873. The peacock motif was copied directly from an heraldic crest that appeared in a book of Japanese prints. Originally the pattern was printed on a bright blue ground but the manufacturers, Jeffrey & Co., preferred the more commercially successful, Aesthetic green. Much to his landlady's dismay, Godwin used this wallpaper in the decoration of his London lodgings in the early 1870s.*

117. (*opposite, right*) *E. W. Godwin*, SPARROWS AND BAMBOO, *block-printed wallpaper, 1871–2. It was not only oriental motifs that appealed to designers in the late nineteenth century but also those qualities of spontaneity and naturalism that characterized much Japanese art. The asymmetrical arrangement of figures and forms proved particularly popular and Godwin's design represents an early example of its use within a wallpaper.*

118. (*below*) *E. W. Godwin*, ANGLO-JAPANESE DRAWING-ROOM FURNITURE, *1877. Plate 8 from William Watt's* Catalogue of Art Furniture *illustrating several examples of Godwin's most obviously Japanese-style pieces. The coffee table was an especially popular design. It was illustrated in Rhoda and Agnes Garrett's* Suggestions for House Decoration *and in Harriet Spofforth's* Art Decoration *and was copied by several commercial firms on both sides of the Atlantic.*

Japanese art and their homes, described in the following chapter, were filled with examples of oriental ceramics and ornament. The most important of the early collectors, however, was Edward William Godwin, who was not only a major exponent of Anglo-Japanese styles, but whose pioneering designs for furniture, wallpaper and interior decoration played a leading role in shaping Aesthetic taste in the 1870s and 1880s.

Godwin and Artistic Japan

Born in Bristol in 1833, Godwin was described by Max Beerbohm as "the greatest Aesthete of them all". He combined an interest in antiquarianism and scholarship with a love of literature and plays and, in addition to being a celebrated architect and designer, he was also a successful journalist and authority on artistic dress. A much-liked figure in society, he was the intimate of Whistler and Wilde. His mistress was the famous actress Ellen Terry, and he was at the forefront of advanced taste. His work, moreover, exemplifies the more artistic elements within the Aesthetic Movement and was highly respected both by other designers and within the trade.

He trained firstly as an architect and his earliest commissions for commercial buildings and church schools were executed in a fairly conventional Ruskinian Gothic mode. During the late 1850s, however, he began acquiring oriental china and prints and shortly afterwards he became the first person in England to decorate his home in a Japanese manner. Dudley Habron, his biographer, describes how the walls of his house at 21 Portland Square were covered with plain, pale colours

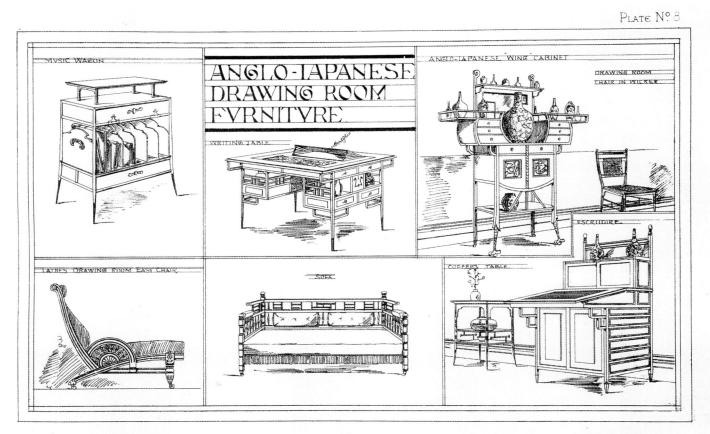

PLATE Nº 8

ART FVRNITVRE WAREHOVSE,
21. GRAFTON STREET. GOWER STREET, LONDON

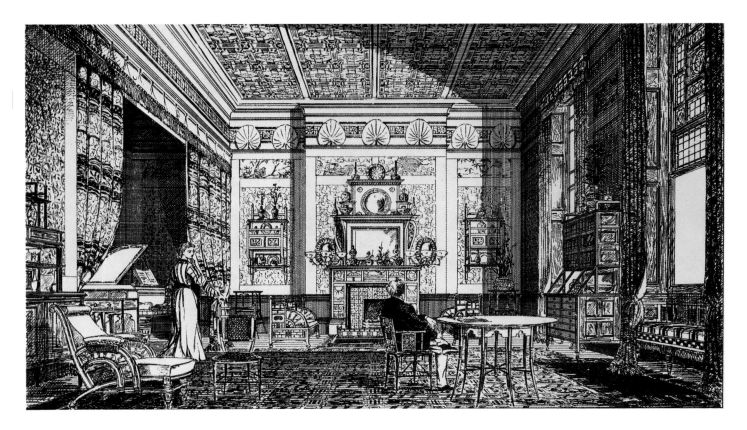

119. *E. W. Godwin*, INTERIOR SCHEME, *1877. Plate 14 from* Art Furniture. *In addition to the Anglo-Japanese furniture Godwin also designed the wallpaper, painted decoration and stained glass for this scheme. While Japanese motifs abound and the furnishings are light and highly rectilinear in appearance, the preponderance of rich pattern covering the ceiling, walls and floor, gives the room an unmistakably Victorian feel.*

and hung with Japanese prints, while his collection of blue and white vases stood on straw matting that covered the floor. His next home, at Fallows Green, Harpenden, was arranged in much the same way, and Habron again records the Aesthetic life-style of the Godwin ménage, where Ellen Terry "wore blue and white cotton and her daughter was dressed in a kimono in which she looked as Japanese as everything that surrounded her".

Japanese art rapidly became not simply a matter of intense personal interest but also a rich source of inspiration in Godwin's work. As early as 1867 he was using oriental colours and forms in his designs for the wall decorations at Dromore Castle, the Earl of Limerick's Irish home, and a scheme for the dining-room includes a frieze of Japanese-style figures and fruit trees interspersed amongst panels of Morris's Trellis wallpaper. Other designs for this commission – notably those for the furniture – illustrate a more eclectic approach, and Godwin was clearly still somewhat divided during this period between his new-found enthusiasm for Japanese art and his earlier commitment to more orthodox Gothic forms. No such confusion appears in his designs of the 1870s, by which time he had evolved a highly personal and original Anglo-Japanese style. This development can be seen most clearly in his designs for wallpaper.

Godwin began designing wallpaper in 1871–2 and many of his papers employ motifs based upon Japanese crests and badges. The Peacock pattern of 1873, for instance, includes medallions containing stylized forms that were copied directly from examples that he had found in a book of oriental prints. The peacock subsequently became a favourite motif with artists associated with the Aesthetic Movement. Its most dramatic application was in the Peacock room, painted by Whistler for F. R. Leyland in 1877, but by the 1880s it could be found adorning a plethora of domestic fittings, ranging from furnishings and fabrics to ornaments and prints. Literally thousands of suburban homes were given a fashionably artistic touch with the introduction of peacock feathers arranged over the mantelpiece or placed in oriental jars on the floor.

Godwin's work, however, involved more than just a superficial grafting of Japanese forms on to essentially Western designs, and his Sparrows and Bamboo pattern of 1872 demonstrates a thorough understanding of the principles underlying oriental art. Like the Peacock, its motifs were adapted from heraldic crests but its style is more naturalistic and its mood altogether more lively and spontaneous than that of its somewhat sombre counterpart. Moreover, the birds are arranged in an ambitiously informal and asymmetrical manner that was typical of Far Eastern art. In time, asymmetry was to become one of the hallmarks of Aestheticism in both the fine and decorative arts but Godwin was the first to employ it within pattern design. This fact did not pass unnoticed by contemporaries and the critic for the *Building News* declared the pattern to be "the only irregular arrangement that we are acquainted with". Moreover, to a generation raised on the strict formality of pattern repeats advocated by the neo-Gothic school, its asymmetry appeared little short of revolutionary and suggested new and exciting possibilities for two-dimensional design.

Even more revolutionary to modern eyes is the Anglo-

Japanese furniture that was produced by Godwin from 1867. Like Morris, Godwin began designing furniture because he could find no commercially produced work that was to his taste, and his earliest pieces, made shortly after he had moved his architectural practice from Bristol to London, were created exclusively for his own use. Inspired by Japanese principles of economy and functional simplicity, he described this work as an attempt to design pieces "by the mere grouping of solid and void and by more or less broken outline". The result was a collection of strikingly simple buffets, tables and chairs, whose highly rectilinear style owed much to the appearance of the domestic fitments and woodwork illustrated in Japanese prints. Each piece was constructed on the basis of an arrangement of straight vertical and horizontal lines, and surface decoration was kept to a minimum with no elaborate carving, ornament or mouldings employed. For reasons of cheapness, the earliest designs were made in deal but all were ebonized in imitation of Japanese work. Later, Godwin's approach to ornament became less severe and the furniture of the 1870s shows a slight move away from the strict vertical and horizontal emphasis. Polished walnut and mahogany sometimes replaced the ebonized finish and occasionally carved boxwood panels, imported from Japan, were introduced. Nevertheless, the early insistence upon economy and simplicity was always maintained and beside the fussy, elaborately decorated furniture produced by commercial firms, Godwin's designs appear remarkably light and restrained.

Throughout the 1860s and 1870s Godwin worked with a number of successful cabinet-making firms, including Collinson & Lock, Gillow's and W. & A. Smee, but it was with William Watt that he forged his most long-lasting and productive relationship. The two began working together in 1867 after the demise of Godwin's short-lived Art Furniture Co. that had been set up to manufacture his private designs. Shortly afterwards, Watt was making the furniture for many of Godwin's interior schemes and over the course of the next decade a wide range of Godwin's designs were sold through the firm's showrooms in Grafton Street. The collaboration between the two men culminated in the publication of the catalogue "Art Furniture designed by Edward W. Godwin FSA and manufactured by William Watt, 21 Grafton Street, London, with hints and suggestions on domestic furniture and decorations", which was issued in 1876. This catalogue illustrates the full range of work with which Godwin was involved and included designs for tables, desks, mantelpieces and armchairs, as well as wallpapers, textiles, toilet sets and pottery. It also illustrates some imaginary views of interiors which showed how these items might be arranged. Plate 14 is particularly interesting, accompanied as it was by the note, "the furniture and decoration throughout have been the result of a study of Japanese form adapted to modern English wants", and underlines the characteristically Western orientation of Anglo-Japanese styles. The light, angular ebonized furniture, hanging wall-cupboards and accessories such as paper fans, are quite authentically Japanese, but, combined with more conventional features such as heavy drapes, richly patterned walls and ceiling, and leaded and stained glass, the interior has an unmistakably Victorian feel.

The fact that Godwin, an architect, should feel equally empowered to produce patterns and furniture as he was to design buildings was entirely in keeping with the Aesthetic Movement's interest in maximizing the artistic potential of the home. Only with the contribution of painters or architects could the objects within an interior be made truly beautiful and harmonious, and the Movement was always one that primarily attracted practitioners whose main specialism was not domestic design. This tendency is exemplified in the Butterfly Suite of 1877, which was also the most influential of the work produced by Godwin for William Watt. Designed as the central feature of the firm's stand at the Paris International Exhibition of 1878, the Suite consisted of a section of an interior and included a cabinet, sofa and chairs, set against walls decorated in pale yellow. It represented a combined effort on the part of Godwin and Whistler, whom Godwin had met in 1863, and with the furniture made in light mahogany to complement the colour of

120. *E. W. Godwin,* THE BUTTERFLY CABINET, *mahogany, 1877–8. Designed by Godwin and decorated by Whistler, this cabinet was the central feature of "The Harmony in Yellow and Gold" exhibited by William Watt at the Paris Exposition Universelle of 1878. Its design is somewhat less severe than those for Godwin's earlier pieces and the broken pediment, in particular, is typical of the Queen Anne style. The oriental cloud motif derives from Whistler's decorations in the Peacock Room.*

the background, the whole ensemble was described as "A Harmony in Yellow and Gold". Godwin designed the furniture and Whistler provided the decoration on the individual pieces and on the walls.

The combination of a painter and an architect was not particularly unusual by this date. Artists such as Henry Stacy Marks and Edward Burne-Jones were regularly employed by commercial firms in painting figures or animals on ebonized cabinets. However, in the majority of cases these decorations were figurative. The Butterfly Suite, by contrast, included semi-abstract devices based upon butterflies and Japanese clouds and, for the first time, the decoration was designed to complement and echo the design of the furniture, not simply to embellish or adorn it. Critical responses were somewhat mixed – one observer described the exhibit as "an agony in yellow and gold" – but on the whole it was well received and it represents one of the most influential and innovative examples of Japanese-inspired design.

Godwin's designs for interior schemes were equally original. He had started working on interior decoration during the 1860s, but it was not until the 1870s that he began devising complete interiors in which he was responsible not only for designing the furniture and

---

121. *James Shoolbred & Co.*, BEDCHAMBER FURNITURE IN THE JAPANESE STYLE, *c.1874. Designed by Owen W. Davies and illustrated in Shoolbred's catalogue from 1874 to at least 1882, this range shows the application of Anglo-Japanese styles to commercially produced furniture. Note the liberal use of oriental surface ornament, and particularly the fondness for painted panels featuring Japanese figures and motifs.*

choosing the wallpapers but also for mixing the paints and selecting the fabrics and ornaments. The keynote of these schemes was an air of spaciousness, simplicity and calm. In a discussion of the requirements of furniture he had remarked, "it is essential for domestic comfort in these high-pressure, nervous times, that the common objects of everyday life should be quiet, simple and unobtrusive in their beauty", and the same principles were brought to bear upon the interior as a whole. The walls and woodwork within his houses were painted subtle shades of yellow, white and grey, the furnishings were light and undecorated, the floors were bare, and the draperies were neither stiff nor festooned but were hung in elegant, loose folds. Such artful economy was almost unheard of in late Victorian rooms, and the radically simple and uncluttered appearance of his interiors is vividly recalled by the actor, Sir Johnston Forbes Robertson, in his description of Godwin's London home:

The floor was covered with straw-coloured matting and there was a dado of the same material. Above the dado were white walls and the hangings were of cretonne with a fine Japanese pattern in delicate grey and blue. The chairs were of wicker with cushions like the hangings and in the centre of the room was a full-sized cast of the Venus de Milo . . .

Godwin died in 1886 at the comparatively young age of 55, but his influence was not inconsiderable. His furniture was admired on both sides of the Atlantic, with copies being produced by the trade, and his interiors were hailed as being in the vanguard of Aesthetic taste. Moreover, his effect upon public taste was thought to be

highly significant and an anonymous obituarist in *The British Architect* observed:

Long before any attempt was made to popularise art, he recognised that houses need not be ugly to be comfortable. We are still, alas! in an age of stucco and bastard art but the little that has been done to beautify our domestic surroundings is mainly due to him.

Godwin was not, however, the only designer concerned with beautifying the home, or with evolving new forms, and before long other leading figures within the design establishment began to produce work in an artistic Japanese style. Christopher Dresser, for example, designed several pieces of furniture whose simplicity of line echoes that to be found in Japanese forms, while Bruce Talbert's wallpapers and textiles adapted a number of oriental motifs. Similarly, Thomas Jeckyll, who is principally remembered as a designer of metalwork, was also responsible for some strikingly authentic Anglo-Japanese interiors.

Jeckyll's first major commission was for the collector, Alexander Ionides, whose house in Holland Park was built by Philip Webb and decorated by Morris & Co. (see previous chapter). Jeckyll designed a sitting-room, a billiard-room, a bedroom and a servants' hall and was also responsible for much of the furniture. The billiard-room was a particularly successful adaptation of oriental forms to European use. The ceiling and walls were covered by a rectilinear system of ebonized oak framing, the cornice, dado and ceiling were made of lacquered Japanese trays, and the openings in the walls were set with Japanese prints and paintings of birds and flowers.

This scheme was the antecedent of the more well-known billiard-room designed for the ship-builder Frederick Leyland in 1877. Now the most famous of Aesthetic interiors, this room was originally intended to provide display space for Leyland's collection of oriental porcelain and a setting for Whistler's painting *The Princesse de la Pays du Porcelain*. However, despite its highly Japanese appearance, the only truly oriental element within the room was the sunflower motif on the cast-iron fire-dogs, and the rest of the decorations represent an ingenious blending of elements from a variety of historical sources. The fan-vaulted ceiling, for example, was an almost exact copy of the Tudor ceiling in the Watching Chamber at Hampton Court, while the walls themselves were lined with antique Spanish leather subsequently overpainted by Whistler with a dramatic arrangement of peacocks and cloud-forms in blue and gold. Nevertheless, the strong vertical emphasis of the ebonized black shelving give the room an extremely oriental feel and it survives today as perhaps the most splendid manifestation of Anglo-Japanese taste.

Liberty and Commercial Japan

If the designs and interiors produced by Godwin and Jeckyll represent a purist interpretation of Japanese styles, then the work made by designers working within the trade illustrates the more commercial applications of Far Eastern art. For these designers it was not so much the forms as the surface decoration of Japanese art that

122. *H. W. Batley*, A SERIES OF STUDIES FOR DOMESTIC FURNITURE, *1883. Batley's work embraced a number of different styles including Egyptian and Gothic as well as Anglo-Japanese. Here, however, the influence is predominantly oriental, and the sideboard includes panels of boxwood carving, the wallpaper features an asymmetrical pattern of swallows and fruit blossom, and Japanese fans and vases stand in compartments, on shelves and on the projecting dado-rail.*

appealed, and with the more widespread interest in the East came a growing enthusiasm for the rich new source of motifs with which it was associated. Before long Japanese-style decoration proliferated, and peacocks, hawthorn blossom, and variations on the ubiquitous sunflower could be found adorning a wide range of different items produced for the home. This development is especially evident in the designs that appeared under the label "Anglo-Japanese Furniture" during the 1870s and 1880s.

Japanese-style furniture was taken up by large numbers of commercial firms and examples were produced by makers at both ends of the market. James Shoolbred, for instance, who had a large department store in Tottenham Court Road, employed the designer H. W.

Batley, whose drawings of overmantels and hanging cupboards show an enthusiastic commitment to oriental art. Jackson & Graham, another respected firm, also produced several Japanese-inspired designs, as did Collinson & Lock and A. Jonquet, and by the last quarter of the century, beds and chairs featuring fretwork, carvings, and panels of leather paper, and cabinets and overmantels containing a large number of brackets and shelves for the display of porcelain, had become a standard part of most commercial manufacturers' ranges. At the top end of the market, much of this work was elegant and well-made, but, inevitably, with the manufacture of cheaper goods, fine craftsmanship was replaced by shoddy work and forms showed a tendency towards flimsiness and instability. Many firms involved in mass-production simply embellished very ordinary pieces of furniture with oriental details and decoration.

A similar process of assimilation and decline was also taking place within the sphere of pattern design. The pale colours so beloved by the early enthusiasts of Japanese art were replaced, at the popular level, by a taste for richer and darker hues while asymmetry became something of a cliché. Thus large numbers of machine-printed fabrics and wallpapers appeared in sombre greens, browns and golds and adopted irregular arrangements with little regard for the balance or style of the design.

Nevertheless, during the 1880s enthusiasm for Japanese art and accessories still ran high, and amongst the public an interest in oriental forms was no longer confined to the wealthy or avant-garde. Japanese-style goods were avidly acquired by anyone with pretensions to fashion or taste, and a multitude of Aesthetic interiors were filled with blue and white china displayed on elaborately bracketed overmantels, and cheap Japanese paper fans that were arranged upon the dado-rail or pinned to the wall. In fact, so pervasive did the vogue for Japanese art become that in 1887 a writer in *The Woman's World* was prompted to declare:

There is hardly a drawing room in the kingdom in which the influences of Japanese art are not felt. Walls are draped and tables covered with rich brocades of the land of the dragonfly; brilliantly enamelled plaques have been found a cheap and effective substitute for china, always costly and of doubtful antiquity. We put our flowers in Japanese bowls; serve tea from Japanese trays; and in the hot summers that have become the fashion, fan ourselves, without regard to sex or condition, with Japanese fans.

Many of these items could be purchased from the new oriental warehouses that sprang up in all the major cities in Europe and America during the last quarter of the century. In New York, Tiffany & Co. sold Japanese and Chinese curios alongside native jewellery and silverware, while in London, many of the larger department

123. THE PEACOCK ROOM, 49 PRINCE'S GATE, *1876–7. The system of ebonized shelving was designed by Thomas Jeckyll to provide display space for Leyland's collection of oriental porcelain and a setting for Whistler's* Princesse de la Pays du Porcelain. *Whistler subsequently overpainted the walls, shutters, dado, ceiling and cornice with a design of Antwerp blue and gold peacocks and peacock feathers. The result outraged his patron and ultimately drove Jeckyll mad.*

stores stocked a range of Japanese goods. The most famous of the oriental emporiums was Liberty, the shop founded by Arthur Lasenby Liberty in Regent Street in 1875.

Liberty's played a leading role not only in stimulating a taste for Aesthetic fashions but also, later, in disseminating Arts and Crafts styles. During the 1870s the shop was the veritable epicentre of fashionable Aestheticism. Much of the credit for its success was due to the energy and enthusiasm of its founder. The friend of Godwin and Whistler, Liberty combined a shrewd business sense with a keen interest in art. He was a regular visitor to artists' studios and he travelled extensively in the Far and Middle East in search of new work. Moreover, his passionate commitment to improving public taste through the provision of artistic goods and his uncompromising insistence upon quality informed all the activities with which the shop was involved gaining it a reputation for excellence that still pertains today.

Born in 1843, the son of a Chesham draper, Liberty worked firstly for Farmer & Roger, whose Great Shawl Emporium was founded in 1854. As its name suggests, this firm specialized in the sale of cashmere and paisley shawls, but in 1862 they acquired a quantity of items from Rutherford Alcock's Japanese display and shortly afterwards they opened an Oriental Warehouse at 176 Regent Street, next door to the main store. Liberty was the junior of the two men employed there. Two years later he became the manager. Under his guidance the warehouse quickly became the most profitable branch of Farmer & Roger's business, and in 1872 Liberty approached the directors with a view to being made a partner. His request, however, was turned down, so encouraged by his artist friends, he decided to branch out on his own. He purchased a half-shop at 218A Regent Street, called East India House, and on 15 May 1875, trading began.

During its early years, East India House was comparatively small and its operations were restricted to the sale of oriental silks and embroideries imported from Japan. Liberty took pains, however, to ensure that these were of the highest quality; much admired by artists, an employee of the firm remembered them as "the sort of thing that William Morris, Alma-Tadema and Burne-Jones and Rossetti used to come in and rave about". During the later 1870s the business began to expand. Liberty took over the other half of the shop and began stocking a far wider range of goods, including oriental bronzes, Japanese lacquer and Satsuma ware. Also during this period the shop became a meeting-place for poets, painters and Aesthetes, and like its counterpart in Paris, La Porte Chinoise, it became a mecca for fashionable society as a whole. In 1876 Godwin described the queues that formed outside prior to the arrival of a new consignment of Japanese fans and noted that the prospective clients included "a distinguished traveller", "a well-known baronet", "two architects of well-known name", "three distinguished painters", and a "bevy" of ladies from the fashionable world. He went on to review the contents of the shop, and his comments, recorded in *The British Architect*, provide not only a useful account of the merchandise for sale, but also an interesting guide to

the range of oriental goods available to the artistic home:

If only it had a little decent furniture, an artist might almost decorate and furnish his rooms from this one shop. There are matting and mats, carpets and rugs for the floor; Japanese papers for the walls; curtain stuff for windows and folding screens, chairs, stools and so forth. There are faience flower-pots, garden seats, vases etc. . .

The lack to which Godwin refers was soon remedied, and during the 1880s the firm's operations expanded to include furniture. Prior to this time the shop had stocked a range of small stools and chairs imported from the East but it now began to develop home-grown designs inspired by oriental forms. Much of this was designed by a Frenchman, Ursin Fortier, who specialized in bamboo work. Cheap, light and conveniently portable, bamboo and wicker furnishings enjoyed a considerable vogue during the last quarter of the nineteenth century and were particularly well-suited to the adaptation of Anglo-Japanese styles. Much was made in Birmingham, the Mikado Bamboo Co. and William Frederick Needham offering the widest selections, whilst in Leicester the firm of W. T. Elmore and Son claimed to be "the largest manufacturers in willow and cane in Europe". Fortier's designs included light-weight cabinets, pedimented hat-stands and small writing-tables.

In 1883 Liberty opened its own Furnishing and Decorating Studio. This section of the business was under the supervision of the painter and Royal Academician, Leonard Wyburd, whose sympathies were allied more closely to Moorish, than to Japanese design. The late nineteenth-century interest in Moorish and Islamic styles of design represents an interesting parallel to that in Japanese art. It began somewhat earlier, during the mid-century, when views of Middle Eastern architecture and interiors became known through contemporary travelogues and the paintings of orientalists such as John Frederick Lewis. Also during this period, designers like Owen Jones did much to popularize Moorish patterns and the strong colours and abstracted forms characteristic of Islamic decoration were admired

by many of the leading exponents of design reform. Somewhat surprisingly, though, it was not until the 1880s, when firms such as H. & J. Cooper and Rottmann, Strome & Co. began importing goods made in Cairo and Damascus, that Moorish-style furnishings and interiors became important. Once again, Liberty's were at the forefront of this trend.

Middle Eastern rugs and textiles had been available in the shop since its earliest days and in 1883 Liberty opened an Eastern Bazaar and Arab Tea-rooms where customers could purchase Indian condiments and preserves along with Eastern pottery and curios. With the introduction of Wyburd's furniture, they were now also able to acquire "Arabian" tables, wardrobes and writing-tables as well as the ubiquitous Koran stands and Cairene screens that were endemic within late Victorian artistic homes. The Decorating Studio also designed complete interiors in the Arab style, and one of their most important commissions was the dining-room for the Earl of Aberdeen's house in Grosvenor Square, which had Moorish arches and old Persian tiles. Wyburd's speciality, however, was cosy corners and Damascene niches and screens. Fixed over doorways and across passageways, and hung with Eastern fabrics, these provided an attractively exotic touch, at comparatively little cost, with which to enliven the most ordinary of London terraces. Today, however, Liberty's are remembered not so much for their Japanese or Moorish furniture as for their fabrics and it was with these that the firm achieved its greatest renown.

During the late 1870s, the standard of Far and Middle Eastern imported fabrics had declined and the colours, in particular, became cruder as foreign suppliers

---

124. (*opposite*) *Louis Comfort Tiffany,* THE MORNING-ROOM, *1881. The son of Charles C. Tiffany, the founder of Tiffany & Co., New York, Louis Tiffany became a leading exponent of the American Aesthetic Movement. He was also famed as a producer of stained glass, much of which was designed in the Art Nouveau style. During the 1880s, however, he favoured a more conventionally artistic style and his interiors featured gilded leather papers, exotic fabrics, coloured glass and drab woodwork.*

125. (*below*) DRAWING-ROOM DECORATED WITH ROTTMANN, STROME & CO.'S JAPANESE LEATHER PAPERS, *1884. Japanese leather papers, imported firstly by Liberty's and later by firms such as Rottmann, Strome & Co., represent one of the most successful of the commercial applications of Japanese art to English and American tastes. Long lengths were used as wallcoverings while smaller panels were employed as decoration in ebonized cabinets and chairs. The patterns illustrated here reflect the increasing Westernization of Japanese styles and owe more to the example of sixteenth-century stamped and gilded leathers than to authentic oriental designs. Note also the fashionable black wood display cabinet and Japanese screen.*

adapted their work to meet the demands of European tastes. Disturbed by this development, Liberty began to look around for British firms who could reproduce the subtle combinations and hues of the originals. This search led to his collaboration with the manufacturer Thomas Wardle of Leek, who had earlier worked with William Morris. Together, Liberty and Wardle perfected new techniques of dyeing that enabled them to develop a range of delicate pastel tints including blue-greens, corals, yellows, and golds. Initially, the fabrics were sold plain but by the 1880s the shop was reproducing old Indian patterns and shortly afterwards, designers such as Walter Crane and Arthur Silver were employed to print Anglicized versions of Eastern designs. Phenomenally popular, these patterns were highly acclaimed and "Liberty Art Fabrics", as they were called, were awarded a gold medal at the Amsterdam Exhibition in 1883. The plain silks were also much in demand and were used extensively as draperies within artistic homes. Some years later a member of the firm's staff recalled:

They "caught on" with the public and literally miles of them were sold for draping purposes, often caught up and otherwise mingled with fans and handscreens. In summer, the heavy poles and curtains were taken down and windows draped with silks in different shades of the same colour, hung in festoons. Sometimes the large chimney glasses were lowered to the floor, and when draped with the silks the result was a

not unpleasing illusion of the entrance to another room. People found that an ugly Victorian room, with its gilt chimney glasses, walnut furniture of bastard French design, repp curtains and crochet anti-macassars, which could boast nothing but an intense respectability, could be made comparatively interesting and brightened at a very small outlay, and East India House was besieged.

Art at Home

Aestheticism was not, of course, simply a matter of Anglo-Japanese styles. As has been shown earlier, the Movement bred an interest in the design and decoration of many different cultures. It also drew liberally upon the art of other periods. Indeed, to a large extent, the very principles upon which Aestheticism was founded encouraged an eclectic and almost ahistorical approach to design. The notion of "Art for Art's Sake" fostered the belief that decoration and design – be they from the Far East or from the distant past – were to be appreciated for their intrinsic beauty rather than for their extrinsic associations, and it validated both the appropriation and the mixing of disparate styles. Thus, in addition to the work produced in his favourite Anglo-Japanese style, Godwin also designed interiors and furniture in the Elizabethan and Jacobean modes, and his advice to students was to study the art of every age and country so as to evolve a style that was distinctively their own. The important thing, within this context, was

126. (*opposite*) THE BILLIARD-ROOM AT NEWHOUSE PARK, HERTFORDSHIRE, *1890s. Moorish styles were especially popular in billiard- and smoking-rooms, and this particularly flamboyant example includes many features, such as flat patterns, fretwork and horseshoe-arched alcoves, that were typical of the genre.*

127. (*above*) *Georges Groegaert,* LA LISEUSE, *1888. Few Victorian interiors would have been as thoroughly Japanese as the boudoir of this Parisian enthusiast. It includes not only the obligatory peacock feathers, parasol and paper fans but also a striking collection of Nō masks, Japanese prints and paintings, samurai weapons, embroidered silk cushions and a costly lacquer cabinet.*

for the designer to select judiciously, to combine the different elements harmoniously, and to create a coherent and beautiful whole.

The eclecticism of this approach is demonstrated most clearly in the myriad range of styles associated with the "Art" furnishings and decorations that emerged in the late 1860s and which were a typical feature within many Aesthetic homes.

The term "Art" was first applied to furniture, and appeared in Charles Eastlake's *Hints on Household Taste*,

and the first maker to be listed in the *Post Office Directory* was Julius Jacoby in 1869. Elizabeth Aslin, the twentieth-century historian of the Aesthetic Movement, has described how it originated in a desire on the part of the design reformers to apply art to industry. If an object had its name prefixed with the word "Art" it indicated that rather than being simply the product of mass manufacture, the item had undergone that special process whereby its design was formulated according to artistic principles. "Art" was in this sense an adjective that set the object apart from other products and it was initially employed in connection with work that was not only architect-, or artist-designed, but also where a strong element of craftsmanship was involved. Inevitably, though, these early associations lapsed and during the 1880s, the word was being used by many commercial manufacturers to describe work that was very little different from that produced by ordinary cabinet-makers and furnishers. In 1885, the editor of *The Cabinet Maker* declared, "Modern furniture is now indiscriminately called art furniture."

In addition to this range in quality, the term also encompassed a wide variety of historical and contemporary styles. Collinson & Lock, for example, issued a catalogue of *Sketches of Artistic Furniture* in 1871; A. Jonquet produced his *Original Sketches for Art Furniture in the Jacobean, Queen Anne and other styles* in 1877–9; and

---

128. (*opposite*) *Arthur Silver*, PEACOCK FEATHERS, *printed cotton, 1884. The peacock feather became the favourite emblem of the Aesthetic Movement, but as early as 1880 the author of* The Artistic Home *declared "peacock feathers are very beautiful in their proper place, but the omnipresent stork of Japan will soon grow as tiring to the ordinary mind as de Quincy found the company of the 'Heathen Chinese'." By the 1890s its appeal had begun to pall. Nevertheless, this design – printed by Liberty's – was one of the most popular of the period and it remains in production today.*

129. (*below*) *Bruce Talbert*, EXAMPLES OF ANCIENT AND MODERN FURNITURE, *1876. Talbert's early work is firmly rooted in the Gothic tradition but, like many design reformers, he was increasingly influenced by Japanese forms and this interior represents a popular synthesis of "Old English" and Aesthetic styles.*

James Shoolbred published their *Designs for Artistic Furniture* in 1874. However, much Art furniture of this period had a number of features in common. The legs, supports and uprights were slender and turned and cabinets and desks contained a great many brackets and shelves. The favoured woods were basswood and walnut – ebonized, or stained black or bottle-green – and decoration was limited to the use of gilt, incised patterns and panels containing painted figures or foliage, which replaced the ornate carving that had been common in the previous decades.

Black or ebonized furniture was an especially important feature within more fashionable, Aesthetic homes and remained in vogue for ten to fifteen years. The fashion was originally inspired by the traditionally styled furniture shown by the French ébénistes at the International Exhibition of 1867, but the taste for such work was also much encouraged by the appearance of oriental lacquer and the domestic fitments to be seen in Japanese prints. The most influential of the early ebonized pieces was the cabinet designed by T. E. Collcutt, exhibited in London in 1871, which displays all the features of the nascent "Artistic" style. It inspired a plethora of imitations, and so widespread did the demand for ebonized work become that in 1880, Max Beerbohm talked of "aesthetes hurling their mahogany into the streets", while, for another authority, ebonized cabinets were "legion and so like each other that none can claim special merit over the others".

Both the richness and the stylistic diversity of Art furniture were also characteristic of the Aesthetic interior as a whole, which, contrary to popular belief, was

The widespread use of chemical dyes in the 1840s and 1850s had encouraged a liking for primary colours, including harsh shades of red, yellow and blue, that were generally considered to be both crude and inharmonious by the 1870s. Disciples of Aestheticism thus favoured more subtle tones, and variations of blue-greens, olives and khakis were used not only in fabrics and wallpapers but also in the paintwork around windows and on doors and on the woodwork throughout Aesthetic rooms.

The rich mixture of pattern within these interiors derived from a different source; namely the revival of the tripartite wallpaper scheme known as the frieze–filling–dado. First described by Eastlake, who had called for a return to horizontal divisions as a means of breaking up the monotony of a single pattern on the

130. (*left*) DETAIL OF THE DINING-ROOM AT 18 STAFFORD TERRACE. *Owned by the illustrator and cartoonist, Edward Linley Sambourne, 18 Stafford Terrace was furnished in the mid-1870s in a fashionable, Aesthetic style. The dining-room was papered with Morris's Pomegranate pattern below a frieze of Japanese leather and above an olive dado. The sideboard is in the style of Bruce Talbert. Its painted panels reflect the maxim: "One good painted panel is worth ten thousand times more than all the meretricious carving with which so much of our modern furniture is filled" (J. Moyr Smith).*

131. (*below*) T. E. Collcutt, EBONIZED WOOD CABINET, 1871. *One of the first and most influential of the many hundreds of ebonized cabinets that appeared under the label "Art" Furniture. By 1881, such cabinets were said to be "legion and so like each other that none can claim special merit over the others".*

anything but uncluttered and simple. Godwin, as has previously been described, produced several light and understated schemes, but the typical artistic room of the late 1870s and early 1880s was richly decorated in deep, dark tones. Its appearance was admirably chronicled by George du Maurier, and, when asked to describe a general Aesthetic interior to be used as a stage set in Frank Burnand's play, *The Colonel*, he advised:

Try to have a room papered with Morris' green daisy, with a dado six feet high of green-blue serge in folds – and a matting with rugs for floor (Indian red matting if possible), spider-legged black tables and sideboard – black rush-bottom chairs and arm chairs; blue china plates on the wall with plenty of space between – here and there a blue china vase with an enormous hawthorn or almond blossom sprig . . . also on mantelpiece pots with lilies and peacock feathers wanted. Japanese sixpenny fans now and then on the wall in picturesque unexpectedness.

Du Maurier's comments conjure up an image of an Aesthetic ideal and actual interiors were obviously rarely as consistently devised as the one he describes. Nevertheless, the passage highlights the dominant elements – slender, ebonized furnishings, oriental accessories, subdued colours and rich pattern – that were to be found in many Aesthetic rooms. The taste for the first and second has already been discussed but the fashion for the third and fourth needs examining in more detail.

The vogue for dull, tertiary hues became the hallmark of Aesthetic taste and arose originally as a reaction to the bright, virulent colours popularized in the mid-century.

132. *Norman Shaw*, EBONIZED WOOD AND GILDED LEATHER CHAIRS, c.1872. *Two of a set of chairs designed by Shaw and made by Gillow's of Oxford Street for the library at Cragside, Northumberland. Their style is reminiscent of Godwin but similar pieces were produced by a number of commercial firms, and lightweight, black, rush or wicker-seated chairs were a popular feature within many Aesthetic rooms.*

wall, this scheme was extremely widely used and by the late 1870s it had become the obligatory form of decoration within every fashionable home. The dado occupied the space between the chair-rail and the skirting and rose to a height of approximately three to four feet from the floor. Its principal function was to provide a background for the furniture and to lend stability to what might otherwise have been a restless decorative scheme. Above the dado came the filling, and surmounting this the frieze, which together covered the remaining sections of the wall. In artistic homes the filling was generally regarded as the most suitable space for paintings and as a result its patterns tended to be flat, conventionalized and small. No such constraints applied to the frieze, which, uninterrupted by furniture or ornaments, might contain birds, animals or figures, or sometimes a pictorial scene.

Many variations were possible within this scheme, some involving high dados and others a wide frieze, and the frieze–filling–dado was discussed at length by writers on decoration in contemporary journals. One authority enjoined, "Have a plain frieze with a much patterned filling"; while another advised, "the frieze should be light and lively; richer colours should be employed than in the filling, and it should be as striking to the eye as the dado". In general, though, most commentators agreed that the patterns should be complementary and that the dado should be darkest with the colours becoming progressively lighter up the wall.

Manufacturers like Jeffrey & Co. produced matching

133. (*left*) *Bruce James Talbert*, FRIEZE-FILLING-DADO WALLPAPER, *c.1877. An example of the tripartite wallpaper decoration popularized by the Aesthetic Movement during the 1870s.*

134. (*above*) *English Anon*, ANGLO-JAPANESE WALLPAPER, *1886. Sold by the Leeds merchants, Firth, Ray & Prosser, this is a good example of the use of "Art" colours and asymmetrical arrangements. By the late 1880s both features had become so commonplace as to appear neither progressive nor even particularly fashionable.*

frieze–filling–dado patterns designed by artists and architects such as Bruce Talbert and Walter Crane. These were advertised as Art decorations and, hand-printed in complementary colours, many of those that survive include striking and harmoniously balanced designs. However, the ever-present danger in even the most artistic of such schemes was that they led to a confusion of pattern and created an impression of heaviness and overcrowding. Ultimately, this was to be the fate of many Aesthetic rooms. The proliferation of ornament within the decorations was matched by the fussiness of much Art furniture and both were symptomatic of a tendency to fill every corner of the interior with objects – albeit *objets d'art*. This trend was equally noticeable both in the houses belonging to wealthy collectors and connoisseurs and in those rented by fashionable members of the middle class, and it reached its zenith in the more sumptuous of those artists' studios that are discussed in the next chapter. Thus, the reforming simplicity espoused by the artists and architects associated with the Aesthetic Movement in its earliest

135. *Kate Greenaway,* SUMMER, *earthenware tile, 1883. Kate Greenaway's illustrations proved the most popular and accessible of all the goods associated with the Aesthetic Movement. The original blend of late eighteenth-century, and early nineteenth-century-style dress worn by the children in her designs for books, wallpapers and tiles exercised a strong influence on contemporary fashions and inspired a host of imitations worn by budding Aesthetes.*

phase was, in practical terms, increasingly overlaid by a taste for eclecticism, elaboration and clutter.

The influence of the Aesthetic Movement was quite short-lived. At least one writer of the next generation was pleased to proclaim, "happily we have survived the art muslin and Japanese fans craze – that age of trash when the 'greenery-yallery' element was allowed to run riot under the name of high art", and by the end of the 1880s the main force of the Movement was largely spent. Nevertheless, the impact of Aesthetic ideas and styles could not so easily be dismissed and was felt in a number of ways. Firstly, although the Movement was primarily of importance within progressive circles, the taste for Aesthetic colours and oriental accessories spread to a much broader section of society and its effects could be seen in a range of middle-class homes. Secondly, the formal characteristics of Aestheticism, notably the use of asymmetry and an elegant fluidity of line, were to provide the basis for a stronger development of these themes within Art Nouveau. And finally, and perhaps most importantly, the ideological basis of the Movement, with its emphasis upon the need for art in every area of life, raised public taste to new levels of self-consciousness and made the notion of beauty an important one in the discussion of the interior as a whole. "The call for art was heard", wrote Hermann Muthesius, a contemporary historian, "and the house emerged from the process greatly improved . . . the furnishings, the wallpapers and materials, which the artists had devised and which previously had been appreciated by a small circle, had now become the property of all cultivated people."

PALACES OF ART

There are studios and studios. There is the studio of the ostentatious Bohemian arts,
whose fire-grate is chocked with ashes, his floor covered with litter, his coat a rag
upon which he wipes his brushes. There is the studio of the very practical man
which looks like a carpenter's shop, or the packing warehouse of a factory. There is
the studio of the painter who makes a compromise with art, and ventures to suggest
in a few rugs and draperies, vases and plaques, keys for colour. Then there is the
studio of the travelled artist, who brings his heart and soul to his work, and
surrounds himself with beautiful things, who feels that his studio is the place in
which he lives the best part of his life, and who makes it his home, worthy of his
labours and his hopes, . . . [a] fitting scene for the development of his highest
creations.
(Journal of Decorative Art, *1889*)

ARTISTS' HOUSES, built in England during the last quarter of the nineteenth century, represent a fascinating and much-neglected area in the history of Victorian decoration and design. For the first time, painters, as well as architects, were commissioning homes designed and furnished entirely to their tastes, and architecturally the model of the studio house established a fashion in domestic building whose popularity has lasted up until the present day. The interiors, moreover, were the subject of widespread public interest and acclaim and their decorations were painstakingly described in a plethora of publications that ranged from large, illustrated monographs to short, gossipy articles in more general magazines. Part of this interest stemmed from a growing fascination with artists themselves, the more successful of whom came to enjoy a social and economic position equal to that of the most wealthy scions of the aristocracy. Part, too, was due to the increasingly widespread preoccupation with all things artistic that dominated discussion of design in the late Victorian period. And finally, Maurice Adams' view, quoted in the *Building News* of 1884, that "the public looked with reason to Artists to show them how best to profit from the first workers in our modern Art Revival", expressed a widely held belief that artists' houses represented not only exotic and beautiful interiors, but also the most exemplary and innovative manifestations of artistic taste.

Artists' houses were not, of course, peculiar to England alone. Equally splendid residences were commissioned by painters abroad and Frederick Church's Moorish palace, Olana, in New York State, and Gustave Moreau's Art Nouveau studio-home in Paris represent two of the more acclaimed examples built in America and Europe during the second half of the nineteenth century. This chapter, however, concentrates upon those houses built in London from the mid-1860s, which not only exemplified contemporary trends in decoration and design, but also, perhaps more than any other examples of the genre, helped to form and reflect progressive Victorian tastes.

The extent to which large, purpose-built artists' houses were a new phenomenon in England in the mid-nineteenth century cannot be overemphasized. The architectural historian Mark Girouard has documented their development and has described how, during the eighteenth century, painters had occupied buildings that were not substantially different from those owned by other members of the professional classes and, where studios were required, they were either adapted from existing rooms or were added on to the main body of the house. Sir Joshua Reynolds, for example, extended the house that he bought in 1760 near Leicester Fields (now Leicester Square) to accommodate an octagonal room used for painting, and a picture gallery. The painting room measured approximately 20 feet long and 16 feet wide and was lit by one small window whose sill stood 9 feet 4 inches above the floor. By the early nineteenth century, it had become more usual for artists to erect

136. *Anna Alma-Tadema*, THE GOLD ROOM AT TOWNSHEND HOUSE, *1880s. Many Victorian painters expended vast sums and enormous care upon the decoration of their homes. A painter of classical subjects, Lawrence Alma-Tadema was inspired mainly by Pompeian styles but the decoration of the Gold Room reflects his interest in other periods and more colourful styles. It includes a painted Byzantine ceiling, Moresque lacquer work alcoves, Musharabyeh tables and costly embroidered silk hangings. An explosion on a barge on Regent's Canal on 2 October 1874 destroyed almost all the interiors but the decorations were painstakingly restored over the course of the next two years.*

large, free-standing studios in their gardens, but these, by all accounts, were fairly utilitarian structures, hidden away from public view. The development of the Victorian artist's house as a large detached residence including a vast studio that occupied most of the first floor, was therefore without precedent, and its emergence in the 1860s and 1870s was due to several factors, both aesthetic and socio-economic.

Firstly, styles of painting changed. Girouard, again, describes how the eighteenth-century academic tradition, with its emphasis on chiaroscuro, broad effects and invented backgrounds increasingly gave way to more naturalistic treatments in which all the details of the figure and the landscape were observed, and verisimilitude, not the Grand Manner, became the nineteenth-century painter's priority. Within this context, the need for daylight became more pressing, and, with the final repeal of all taxes on windows in 1851, the idea of introducing the large north-facing windows that are now synonymous with artists' studios became, for the first time, not only desirable but also economically viable.

Secondly, many of the more successful painters of the late nineteenth century earned incomes that, by previous standards, were spectacularly high. For many years painters and critics had complained that patrons only bought Old Masters, but from the 1850s the demand for works by living painters began far to exceed that for art of the earlier periods. Saleroom prices for contemporary paintings reached unprecedented

heights, and a record was set by Edwin Long's *Babylonian Marriage Market*, which was sold to Thomas Holloway for £6,615 in 1882. Some years earlier, Holman Hunt had received 5,500 guineas for his *Finding of the Saviour in the Temple* of 1860, and in 1862, W. P. Frith was paid £5,250 for the oil sketch and copyright of the painting *The Railway Station*. John Everett Millais, moreover, was rumoured to earn in excess of £30,000 a year. A contemporary description of a dinner party given in 1885 records a discussion about incomes that he had with the Prince of Wales, in which the doctor Sir Henry Thompson and the barrister Sir Henry James also took part. The doctor and the barrister claimed that the most eminent men in their professions could make £15,000 and £20,000 a year respectively. Millais countered that a painter could expect to earn at least £25,000 and continued, "For the last ten years I should have made £40,000 had I not given myself a holiday of four months in the year: what I did actually make was £30,000, so that I gave an estimate considerably under the fact." In today's terms, these figures suggest that Millais was not simply rich, but a millionaire, and the house designed for him in 1878 in Palace Gate, into which Lethaby claimed, "the aestheticism of the day does not enter: no, not by so much as a peacock fan", was a veritable mansion. Few other painters could afford such splendour, but with successful Royal Academicians earning, on average, between £5,000 and £10,000 a year, many were able to consider building imposing new homes.

Finally, Victorian artists were also more fêted and

137. (*opposite*) *Leonard Wyburd,* THE STUDIO, *1880s. Late Victorian painters' homes were characterized by an accumulation of collected treasures, artists' properties and bric-à-brac. Contemporaries deemed them pre-eminently "artistic", and increasingly they came to be regarded as an exotic and enticing alternative to the more mundane settings of everyday life. This studio, clearly that of "the travelled artist . . . who surrounds himself with beautiful things", may well have been Wyburd's own and its contents reflect his fondness for Far and Middle Eastern curios and ornaments.*

138. (*above*) *John Ballantyne,* W. P. FRITH IN HIS STUDIO, *late 1850s. With the exception of the large canvas and the raised platform for the model, there is little in this room to distinguish it from other affluent middle-class rooms of the period, and it clearly pre-dates the notion of artists' studios as places that were distinct from ordinary interiors. The strong colours, heavy curtains with their deep pelmet, and plush, comfortable seating reflect the taste of the mid-century. The setting is a house in Pembridge Villas, Kensington, where Frith was living c.1858.*

139. ENGRAVING OF THE EXTERIOR OF LEIGHTON HOUSE, KENSINGTON, *1876. Modelled upon a Renaissance artist's palazzo, Leighton House was the first of the large, detached houses commissioned by wealthy painters during the late nineteenth century. The vast north-facing studio window that dominates the garden front was an innovative feature in the 1860s when the house was built, but by the 1870s, such designs had become characteristic of purpose-built artists' homes.*

more honoured than any that had gone before. Whereas previously artists had been regarded as the servants of the aristocracy, during the nineteenth century knighthoods and baronetcies were showered on painters of repute and, unlike their Continental counterparts, English artists enjoyed a status equal to that of the very highest ranks of society. Millais, Lawrence Alma-Tadema and Luke Fildes were amongst the many to be knighted, and a host of lesser stars received honours that included OBEs, doctorates and honorary degrees.

Alongside this rise in income and social status went a change in life-style. The Bohemianism and unconventionality associated with Parisian artistic life was unthinkable in London, and wealthy painters were the very image of respectability. Many also entertained on a lavish scale. Frederic Leighton, for example, played host to royalty and Prime Ministers, and his annual musical evenings, at which celebrities such as the pianist Clara Schumann and the composer Charles Hallé performed, were a high-point in the London Season and much-publicized in the Court pages of contemporary newspapers and magazines. The need to provide an appropriately magnificent setting for occasions of this kind was not inconsiderable and acted as a powerful incentive in the building and furnishing of his and many other artists' homes.

Artists' houses were not simply, however, places in which to work and entertain. They were also an important means of advertising a painter's success and in the large, detached houses built by Royal Academicians in Melbury Road, the public was offered visible proof of their owners' status and prosperity. The studios, moreover, also functioned as a kind of picture gallery and saleroom. Once a year, on "Show Sundays" – a Sunday before the private view of the Royal Academy Summer Exhibition – they were thrown open to the public, who flocked in their thousands to see the artists' newest offerings. Luke Fildes' biography provides a particularly informative account of these days and records how his wife's parlour maid used to stand outside the studio door and drop a coffee bean into a brass bowl for every visitor. In April 1883, the year in which he exhibited his *Village Wedding*, nearly 700 beans hit the bowl and in subsequent years the number seldom fell below a thousand.

Patrons came more frequently and many made regular visits to the artist's studio to view work in progress or prospective purchases. For them, the vast rooms filled with artists' "properties" were both evidence of professional efficiency and a guarantee of the commercial worth of the work on show. Furthermore, an opulent setting was not only admired for its own sake, but also, to quote the historian William Gaunt, "induced the humble frame of mind in which a cheque might be reverently offered". As a result many painters laboured long and hard to create suitably impressive interiors in which they might encourage visitors to buy.

Stylistically, these interiors were quite diverse, and to some extent the variety of furnishings and decorations reflected the growing eclecticism of late nineteenth-century and particularly Aesthetic tastes. Marcus Stone's house in Holland Park, for example, was decorated in "the spirit of an Old English Home", while Hubert Herkomer's home, Lululand at Bushey, Hertfordshire, was fitted out as a Northern Renaissance palace. Other painters commissioned interiors that corresponded to their styles of painting, a feature that is demonstrated most clearly in the Roman villa designed by the classical artist, Lawrence Alma-Tadema, in St John's Wood. Tadema's homes also demonstrate the increasing elaboration of many wealthy Victorian artists' interiors. His first house in Regent's Park was an exotic mixture of international styles, combining a Gothic library and Dutch bedrooms with a Pompeian studio. Its high-point was an exceptionally lavish music-room decorated in the newly fashionable Byzantine mode. This room featured gold walls, Chinese lacquer and rich hangings, and its

décor culminated in a painted ceiling modelled on the celebrated three-dimensional ceilings designed by Owen Jones for Alfred Morrison's residence at 16 Carlton House Terrace. Tadema's second house at 34 Grove End Road was even more extravagant. It was purchased in the early 1880s from the French painter James Tissot and the interiors were extended and refurbished at the reputed cost of around £70,000! Two studios were provided, one designed in the seventeenth-century Dutch style for Tadema's wife, Laura, and the other, incorporating a vast semi-domed ceiling made of polished aluminium, for the artist himself. The entrance hall was decorated with fifty panels containing paintings by figures such as Leighton, Sargeant, Sir Frank Dicksee and Sir Edward Poynter, and precious metals, including Mexican onyx, marble and mosaic were employed throughout. In fact, so rich was the appearance of the interiors that one observer mistakenly assumed the polished brass staircase to be made of gold, a misapprehension that subsequently brought a torrent of begging letters to Grove End Road!

Nevertheless, despite the individuality of particular artist's homes, many were surprisingly similar in appearance and the 1880s saw the gradual evolution of a distinctive studio style. This was characterized by a profusion of antique carved furnishings, exotic hangings, curios and bric-à-brac, all arranged to appear the work of chance rather than careful artifice, and the

---

140. *Thomas Matthew Rooke*, THE STUDIO AT 6 MELBURY ROAD, *c.1890. A view of G. F. Watts's studio, illustrating the design and scale of such rooms from the interior.*

141. *Dewey Bates,* THE PORTRAIT, *1880. The artful disorder of this interior, with its discarded bottles, playing cards and unsorted paints, suggests a careless Bohemianism not usually associated with London artistic life. Moreover, features such as the oriental prints and screen proclaim this to be the studio of a dedicated Aesthete rather than the reception room of an established Royal Academician. While such studios were undoubtedly admired in progressive circles they were unlikely to impress patrons with more conservative tastes.*

effect can be seen most clearly in photographs of the painting-room at Leighton House. Much admired by contemporaries, this style exercised an important influence on contemporary tastes. Features such as the rich draperies, collections of ornaments and antiques, and the device of displaying paintings on easels proved especially popular, and in a period when artists' studios came increasingly to be regarded as an exotic and enticing alternative to the more mundane settings of everyday life, "swell studios", as they were called, provided a much-vaunted model for the decoration of many wealthy, Aesthetic collectors' homes.

Successful Victorian painters were, therefore, wealthy and respectable, with expensive and semi-public lifestyles to maintain. They built large, imposing houses in fashionable areas such as Kensington, Chelsea, St John's Wood and Bedford Park. Kensington and Chelsea, in particular, attracted a veritable galaxy of artist-stars and it is to the two colonies that grew up around Holland Park and the Embankment that attention will now be turned for a closer inspection of some of the more significant nineteenth-century artists' homes.

The Holland Park Colony

The origins of the artists' colony that grew up around Holland Park lay in the fashionable circle of literary and artistic figures who met regularly during the 1850s and 1860s at Little Holland House. This house, which lay in grounds adjacent to the main Holland estate, was situated in Kensington, an area that lay to the west of London.

At the outset of the nineteenth century, Kensington had been little more than a village, but periodic building booms pushed the metropolis ever outwards, and from the 1840s developers made large fortunes in building huge new residential estates. In the main, these consisted of substantial, stucco-fronted terraces, designed in the neo-classical style, and by the 1860s the borough was well-established as a smart suburb, very popular with the rising professional classes. Large new shops lined the recently widened High Street and communications were excellent. Mayfair and the City were not far away by cab and the Metropolitan Railway (which opened a station here in 1868) made a valuable connection with the important mainline stations of Paddington, Marylebone and Euston, as well as giving easy access to theatres and restaurants in the centre of town. The area was therefore fashionable and affluent, and as a setting for London's most prominent and wealthy painters, its credentials were excellent.

Little Holland House was originally owned by Lord Holland, and members of the Holland family had lived there since 1744. From 1844, however, the house was rented and in 1850 the lease was taken over by Thoby Prinsep, a retired Indian civil servant and a director of the East India Company. Prinsep's wife, Sarah, was one of the famous Pattle sisters whose beauty and talent dazzled several generations of London society. A gifted and indefatigable hostess, she held open house for artists, musicians, poets, authors and philosophers. Mrs A. M. W. Stirling, the biographer of the Pre-Raphaelite painter Roddham Spencer Stanhope, recalled the

atmosphere of her famous Sunday afternoon "at homes":

A breezy Bohemianism prevailed. That time of dread, the conventional Sunday of the early Victorian era was exchanged for the wit of cynics, the dreams of the inspired, and the thoughts of the profoundest thinkers of the age. Throughout the sunny summer afternoons, under the shade of the fine old trees, were placed big sofas and seats, picturesque in their gay coverings, and the desultory talk around the tea table was varied by games of bowls and croquet on the lawn beyond.

The regular habitués included the authors Thomas Carlyle, Tennyson, Thackeray and Dickens, and the artists Rossetti and Burne-Jones, but perhaps the most enduring of Mrs Prinsep's conquests was the painter George Frederick Watts, who "came to stay for three days and stayed thirty years". Watts' presence in the house gave it an added artistic "cachet", and by the 1870s it had become a much-publicized centre for a cultured and intellectual élite.

Initially, the Prinseps' tenancy was for twenty-one years, and when this period expired they clearly hoped to be able to renew their lease. Unfortunately, though, their landlord, Lady Holland, was facing bankruptcy, and in 1872 the administration of the estate was turned

142. MARCUS STONE IN HIS STUDIO, *1884. Built by Norman Shaw in 1875, Stone's house was designed in the fashionable Queen Anne style, the interior was decorated, however, "in the spirit of an Old English Home". It features a large Flemish tapestry and an angled Renaissance chimney-piece, and exemplifies not only the mixture of styles typical of late nineteenth-century artistic interiors, but also the tasteful affluence characteristic of successful Victorian painters' homes.*

over to Lord Ilchester, who made plans to demolish Little Holland House and to dispose of the land for the development of Melbury Road. Watts was devastated by this turn of events. His fondness for the house was matched only by his affection for the Prinsep family, and with the prospect of homelessness approaching fast, he assiduously applied himself to portraiture in order to raise the money with which to build his own home. He leased some land at 6 Melbury Road and commissioned F. P. Cockerell to design a house, which, after long delays caused by the "drunkenness, idleness and dishonesty" of the builders, was finally ready for occupation in February 1876.

According to the *Building News*, Little Holland House, as Watts's new house was also confusingly called, was "unpretending, like its owner, and mostly devoted to work". Watts had apparently stipulated that there should be no spare bedrooms, "to avoid complications", and the main accommodation consisted of a sitting-room, the artist's bedroom, and not one, but four

studios, as well as a lumber-room for "artists' properties". In 1879 he engaged George Aitchison to remodel sections of the interior. Aitchison was already well known for his work on other artists' homes, having designed the trend-setting Leighton House in 1864, and his alterations at new Little Holland House included turning the double studio on the first floor into one large room, measuring 28 by 24 feet, with recesses at either end. The need for extra space was almost certainly determined by the size of Watts's paintings, which seemed to grow with each successive year; a photograph of the artist taken in 1884 shows many of his vast canvases piled up high against the walls. Aitchison's improvements also included a top-lit picture gallery which was added on to the west end of the house in 1879. A firm believer in the spiritually regenerative properties of art, Watts hung this room with a selection of his most high-minded allegories and on Sunday afternoons, the room was opened up to the general public.

It was probably Watts's presence at the original Little Holland House that attracted Frederic Leighton to the area – the two had met in 1855 and remained close friends until Leighton's death in 1896 – and in 1864 he purchased a plot of land close to the Prinseps' house at 2 Holland Park Road.

Leighton epitomized the kind of nineteenth-century artist whose prosperity and status have been described earlier. Born in 1830, the only son of a wealthy doctor, he achieved a meteoric rise to fame with the exhibition

143. *James Jacques Joseph Tissot,* HIDE AND SEEK, C.*1877. Alma-Tadema's second home at 34 Grove End Road was originally owned by the French painter James Tissot whose liking for exotic accessories is admirably demonstrated in this view of his drawing-room. The* *comfortable Victorian seating is covered with furs, a painted screen stands in the window, an Indian brass ewer stands on a Chinese table, a tribal mask hangs from the easel and white sun blinds protect the heavy velvet curtains and handsome Persian rugs on the floor.*

of his painting, *Cimabue s Celebrated Madonna Being Carried in Procession through the Streets of Florence*, which was purchased by Queen Victoria in 1855. There followed a short period of critical adversity, but in 1864 he was elected an Associate of the Royal Academy and from this time on his work was avidly collected by wealthy industrialists and aristocrats alike. Described by a less admiring colleague as a "cross between a head waiter and Olympian Jove, a superb decorator and a superb piece of decoration", he was nonetheless cultivated and urbane and mixed freely with the most select members of society. He was also extraordinarily successful. He became a full Academician in 1870, was elected President in 1878, was knighted in 1885, and in 1895 became the first and only painter ever to be raised to the peerage. His biographer recalled that "he liked pomp and graceful ceremony, and was of the opinion that great artists should lead a Princely life, so that in their manners and method of existence they might furnish models to mankind in general, and elevate the tone and taste of nations". His house was a monument to these beliefs, and, a testimony of his prowess and success, it exemplified the most Aesthetic and artistic of tastes.

Built from 1864 of red Suffolk brick with mouldings of Caen stone, the exterior was essentially classical in style. With the exception of the large studio window which dominated the garden front, there were few embellishments to attract the eye and, initially at least, its appearance was quite restrained. The accommodation consisted of three reception rooms, studio and one

bedroom – Leighton, like Watts, did not want to encourage overnight guests – with rooms for servants in the basement and on the attic floor. Both the artist and Aitchison, the architect, however, had always intended to extend, and in the early 1870s there began the first of a series of additions that were eventually to include the Arab hall, a library, a winter studio and a picture gallery. Thus, from having been a modest Italianate villa, it became a large imposing house, and contemporaries described it as an "Italian Renaissence Palace".

On entering the house the visitor was struck firstly by the profusion of boldly contrasting colours. Decorative polychromy was a distinctive feature of all Aitchison's interiors and can be seen in many other examples of his work. At Leighton House its application was particularly dramatic. Iridescent turquoise blue tiles, produced by William de Morgan in 1879–81, covered the walls of the staircase and hall, and black and gold ebonized doors – a fashionably Aesthetic feature employed throughout the house – led through to the dining-room and drawing-room sumptuously decorated wth deep Indian red and brown wallpapers and richly patterned Persian-style carpets. The drawing-room was especially elegant and contained the choicest examples of Leighton's collections of French art, including four paintings by Jean-Baptiste Corot of the *Times of the Day* and a sketch by Delacroix of a ceiling in the Palais Royal, that Leighton had purchased in Paris in the 1850s. A white marble fireplace was placed directly underneath the window and, at night, a sliding shutter was drawn across to form

144. (*opposite*) ALMA-TADEMA IN HIS STUDIO, *1884. The studio at 34 Grove End Road was famed for the extravagance and elegance of its décor. A visitor described it as conjuring up "visions of all the luxury, the ivory, apes and peacocks of the Roman civilisation with which his art was largely preoccupied", and the light-reflecting aluminium ceiling was a feature that even left its mark on its owner's style of painting. In this view it is details such as the portrait bust of Laura Alma-Tadema, the rich gold tissue above the pedimented fireplace and the variety of masks, pots and animal skins that catch the eye.*

145. (*above*) GEORGE FREDERICK WATTS IN THE PICTURE GALLERY AT 6 MELBURY ROAD, *1884. Described as "unpretending, like its owner, and mostly devoted to work" Watts's house contained few of the costly accessories and curios normally to be seen cluttering artists' homes. His studio was extended in 1879 to accommodate the increasingly large scale of his paintings and in this view of the picture gallery he is shown almost dwarfed by the vast allegorical canvases that became his speciality during the last decades of the century.*

a mirror in whose reflection could be seen the sparkling glass of the ornate Venetian chandelier.

Upstairs, the studio was a veritable Aladdin's cave, filled with antique furniture, easels, bric-à-brac and *objets d'art*. Leighton was a tireless bargain-hunter and collector of foreign souvenirs and, in the grand manner of Rubens, he disdained to work in an atmosphere of functional simplicity, and surrounded himself with beautiful things to inspire his own creations. Opposite the window hung a plaster copy of the Parthenon frieze and a cast of the Michelangelo *Tondo*, now owned by the Royal Academy, and scattered about the room, draped over furniture and on the floors, were a quantity of costly Persian rugs and prayer-mats. At the east end of the room a galleried screen, painted peacock blue, concealed a back staircase used by models and contained a number of compartments and cupboards especially designed to house the artist's brushes and paints. The walls were painted a deep terracotta, Leighton's preferred colour for the display of paintings, and an apsed semi-dome was decorated with gold leaf. Few could fail to be struck by the richness of this interior and Leighton's own account of a concert held there in 1871 provides a vivid evocation of the sensations that the decorations aroused:

To me perhaps the most striking thing of the evening was Joachim's playing of Bach's "Chacone" up in my gallery. I was at the other end of the room, and the effect from the distance of the dark figure in the uncertain light up there, barely

relieved from the gold background and dark recess, struck me as one of the most poetic and fascinating things that I remember. At the opposite end of the room in the apse was a blazing crimson rhododendron tree, which looked glorious where it reached up into the golden semi-dome.

Even more striking than the studio, however, was the Arab hall, which was added on to the west end of the house in 1877 to accommodate Leighton's priceless collection of sixteenth- and seventeenth-century Syrian and Isnik tiles. Leighton had first become interested in Middle Eastern pottery in 1867 when he visited Rhodes, and he purchased a quantity of Persian and Lindos-ware plates, which were displayed on the walls of the dining-room at Leighton House. The following year he travelled to Egypt and Syria and, much impressed by the architecture and colourful style of decoration, he began acquiring tiles. As his collection grew he enlisted the help of friends in making additional purchases. Sir Richard Burton, the explorer, was a particularly useful contact and in 1871 he wrote to Leighton from Cairo that he was pulling down derelict Mamluk houses in search of rare and valuable examples. Two years later, Leighton travelled to Damascus visiting kiln-sites with the missionary, the Reverend William Wright, and in 1876 Burton secured for him an important collection of tiles from the tomb of Sakhar on the Indus. These included several panels that were too large to be display-

146. (*above*) THE STAIRCASE HALL AT LEIGHTON HOUSE. *The dramatic, polychromatic style of the hall is typical of both Leighton's and Aitchison's Aesthetic tastes. The walls are lined with William de Morgan tiles, the woodwork is ebonized, and the floor has a black and white mosaic design inspired by examples at Pompeii. The Turkish screen dates from the eighteenth century and was purchased in Damascus.*

147. (*opposite*) George Aitchison, DESIGN FOR THE ARAB HALL, *1879. Based on the design of an existing Arab room in Sicily, the Arab Hall was built to house Leighton's extensive collection of sixteenth- and seventeenth-century Syrian and Isnik tiles. It contains a fine display of painted decoration in the Moorish style, a wooden alcove inset with fourteenth-century tiles, and a mosaic frieze designed by Walter Crane. Much admired by contemporaries, one author compared it to "an Arabian dream", while another praised "that peculiar sense of repose and stateliness of colour characteristic of the true East".*

142

ed in the existing body of the house and faced with the problem of how to store these acquisitions, Aitchison offered "to furnish Leighton with a design that would be suited to their employment". The result was the Arab hall where the large panels were fitted into the walls and the room was entirely encased with patterned tiles in the manner of a Moslem mosque.

Arab rooms were not an entirely new phenomenon in the 1870s, and during the late nineteenth century, Moorish-style decorations, deemed particularly suitable for smoking- and billiard-rooms, added an exotic touch to many Victorian homes. Up until the 1860s, however, the effects in these interiors were largely picturesque and it was not until the decoration of Owen Jones' Alhambra Court, produced for the Crystal Palace Exhibition of 1851, that the first example of truly authentic Islamic architecture and patterning appeared. Leighton's Arab hall reflects this more archaeological approach to Moorish design and, while it was not directly influenced by Jones's work, the style of decoration clearly owes much to the colours and patterns popularized in source books such as his *Plans, Elevations, Sections and Details of the Alhambra* (1836–45).

The building itself was modelled on an existing hall at La Zisa, near Palermo in Sicily, which Aitchison had drawn whilst on an Italian tour in the 1860s. Its typically Moorish features include the arched window recesses, squinches and the large pendentive dome. Carved lattice wood covers the windows and an eighteenth-century zenana-, or harem-screen, purchased in Damascus, hangs above the entrance to the hall. The central pool was Aitchison's invention, as was the vertiginous copper and wrought-iron chandelier which, like the rest of the lighting in the house, was converted to electricity in the late 1880s. Leighton also, however, wished to make the hall a showcase for contemporary art and he commissioned Walter Crane to design the mosaic frieze and Randolph Caldecott and Edgar Boehm to model and carve the marble and gilt capitals of the pillars.

To contemporaries, the Arab Hall and, indeed, Leighton's house as a whole, was a marvel. An anonymous author in the *Strand Magazine* of 1892 declared, "Sir Frederick's [*sic*] Arabian Court is simply a creation; one can only stand and listen to the splashing of the fountain falling beneath the golden dome . . . and conjure up recollections of the finest scenes and grandest of

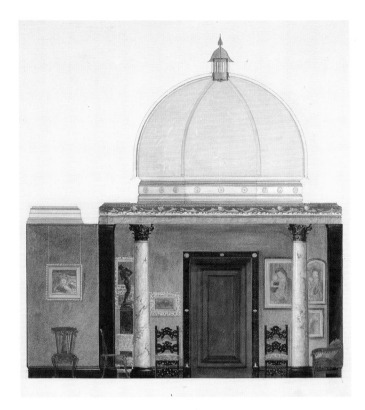

150. *George Aitchison,* DESIGN FOR THE PICTURE GALLERY AT LEIGHTON HOUSE, *1895. The Picture Gallery was the last of Aitchison's additions to Leighton House. It was designed to house items from Leighton's collections of Old Master and contemporary paintings and included a colourful plaster frieze of dolphins below a large glass dome. Decorative though this feature was, it was deemed somewhat overpowering and on Leighton's instructions it was painted white.*

palaces described in the Arabian Nights"; while Mrs Haweis, an influential authority on decoration and design, was no less effusive. Having praised the decorations throughout the house as a model of artistic and elegant taste, she singled out the inner hall as "possessing an imperial stateliness and strength of flavour", and concluded "the silence is like a throne". Nevertheless, the building itself, however, was not to everyone's taste and old Lady Holland, who was still living at Holland House, complained of the "fantastic erections of Watts and Leighton" that threatened to spoil her view, while Godwin pronounced Leighton House "altogether unsatisfactory . . . Mr. Webb's work . . . next door . . . is chiefly admirable for the very things in which its neighbour is so utterly deficient – viz. beauty of skyline and pleasing arrangement of mass."

The house to which Godwin refers was built in 1865 for another painter, Val Prinsep, who had been a pupil of Watts and Rossetti and who had worked on the decorations of the Oxford Union Debating Hall. Prinsep's home, situated on the site adjacent to Leighton House, was designed in the Gothic mould and the simplicity of its architecture recalls elements of Webb's work at the Red House, Bexleyheath. By the 1870s, however, artists wanted homes that were more picturesque and from this time many favoured houses built in the more fashionable, and overtly artistic, Queen Anne style. Two painters' houses, designed by Norman Shaw, exemplify this trend. The first was commissioned by Luke Fildes, and the second by Marcus Stone. Both were

148. (*opposite, above*) and 149. (*opposite, below*) TWO VIEWS OF THE STUDIO AT LEIGHTON HOUSE, *1895. Filled almost to overflowing with antique furniture, carvings, bronze dishes, oriental vases, embroidered fabrics, books, designs and Persian rugs, Leighton's painting room epitomizes the style of "swell studios" and was devised to suggest an air of scholarship and creativity. Plaster copies of the Parthenon frieze and Michelangelo's* Tondo *hang above the door and numerous small landscapes painted by the artist himself cover the walls. The studio was also a setting for Leighton's celebrated "At Homes" and Alice Corkran recalled an evening when "splendid carpets hung from the gallery at one end . . . flowers of perfect bloom brightened every corner. The pictures of the year stood about on easels. Lovely and charming, women, men distinguished in every walk of life, thronged the room . . . the house was filled with the sounds of Joachim's and Piatii's violins, with the accent of perfect voices singing."*

ARTISTS' HOMES
N°9
M.ʳˢ S. LUKE FILDES'
HOUSE·AND·STUDIO·
KENSINGTON
R. NORMAN SHAW R·A· ᴬᴿᶜᴴᵀ

151. *Maurice Adams*, ENGRAVING OF 11 MELBURY ROAD, *1880.*
Luke Fildes's house underlined, in terms of both its size and its cost,
how an artist's home could be an important means of advertising his
status and prosperity.

started in 1875 and both occupied plots on Melbury
Road. Fildes and Stone enjoyed a friendly rivalry and
each considered their own house to be superior to the
other's despite the fact that they were designed by the
same architect and erected by the same builder, Henry
Lascelles. In November 1876 Fildes wrote, "The house
is getting on famously and looks stunning . . . it is a long
way the most superior house of the lot; I consider it
knocks Stone's house to bits, though of course he
wouldn't have that by what I hear he says of his, but my
opinion is the universal one." Despite the lighthearted
tone of these remarks, they underline the fiercely competitive nature of the Victorian art world and highlight
the importance of artists' houses in confirming their
owners' status and success.

Along with Fildes and Stone, other artists also came to
Holland Park. In 1876, the sculptor Hamo Thornycroft
and the painter Colin Hunter built houses at 2 and 14
Melbury Road, and during the 1890s, the portrait-
painter Sir James Shannon and the cartoonist Phil May
moved to Holland Park Road. By the end of the century
the area had become the focal point of London's
fashionable artistic life. However, not all the houses built
there were "Palaces of Art", and Walter Crane's home at
13 Holland Street serves as a useful corrective to this
view of artists' homes.

During the 1870s Crane had lived in Shepherd's Bush
and his move to Kensington in the early 1890s shows
him to have been going up in the world. Nevertheless,
his house was rented, not owned, and unlike those of his
contemporaries, it was furnished in a markedly homely
and comfortable style. This was not because Crane was
unable to devise elaborate decorative schemes. His work
at Clare Lawn and Coombe Bank executed in 1888 and
1879, had included lavish use of gilded and painted
plasterwork and, with far greater experience of design,
he was in many ways much better placed than most
other painters to provide an ornate "artistic" home.
Crane, however, was not as wealthy as his neighbours in
Melbury Road and, a committed socialist, his personality
did not lean towards self-advertisement or extravagance. More important still, his taste in interior decoration was for simple and more homely styles. A follower
of Morris, he espoused the same ideal of furnishings
that were not only beautiful and well-made, but also
functional and restrained. In decoration, he favoured
the Queen Anne and Arts and Crafts styles. The historian Charlotte Gere has pointed out how neither of
these styles proved popular in wealthy Victorian homes.
Queen Anne, as practised by the most progressive
exponents of the style, gave little scope for conspicuous
consumption while the Arts and Crafts interior can be
said to have totally repudiated the wanton luxury of the
rich. Thus, in place of the opulent gilding and *objets d'art*
to be found at Leighton House, 13 Holland Street was
filled with hand-crafted furniture and wallpapers of
Crane's own design, and his house was closer to the
Home Beautiful of the early twentieth century than to

an Aesthete's "Palace of Art". A writer in the *Ladies Field* noted the distinctions between these two styles and observed, "the beautiful things with which Mr. Crane's house is filled are obviously for use and not for show", concluding, significantly, "It is evidently an artist's home, not an artist's reception rooms."

Artists' Chelsea

Chelsea of the mid and late nineteenth century represented a very different social and artistic milieu to that of Holland Park. During the eighteenth century the Physick Garden on Swan Walk had attracted affluent apothecaries, and rows of elegant Georgian housing had sprung up in the neighbourhood around Cheyne Row and Cheyne Walk. By the early nineteenth century, however, the area had become somewhat run-down, and with the opening in 1832 of the infamous Cremorne Gardens, which advertised mock tournaments,

---

152. THE DRAWING-ROOM AT 13 HOLLAND STREET, *1890s. The comparatively simple and homely style of decorations in Crane's house represents a striking contrast with the opulence and luxury of the interiors at Leighton House. Many of the decorations were designed by Crane himself and include the Marguerite and Dove wallpapers, and a settee exhibited at the Arts and Crafts Exhibition of 1889.*

pony races and balloon ascents, and which was much frequented by prostitutes, pickpockets and drunkards, Chelsea's riverside gained a reputation for being neither prosperous nor genteel. Artists, moreover, had gravitated to localities such as Long Acre and St Martin's Lane which were closer to the centre of the capital and gave easy access to theatres and clubs. However, with the development of interest in landscape painting, Chelsea's picturesque views of the river represented an increasingly significant attraction, and several painters took up residence in the undeveloped areas close to the waterfront. J. M. W. Turner, for example, rented a small house on Cheyne Walk to which he would retreat for weeks or months at a time. Leopold Martin, the son of the painter John Martin, visited him there in 1832 and recorded his impressions of the house: "it was a small, six-roomed house on the banks of the Thames in a very squalid place past Lindsay Row", and "with but three windows in front", he declared it to be "miserable in every respect". Nevertheless, Turner was followed by other artists – including the Martins themselves – and with the influx of literary figures such as Leigh Hunt and Thomas Carlyle in the 1830s and 1840s, the area around Cheyne Walk began to assume an air of Bohemian chic. Two communities of painters took up residence there: the first Pre-Raphaelites, and the second Aesthetes.

The Pre-Raphaelite phase of Chelsea's history began

153. *(opposite, above) Henry Teffry Dunn,* THE SITTING-ROOM AT TUDOR HOUSE, *1882. Contrary to popular belief Rossetti's home was neither the depraved den of an opium addict nor the uncared-for abode of a Bohemian. The interior here represents the taste of a cultivated Aesthete and highlights his interest in exotica and antiques. It is dominated by a large Chinoiserie mirror but also contains a Regency overmantel, Delft tiles and ornaments, an eighteenth-century Italian sofa and examples of early Italian and contemporary art.*

154. *(opposite, below) George Robinson,* THE DRAWING-ROOM AT TUDOR HOUSE, *1882. Running across the entire width of the front of the house, this room was also used as a dining-room, and the heavy patterned drapes and elaborate candelabra provided an appropriately theatrical setting for Rossetti's carefully orchestrated dinners and evening entertainments.*

in 1862 when Dante Gabriel Rossetti moved to Cheyne Walk. Rossetti's wife, Elizabeth Siddal, had died in February 1862, and it was undoubtedly a desire to escape the painful memories of her death that prompted him to move from the rooms that the two had decorated in Chatham Place. He was also becoming increasingly successful during this period, and with financial security at last within his grasp he decided to take over the lease of a large eighteenth-century house, rented from Lord Cadogan, at 16 Cheyne Walk. The house was known as Tudor House in deferrence to the tradition – actually completely erroneous – that it had once been used as a nursery for the children of Henry VIII, and it stood in an acre of garden containing a long avenue of lime-trees and enclosed by a high wall. Here Rossetti kept his menagerie of curious animals and birds, including the peacocks whose shrill cries so incensed the other residents of Cheyne Walk that Lord Cadogan thereafter inserted a paragraph in his lease prohibiting the keeping of these birds.

The house itself was fairly spacious but had been much altered during the late eighteenth and early nineteenth centuries. A large bay window had been added to the street front and the original staircase removed, and by the time of Rossetti's occupation the building had become a labyrinth of passages "so filled with crooks and corners as to bewilder the most ingenious observer". The main rooms consisted of sitting-room, studio and breakfast room on the ground floor with Rossetti's bedroom, the drawing-room and additional bedrooms above. The studio had originally been the dining-room, but at Rossetti's insistence the mullioned window was enlarged to provide useful additional light.

Judging from contemporary descriptions the rest of the interior was rather dark and it was filled with an assortment of curiosities and antiques. Rossetti's passion for collecting is now well known. He had been one of the earliest collectors of Japanese ceramics, purchasing examples from Sir Rutherford Alcock's display at the Great Exhibition of 1862, and the catalogue of the sale of the contents of his house on 15 July 1882 lists an impressive array of sixteenth- and seventeenth-century furnishings, ancient metalwork and statues as well as the more obviously fashionable Turkey rugs, Japonaiserie, cane and Chippendale-style work. His bedroom contained a huge eighteenth-century four-poster bed "bought from an old furniture shop somewhere in the slums of Lambeth" and a "medley assortment of brass repoussé dishes, blue china vases . . . oddly fashioned Early English and foreign candlesticks". These, together with the heavy velvet curtains and seventeenth-century crewel work bed hangings, led one visitor to pronounce the room sombre, concluding that "the very gloom of the place made one feel depressed and sad". Even more gloomy, though, was the bedroom occupied by the critic Theodore Watts-Dunton, who was a regular guest at Tudor House during the 1870s. All the furniture in this room was ebonized or painted black – a fashionably Aesthetic touch – and according to Watts-Dunton it was so "crowded with old carved heads and grinning gargoyles and Burmese and Chinese Buddhas . . . of every degree of placid ugliness" that it acquired the reputation for being haunted.

Like Leighton, Rossetti entertained in style, and Tudor House provided an exotic setting for carefully orchestrated soirées and gatherings of poets, painters and society wits. Unlike Leighton, however, Rossetti never aspired to official status or publicity, and the interiors of his home were not photographed or widely reported in the same way as those at Leighton House. Fortunately, though, several of the rooms were recorded in paintings by his studio assistant, Henry Teffry Dunn, and these, together with Dunn's memoirs, published posthumously in 1904, provide a valuable record of the furnishings and decorations at Tudor House. Dunn's descriptions of the drawing-room and sitting-room are worth quoting at length. Of the downstairs sitting-room he recalled:

On gaining admission I was ushered into one of the prettiest and most curiously furnished old-fashioned parlours that I had ever seen. Mirrors and looking-glasses of all shapes, sizes

155. ENGRAVING OF THE DRAWING-ROOM AT BELLE VUE HOUSE, *1882. The mixture of oriental plates, Persian carpets and neo-classical paintings with an embroidered portière and an Adam plasterwork ceiling in the sitting-room at William Bell Scott's home represents an artful blend of Aesthetic and Queen Anne styles. The painter moved to Belle Vue House in 1876 and remained there until his death in 1890.*

and design lined the walls . . . What space there was left was filled up with pictures chiefly old and of interesting character. The mantel-piece was a most original make-up of Chinese black lacquered panels bearing designs of birds, animals, flowers and fruit in gold relief . . . On the other side of the grate were inlaid a series of old blue Dutch tiles mostly of Biblical subjects done in the serious comic manner that existed at the period. The firegrate was a beautifully wrought specimen of 18th century design and workmanship of brass with fire-irons and tender to match. In one corner of the room stood an Old English china cupboard: inside was displayed a quantity of Spode ware. I sat myself down on a dear little cosy sofa with landscapes and figures painted on the panels of the Cipriani [late eighteenth-century] period.

The drawing-room on the first floor was a large rectangular room, 40 feet long, that extended across the entire width of the front of the house. On formal occasions it was used as a dining-room, and Teffry Dunn remembered it as:

A beautiful room by day when the sun streamed in and lit up all the curious collection of Indian cabinets, couches, old Nankin and miscellaneous odds and ends with which it was crowded almost to superfluity, but at night when the heavy Utrecht velvet curtains were drawn and the dining table extended to its utmost length, when the huge Flemish brass wrought candelabra with its two dozen wax lights that hung suspended from the ceiling midway over the table was lit up and the central old-fashioned silver epergne filled with flowers, then the room was filled with a pleasant glow and warmth, anticipatory of the company expected.

It is interesting to compare these rooms with those in houses belonging to Morris and Burne-Jones, with whom Rossetti was closely associated during the late 1850s and 1860s. There are certain obvious affinities with the Morris style. The deep green colour of the

panelling in the sitting-room, for example, was a characteristic feature of Morris & Co. interiors and was used in the Green dining-room at South Kensington and in the rooms at 1 Holland Park, while the lyre-back chair that appears in the background of Dunn's painting was one that Rossetti designed for the firm in 1866. Similarly, the light antique furnishings in the drawing-room echo the style of furniture favoured by Morris from the 1870s. Nevertheless, the hand-painted furniture and woven hangings that play so prominent a role in the decorations at both The Grange and the Red House are noticeably absent in Rossetti's home and there is little evidence of the medievalizing influence that had exercised so strong a hold on the Morris circle in its formative years. The inspiration at Tudor House was, in

156. (below) E. W. Godwin, REVISED DESIGN FOR THE FRONT ELEVATION OF THE WHITE HOUSE, 1877. Built for James McNeill Whistler, the White House was arguably the most innovative and original of any nineteenth-century artist's home. Godwin's first design contained virtually no ornament and was rejected by the Metropolitan Board of Works. His second design, illustrated here, included changes, such as the addition of panels of decoration between the windows and above the door, but the daringly asymmetrical placing of the openings was retained.

157. (opposite) E. W. Godwin, FIRST DESIGN FOR THE EXTERIOR OF FRANK MILES'S HOUSE, 1878. The first design for Frank Miles's house at 44 Tite Street was possibly even more radical than that for the White House. Once again, however, Godwin was forced to make changes and the stark simplicity and angularity of the façade was later softened by the introduction of a Flemish gable over the studio window and door.

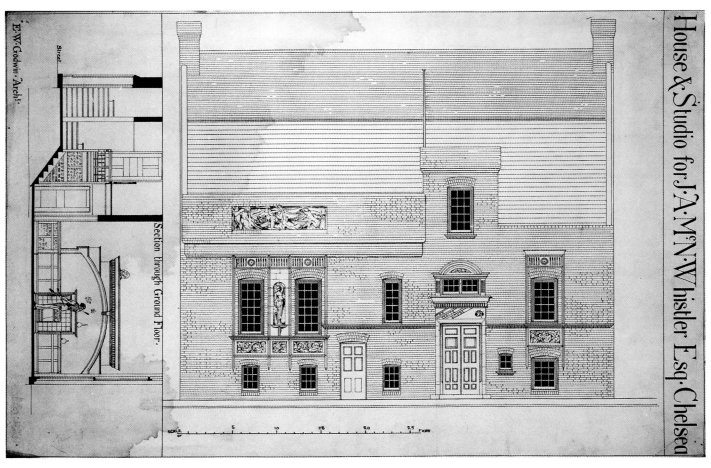

fact, far more Aesthetic than Pre-Raphaelite, and in the pale yellow walls of the drawing-room, the elegant eighteenth-century furniture, the Dutch tiles, and the ebonized and lacquered Chinoiserie mantels and mirrors, can be seen prefigurings of elements characteristic of late nineteenth-century progressive, artistic taste.

During the 1870s several other members of the Pre-Raphaelite circle moved to Chelsea, including the potter William de Morgan and the artist William Bell Scott. De Morgan lived firstly at 30 Cheyne Row and later, from 1887, at 1 The Vale, which A. M. W. Stirling described as "full of unexpected nooks and irregularities, spruce with gay Morris papers and decorated with De Morgan

pots and rich-hued paintings". Scott settled in 1876 at Belle Vue House on Cheyne Walk, and an illustration in Moncure Conway's *Travels in South Kensington* (1882) shows the highly individual blend of Queen Anne and Aestheticism that he contrived. By the late 1870s, however, Rossetti was becoming more reclusive – he was addicted to the drug chloral (a tincture of opium) and he suffered increasingly from bouts of depression, attacks of madness, and general ill health. He died in 1882 at Birchington-on-Sea, Kent, by which time the artistic focus of Chelsea had shifted from Tudor House to Tite Street. At its centre was the American painter James McNeill Whistler.

Tite Street

Whistler was much disliked by the Royal Academicians at Holland Park. His dandy's clothes, "irregular" domestic arrangements and outspoken manner did little to endear him to these pillars of the establishment, and when he engaged Ruskin in the celebrated libel action of 1878, they closed ranks against him, condemning both his "slapdash" painting and his Bohemian life-style. Notwithstanding, Whistler's house at Tite Street was one of the most innovative of any built in the late nineteenth century and was the first of a remarkable series of artists' houses designed by Godwin from 1876–9.

Whistler had first come to live in Chelsea during the late 1850s, when he shared a house in Sloane Street with his sister and her husband, the engraver Francis Seymour Haden. In 1863 he moved to 101 Cheyne Walk and in 1866 to 2 Lindsay Row, a Georgian terrace that had previously been occupied by the painters John Martin, Daniel Maclise and William Dyce. During this period he became increasingly interested in the idea of opening an atelier and it was this, as much as his increasing reputation, that prompted him to commission Godwin to design a new home.

The site that he chose was close to Chelsea Embankment, a new riverside development just over three-quarters of a mile long, constructed by the Metropolitan Board of Works between 1871 and 1874. This body controlled all the leases on the surrounding areas and on 23 October 1877, Whistler signed an agreement to build a studio house on a double plot of land on Tite Street. The building was to be an "ideal" house; a studio, school for pupils and residence all in one, and Godwin's design was revolutionary in its simplicity. A green slate roof surmounted white brick walls, and with the exception of a few mouldings around the asymmetrically placed windows and doors, there was virtually no ornament. The house was called the White House and work on the building began in 1878. Mark Girouard has chronicled its subsequent history: the Metropolitan Board of Works rejected Godwin's designs, declaring the elevation to be "of an ugly and unsightly character", and after a long and bitter wrangle it was finally agreed that he should alter the plain façade, adding stone surrounds to the door and window, and inserting two panels filled with sculpture between the windows and in the roof. Only the first part of this work was ever carried out for in May 1879, following the libel case, Whistler was declared bankrupt. His period of occupation had lasted only a matter of months, and in September 1879 the White House was sold to the art critic Henry Quilter who substantially altered the building and the façade.

Unfortunately, none of the interiors at the White

House survives and given the brevity of Whistler's stay there it is unlikely that they were ever completed. Much, however, can be surmised from contemporary descriptions and from his work at other houses during the 1870s and 1880s. The colour was apparently predominantly light yellow, and Charles Augustus Howell remarked that "to be in Whistler's house was like standing inside an egg". Other features included schemes based upon the "Harmony in Yellow and Gold" exhibited in Paris in 1878, and much of the furniture was ebonized and designed by Godwin in the new Anglo-Japanese style (see previous chapter). Japanese matting was used on the floors and a vast quantity of Nankin china, ornaments and oriental prints stood on shelves and adorned the walls. The critic Malcolm C. Salaman visited a studio that Whistler occupied in the 1880s and remarked particularly upon features such as "plain white-washed walls . . . the vast space unencumbered by furniture, and the large table-palette, . . . [which] all give the appearance of the working-place where serious Art alone is tolerated". A Whistler self-portrait of 1864 suggests the appearance of such a scheme. It shows him standing in a studio where the only decoration is provided by the blue and white china displayed on the elaborately bracketed shelves of an overmantel and if this is taken as a guide to the interiors at the White House, they must have appeared remarkably unfussy and free of clutter.

Whistler's interest in interior decoration was neither casual nor amateur. A letter to Theodore Duret of 1885 included the remark, "For you know I attach just as much importance to my interior decorations as to my painting", and as well as fitting out his own homes, he advised on interiors for Sir Thomas Sutherland, William Heinemann, Mortimer Menpes and Mrs D'Oyly Carte. His most celebrated commission was the Peacock room painted for F. R. Leyland in 1877, whose history has been described in the previous chapter, but an examination of his notebooks reveals many drawings for furniture and he was clearly much interested in all aspects of domestic design. His main concern, however, was with wall treatments and colour schemes and it was here that he made his main contribution to Aesthetic taste. Mrs D'Oyly Carte explained how he worked:

It would not be quite correct to say that Mr. Whistler designed the decorations of my house, . . . what he did do was to design a sort of colour-scheme for the house, and he mixed the colours for distempering the walls himself, leaving only the painters to apply them. In this way he got the exact shade he wanted . . . He distempered the whole of the staircase walls a very light pink colour; the dining room a different and deeper shade; the library he made one of those yellows he had in his own drawing room, a sort of primrose which seemed as if the sun was shining, however dark the day, and he painted the woodwork with it green, but not like the ordinary painters' green at all. He followed the same scheme in the other rooms. His idea was to make the house "gay" and delicate in colour.

Whistler's priority, therefore, was to achieve subtle harmonies of colour and hue, and with the exception of the Peacock room, all his interiors used flat tones devoid of pattern or ornament. At a time when luxuriant pattern, painted for those who could afford it and printed for those who could not, had become manda-

158. *James McNeill Whistler,* THE ARTIST IN HIS STUDIO, *1864. Whistler's studio represents a powerful affirmation of his painting style and suggests the same liking for subtle colour harmonies and Far Eastern ornament. Furnishings were kept to a minimum and the walls were often plain so as not to detract from the effect of the paintings. In comparison with most other Victorian artists' homes his interiors were remarkably uncluttered and their effect was one of understated elegance.*

159. (*above*) and 160. (*opposite*) TWO INTERIORS AT 25 CADOGAN GARDENS, *1895. Designed by A. H. Mackmurdo for the painter Mortimer Menpes, this house represented one of the most authentically Japanese interiors of its time and contained a range of furniture and fitments that had been made specially for the owner by Japanese craftsmen whilst he was on a visit to Japan. However, within a decade Menpes's tastes had changed and in 1900 he exchanged the somewhat dubious comforts of his oriental home for the more prosaic delights of an English fruit farm in Kent.*

tory in fashionable interiors, this emphasis on plain, blank walls was radical to say the least and went against the grain of popular taste. No less extraordinary was his liking for pale colours, and the light yellows, pinks and greys employed throughout the White House must have appeared strikingly fresh beside the deep blues, Indian reds and tobacco browns favoured in Royal Academicians' homes. Both preferences were ones that Whistler shared with Godwin, who advised on all the interiors at the White House, and pale colours, in particular, became the hallmark of Aesthetic taste during the late 1870s. Much-admired, and indeed, much-copied by contemporaries such as Oscar Wilde, it was nonetheless a taste that proved too extreme for general consumption. Even the more avowedly artistic adherents of Aestheticism tended to prefer strong tones, and it was not until the end of the century, when white walls began to appear in certain Arts and Crafts interiors, that lighter, simpler schemes became in any sense popular or influential.

Whistler's presence in Tite Street acted as a magnet for many of his admirers and friends and the area around the Embankment soon became notorious as a stronghold of Aestheticism. The first of the Whistler circle to follow him there were the painters Archibald Stuart-Wortley and Carlo Pellegrini, for whom Godwin designed a double studio house opposite to the White House in 1878. A month or two later Godwin began work on another studio house for Frank Miles, which was situated a little further up the street. When the design for this commission came before the Metropolitan Board, it suffered a fate similar to that of the White House. The Board declared it to be "worse than Whistler's" and once again Godwin was forced to make changes to the exterior. He "introduced a number of reminiscences of a visit to Holland" – that is, he made the façade more obviously Queen Anne – and "the thing was pronounced charming", enabling building to go ahead in 1879. Inside, the staircase had delicate Japanese-style balustrading and in the studio was a deep and capacious inglenook similar to one that had been designed for the White House. Perhaps the most unusual of the Chelsea Aesthetes' houses, however, was that belonging to the Australian painter Mortimer Menpes, which was located not in Tite Street, but in Cadogan Gardens, close to Sloane Square.

Menpes had met Whistler during the 1860s and was a regular visitor to his studios at the White House and 2 Lindsay Row. His first house in Fulham had been decorated with the older artist's help, and at his suggestion Menpes had introduced a number of Japanese fans and oriental embroideries into interiors largely furnished with Sheraton-style tables and chairs. Over the

course of the next few years Menpes' keen, but essentially amateur interest in Japan became much more pronounced, and by 1888, the year in which he purchased the Mackmurdo house at 25 Cadogan Gardens, he had become a passionate advocate of oriental decoration and art. His own account, published in *The Observer* of 1900, provides a full description of the history of this house:

Some twelve years ago, I built the shell of a house – simply the bricks and mortar. Then I proceeded to Japan with a view to preparing the interior. I had taken with me very full plans and I gathered together the best artists and craftsmen that I could command. Altogether I employed for more than a year upwards of one hundred men . . . Ceiling, doors, wall-coverings and windows were finished completely according to plan by these Japanese craftsmen. In two hundred packing cases their work was carried to London . . . [and] so perfectly was everything made that it simply had to be fitted in without the aid of nails and glue.

The result was described as a "dream of Oriental beauty" and contained an unprecedentedly comprehensive range of genuine Japanese furnishings and ornaments. The floor was covered with matting, the lights were Japanese lanterns and the furniture included numerous lacquered tables and chairs. Fretwork wood screens lined the walls, the ceilings were embellished with carvings of Japanese flora – a different example being used in each room – and the colour-schemes throughout were light and clear. The hall, for example, was painted pale apple-green, and the dining-room vermilion, while the reception rooms were decorated in tints of yellow derived from the interiors at the White House. This last feature was considered highly original

by Menpes' friends, and certainly, in comparison with other Anglo–Japanese interiors of this date, his house was a remarkably authentic rendering of oriental decoration and design. Whistler, however, was infuriated by Menpes' unacknowledged copying of his taste. He subsequently broke off all relations with his erstwhile protégé and in a widely-reported public row, he accused Menpes of plagiarism and likened him to "the kangaroo of his country, born with a pocket and putting everything into it"!

With the passing of interest in Orientalism, interest in Menpes' house also waned. Unlike the White House, it inspired no imitations, and by the end of the century even Menpes himself had tired of living in the Japanese style. In 1900 the house was put up for auction, all the contents were offered for sale, and Menpes exchanged the discomforts of his "Oriental dream" for the more conventional delights of a fruit farm in Kent.

Tite Street, and to a lesser extent Tudor House, exemplify the more avant-garde of Victorian artists' houses, the majority of which were ultimately furnished and decorated in a fairly orthodox manner. Whistler's house, especially, represents not only a powerful affirmation of his painting style but also a radical and distinctive new development in nineteenth-century interior design. The fact that its light, uncluttered style of decoration was not to become influential until the end of the century serves to strengthen, rather than weaken, its innovatory status, and both in its individuality and in its claims to originality the White House can be seen as prefiguring the character and ambitions of artists' homes of the modern period.

UNDERGROUND

SANCTUARY.

"'Tis pleasant, through the loopholes of retreat,
To peep at such a world; to see the stir
Of the great Babel, and not feel the crowd;
To hear the roar she sends through all her gates
At a safe distance, where the dying sound
Falls a soft murmur on th' uninjured ear."

William Cowper.

J. R. & CoLTD

THE SOONEST REACHED AT ANY TIME

GOLDERS GREEN
(HENDON AND FINCHLEY)
A PLACE OF DELIGHTFUL PROSPECTS

COTTAGE STYLE

Away, then, to the country – the healthy, the pure, the lovely country! . . . Away to
the uncontaminated country! . . . Let us visit the snug homestead of the farmer, the
good old English yeoman; the old orchard and the old croft; the ancient secluded
path with its antique stiles; the cottage of the labourer and his little garden; the
village inn and the village common – all objects from the loftiest to the most
humble, which, with their living characters, various in station and degree, make
perfect the picture of rural life and rural scenes.
(*Martingale,* English Country Life, *1843*)

Between 1801 and 1911 the proportion of the population living in urban areas in England rose from 20 per cent to 80 per cent. The visible decline of the countryside prompted a rush of nostalgia for rural life. Traditionally the countryside held an ambivalent position in English cultural attitudes, sometimes seen as the abode of joy and tranquillity, more often regarded as dull. Now, with the traditional countryside apparently disappearing for ever, pastoral attitudes were reasserted with intensity. The city was seen as physically and morally corrupting. Health and happiness were only to be found in the countryside, in rural life and agricultural occupations. Love of the country became an article of faith, as essential to respectability as the belief in manners or morality. The "lost" values of the English yeoman were resurrected by those living in cities and suburbs, and as the new century approached there grew a steady procession of urban emigrants to the country.

This anti-industrial impulse had three basic elements: the return to the land, the simplification of daily life and the revival of handicrafts.

The ideological and aesthetic framework of the Arts and Crafts Movement, the dominant force in progressive design in the latter quarter of the nineteenth century, was based on an accretion of related ideas – the unification of the arts, the fitness of design to function, the beauty of rustic art, the happiness of the hand-worker, the ugliness of machine-made products. John Ruskin had first popularized the equation between the ugliness of the modern world and the degeneration of

---

161. LONDON TRANSPORT POSTER FOR GOLDERS GREEN, *1908.*
Behind the Arts and Crafts house in its semi-rural idyll can be
glimpsed an idealized version of what is now the Northern line.

craft skills. As traditional manual skills fell out of use, the machine came to be blamed for the social problems that arose with industrialization. This was soon an accepted "fact" for those with artistic leanings.

Morris had proclaimed that the present social and economic system would have to be abolished for beauty to be produced. The Arts and Crafts Movement, which developed in response to the teaching and practice of Morris and Ruskin, was, in the words of Walter Crane, one of its main propagandists, "a revolt against the so-called industrial progress which provides shoddy ware, the cheapness of which is paid for by the lives of their producers and the degradation of their users". The main things Morris wanted to change arose from the mechanical nature of industry, mechanical not only in the use of machines, but in the unimaginative way in which designs were produced, mostly copied from earlier work and traced out by factory draughtsmen and women. The abuses affected not only the worker, whose role was changing from that of craftsman to machine-minder or copy draughtsman, but also society at large, because of the quantity and ugliness of the products. The machine allowed a wealth of patterning and ornament to be produced at little extra expense, and this could be used to disguise poor construction and shoddy materials.

Morris, as previous chapters indicate, had not attempted to reform industrial practices in the way that other design reformers had done; he had proposed, by his personal example, an alternative to commercial manufacturing, which relied on closely knit communities of workers following the model of medieval guilds in their piety, hard work and closeness to nature. He rejected commercial procedures, in principle, if not always in practice, seeing the ideal client–craftsman relationship

162. *F. L. Griggs*, ENGRAVING OF ERNEST GIMSON'S COTTAGE AT SAPPERTON, GLOUCESTERSHIRE, *1922. The walls are of limestone quarried on the site with dressings of local stone. The constructional timbers and joinery are of larch and oak grown locally. The roof is thatched with wheat-straw.*

as an exchange of gifts, freely given and received rather than the interaction between the impersonal, economic forces of the market. Morris believed that workers could feel pride and pleasure in their work only if they were participants in the design process, or at least had some idea of the physical and creative skills involved.

In their enthusiasm for manual skill and their nostalgia for the pre-industrial workshop where there was, according to W. R. Lethaby, one of the most influential figures in the Arts and Crafts Movement, "no one who directs or merely finances what he cannot practise", Arts and Crafts adherents sometimes overemphasized their opposition to machinery. It was fashionable to dismiss machine-made goods as inferior. In practice, designers were not purist. Like Morris, they recognized that the enemy was not the machine itself, but the industrial system. Most Arts and Crafts workers welcomed machinery which eliminated "drudgery", such as power saws, and did not insist that their metals be mined and smelted by pre-industrial methods.

Related to the belief in the necessity for the integration of design and manufacturing, was the unification of the arts, which similarly derived from contemporary notions of medievalism. A development of the philosophies of Pugin and Ruskin, who viewed it as a fundamental characteristic of the Gothic/Pre-Industrial age, it was a concept that underpinned most progressive design. Although a number of painters of the Pre-Raphaelite circle notably Rossetti and Burne-Jones, designed furnishings, this interchange between the arts primarily involved architects.

Design at the time was deeply rooted in the architectural movement of the day. Architecture was regarded as the "mother art". The most successful designers of the day had had an architectural training. Philip Webb, who was much respected by the younger generation of architects, had believed that the architect should control all aspects of a building, structural and decorative as well as practical and spiritual. These ideas, traceable back to Pugin, had an immense influence on the philosophy and practice of the Arts and Crafts Movement.

There was an element of sincere amateurism involved in this dedication of artists and architects to craft and design. This expresses another key idea in the Arts and Crafts Movement, that of "honesty" in design, which involved the practical application of the Pre-Raphaelite painters' aesthetic concern for another central Ruskinian concept, "truth to nature". Honesty in design was measured by the rule of "fitness of purpose" or function. The manifestation of this varied from the design of two-dimensional patterns for carpets, flat textiles and wallpapers; "truth to materials" and the rejection of sham; to a stylistic emphasis on structure and form.

Many designers believed that symbolic expression was an essential part of the design process; everything we surround ourselves with should possess moral meaning. From the allegorical use of lilies and other flowers to the writing of mottoes from the Bible, literature or proverbs, the Victorian tendency to sentimentalize was carried over into the Arts and Crafts Movement.

A distinction should be made here between a very close copying of natural forms and a more analytical abstraction from nature, in which the essential characteristics of forms were accentuated at the expense of surface details. The first tendency owed a great deal to Ruskin, who always insisted that only the minutest understanding and careful rendering of the details of nature could maintain the values he admired. Apparent from the 1830s, this close copying of natural subjects cannot altogether be dissociated from the Gothic Revival, which strove to imitate the medieval stonemason's understanding of nature. Naturalism as a design principle allowed designers to go beyond the Gothic repertory of forms, selecting new examples to copy and extending the applications to cover everything from table legs to gas brackets. Copying from nature suggested a resolve to avoid copying from the past too rigidly. The second tendency towards an abstraction of nature had its origins in the work of the design reformers, exemplified by Owen Jones's famous book, *Grammar of Ornament* (1856). Jones made it clear that he preferred those styles which came closest to what he called "conventionalisation" of nature: Egyptian, Celtic, Moorish, Gothic, Renaissance. The South Kensington Museum had a rapidly growing collection of oriental and exotic art, which provided plenty of examples for designers to study. Many designers, principally Morris, embraced both ways of approaching nature – close copying and abstraction.

Two main stylistic tendencies can be distinguished in the Arts and Crafts Movement. The first, typified by Morris and Ford Madox Brown, was inclined towards

163. (*opposite*) EMBROIDERED HANGING *designed by Godfrey Blount and worked by the Haslemere Peasant Industries Association in silk and hand-woven linen on linen ground, 1896–7.*

164. (*opposite*) WATERCOLOUR DESIGN FOR A STENCIL *by Walter Crane. Probably drawn at the end of the century when this type of decoration was at its most popular.*

165. (*above*) EMBROIDERED PANEL *designed and worked by Grace Christie, c.1914. Mrs Christie's interest in the revival of embroidery techniques is shown in the great variety of stitches used here.*

simplicity, with strong, elementary forms reinforced by an appeal to traditional vernacular values and a reliance on clearly expressed structure and solid workmanship. The second shows an interest in decoration which varies from the highly ornate naturalistic detail of some of the Guild of Handicraft's work, through a very wide spectrum of medieval or Renaissance motifs, to a style which is almost indistinguishable from that which is now recognized as Art Nouveau.

Some of the decorative forms developed by designers in the Arts and Crafts Movement, such as those produced by Mackmurdo, Voysey and Crane, whose work will be discussed later, provided a stylistic nucleus of Art Nouveau forms, which were extended in their implications and associations by Continental designers in the Art Nouveau style.

For all the castigation of the industrial system, most Arts and Crafts practitioners worked in cities, particularly in London and in Birmingham. In terms of its location, organization and membership the Arts and Crafts Movement was predominantly urban. But it saw itself as anti-urban and much of its iconography is pastoral. Buttercups and daisies adorned the tiles around cast-iron fireplaces, and luxuriant foliage evoked woods and hedgerows in wallpapers and furnishing fabrics for mansion flats and suburban villas.

Those urban designers and craftsmen who removed their workshops into the country mainly sought the benefits of rural life for themselves, though they often believed that their presence was a benefit to the countryside. Other country-orientated reformers were anxious to establish rural workshops to encourage people to stay on the land. To this end a number of benevolent schemes provided hand-craft employment.

One of the ironies of the Arts and Crafts Movement was that, despite Morris's Socialist principles, which were shared by almost all his adherents, hand-made decorative art could only be purchased by the very wealthy. The Movement was concerned with the way things were made, with the craftsman, rather than the client. One consequence of this was the formation of the Home Arts and Industries Association in 1884. Organized into hundreds of classes all over the country by Arts and Crafts supporters, such as the Hon. Mabel de Grey and Mrs G. F. Watts, the Association aimed at the infiltration of cultural values and taste throughout society, giving a great range of people the opportunity to make a little money at home and to learn the joys of creativity. Esther Wood, writing of an exhibition of their work in *The Studio* in 1899, declared:

There should no longer be any excuse for an English lady to clothe herself in shoddy material, or for her lover to buy her engine-turned jewellery at the ordinary trade shop. How far more gracious is the gift that bears the stamp of humanity in all its parts – a free, sincere, and intelligent utterance of the joy of living.

In 1898 the Peasant Arts Society was located in Haslemere, where Godfrey Blount launched a "New Crusade" to unite "all those who feel that the time has come to protest against the materialism of the present day and to try and restore nobler ideals of thought and life". In a publication entitled *The New Crusade* (1903), members were urged to give up "useless, cruel and extravagant fashions" and "dress if possible in homespuns" and generally to admire and use "when we can get and afford them handmade boots, crockery, books and furniture".

"New Lifers" was the name given to all those who embraced alternative life-styles in the late nineteenth and early twentieth centuries. The movement towards greater freedom and naturalism, which accompanied anti-industrial sentiments and the cult of the country-

166. (*above*) THE GREAT HALL, SHIPLAKE COURT, OXFORDSHIRE, 1891. *Designed by Ernest George for Mr Robert Harrison, High Sheriff of Oxfordshire. Such halls were apt to become an auxiliary sitting-room, a room with no very specific function, useful for killing time in rather than settling down. They also served as ballrooms.*

167. (*opposite, above*) and 168. (*opposite, below*) EXTERIOR VIEW AND LIVING HALL OF DEANERY GARDEN, BERKSHIRE, *designed by Edwin Lutyens for Edward Hudson, owner of* Country Life *magazine 1899–1902. The design is more suggestive than imitative of the past. The general impression is of a Tudor manor house, but the features are sparingly used and free from historical detail. It was described as "one of the finest pieces of traditional craftsmanship produced in the twentieth century".*

side, touched on virtually all aspects of life and society: dress, diet, schooling, recreation, transport, architecture and town-planning. Rational rooms were created for rational homes. Vernacular traditions provided the inspiration for Cottage Style.

The Vernacular Tradition

Philip Webb has been hailed as a pioneer of the English vernacular style, which can be traced back to the Red House, built for William Morris in 1860. In 1877 Morris founded the Society for the Protection of Ancient Buildings (SPAB), which provided an important forum for the study and application of vernacular building methods.

The homes built in the suburbs and home counties for the new bourgeoisie were designed in the English vernacular tradition, or "Free English" style as Lethaby called it. In contrast to the homes of the previous generation, ostentation and bombast were eschewed in favour of plainness and simplicity, "sweetness and light". The ideal home was one that looked as if it had always been there rather than one which proclaimed its

new stylishness. The wealth of those who commissioned these houses typically derived from commercial or professional pursuits. When, in 1899, the owner-editor of the hugely successful magazine *Country Life*, Edward Hudson, commissioned a promising young architect, Edwin Lutyens, to build a country retreat on the River Thames at Sonning, Berkshire, he chose a vernacular style residence. Large, but not ostentatious, Deanery Garden epitomizes the restrained manner of this style.

Inside the home densely cluttered and elaborately ornamented Victorian furnishings were rejected in favour of clean lines and bare boards. Cottage style was characterized by a variety of architectural features: low ceilings, lead-lighted casement windows, window seats in bays, polished oak floorboards, panelled walls, exposed beams, and built-in cupboards. The inglenook was revived for homes of all sizes and in larger residences, halls and galleries were sometimes incorporated in emulation of baronial halls. Such buildings looked back to some of the oldest buildings in England, copying half-timbered exteriors, small paned casement windows, uneven gables, rustic porches, tile-hung walls and thatched roofs. In some cases the archaic ambitions of the architect were vetoed by the clients; Edward and Constance Garnett rejected the original plans for their new house in Limpsfield, which contained a great hall with a central open fire, and insisted on a more convenient L-shape, with a conventional arrangement of rooms on two floors.

Wall divisions were reduced to two, breaking at door height. The wall area could be plain, patterned or panelled. The frieze was either colour-washed or filled with a large pattern. Special frieze papers could be purchased. Decoratively, the style relied for its effect upon limited areas of elaborate decoration contrasting with plain surfaces. The focal point of the room was the fireplace. Inlays of wood, metal hinges, stained glass and inscriptions decorated plainly constructed furniture and fitments. Upholstery was banished, apart from closely fitting cretonnes, printed velvets and scattered rugs. Country style furniture, epitomized by the Morris and Co. 'Sussex' chair, was selected to complete the effect.

The fashion for collecting antiques, which developed in the latter part of the nineteenth century, encouraged those who adopted the style to scour the countryside for

---

169. (*below*) THE DINING-ROOM AT SMALLHYTHE PLACE, NEAR RYE IN KENT. *A sixteenth-century house owned by the actress Ellen Terry, it was furnished with a mixture of antiques and new cottage style furniture. The house today belongs to the National Trust.*

170. (*opposite*) DESIGN FOR A SITTING-ROOM IN A TOWN FLAT *by Heal's, 1915. Heal's simply styled furniture can be seen here in an elegant modern setting.*

authentic farmhouse furniture. J. H. Elder Duncan in *The House Beautiful and Useful*, first published in 1878, commented on the irony of this practice:

The business of old furniture vending, comparatively new though it is, is a flourishing trade; our country cottages and farmhouses have been denuded of their old tables, chairs, settles, bedsteads, copper warming pans, brass candlesticks, and willow-pattern plates, and there is a pathos in the alacrity with which the cottager yields up fine old household goods, which are probably replaced by horrors from cheap shops.

The actress Ellen Terry filled her famous cottage at Smallhythe, near Rye in Kent, with pewter dishes and Staffordshire china, typical of such ornaments from modest households in preceding decades.

For those who did not have the time or the inclination to track down the genuine article, modern mass-produced items were available from several furniture firms, the best known of which was Heal and Son of Tottenham Court Road, London. The family firm of Heal's was well established in London's West End when

171. (*above*) QUEEN ANNE'S GARDENS, BEDFORD PARK, *lithograph by H. M. Paget.*

172. (*opposite, above*) INGLENOOK AT A HOUSE IN LETCHWORTH.

173. (*opposite, below*) DRAWING-ROOM AT A HOUSE IN LETCHWORTH. *The building is in vernacular style; the furnishings are a mixture of early Victorian, Aesthetic style and rustic.*

Ambrose Heal, who had trained with a cabinet-maker, launched his first catalogue of designs for plain oak bedroom furniture in 1898. In 1900 a Heal's bedroom was displayed at the Paris Exhibition. The *Architectural Review* described it as "a triumph of craftsmanship". Although standards of workmanship were never less than decent, Heal's "Cottage" furniture was more a triumph of commercial acumen. Critics were silenced with the statement that: "It may be objected that our designs err on the side of excessive plainness. Our answer is that economy has been studied everywhere except at the expense of sound construction."

The movement towards simpler and more rational furnishing received a boost from the well-publicized Cantor Lectures of 1880 given by the architect Robert Edis and published as *Decoration and Furniture of the Town House* in 1881. In this book he praised Morris & Co., Crace, Gillow, Jackson & Graham, Holland & Sons and Trollope & Co., "the best of our cabinet makers", for "having for the most part shown a desire to substitute general simplicity of form and detail for extravagance and eccentricity of design and construction". Edis, like many thinking people at that time when typhoid, cholera and a variety of fevers still regularly took a toll of many lives, was greatly concerned with the health hazards created by furnishings. Household dust was particularly harmful for sufferers of tuberculosis, a major cause of death until the 1940s. In 1884 he published *Healthy Furniture and Decoration*. His concern for the dangers of dust led him to pioneer fitted furniture schemes. Edis was inspired by the Ruskinian concept, "fitted for a place and subordinated to a purpose". In 1884 *The Cabinet Maker* pronounced fitted furniture "a new departure in the history of house furnishing". In the same year the International Health Exhibition was held in London. Amongst the exhibitors was the Century Guild, the first group of Arts and Crafts designers to be formed, who were exhibiting publicly for the first time.

Vernacular architecture and cottage-style furniture and furnishings were an integral part of the so-called "Queen Anne" Movement, which will be discussed in more detail below under the subject of revival styles. "Queen Anne" is not simply a revival style, however. Stylistically it bears little resemblance to the decorative arts of the early eighteenth century, but architectural forms of the period were applied to buildings and much furniture produced from the 1870s. The term created a certain amount of confusion at the time and has subsequently become even more complicated. The architect and writer Robert Kerr, in an essay published in 1884,

explained how, "A popular successor to the style of secular Gothic has . . . been growing up of late years . . . somewhat inexpressively and arbitrarily called by the name of the Queen Anne style". It was, he says, evolved to meet "the public demand, now being satisfied by means of an infinitude of charming picturesque detail, chiefly appearing, however, in the design of small works". "Queen Anne" was more an attitude of mind than a style, since it could embrace features of almost any style that happened to appeal to the architect concerned. As the architect William Burges explained, the recipe for "Queen Anne" was:

to take an ordinary red brick house and to put [on it] as many gable and dormers and bow windows as possible – in fact to cut up the outlines; the great object being to get the picturesque by any and every means. The windows should be long and narrow and filled with lead glazing or with small frames divided by straight bars painted white – the ornamental parts consist of a few scrolls in the brickwork and coarse woodwork occasionally verging on the Jacobean.

The haphazard, irregular arrangement of the picturesque was fundamental to the "style"; Jacobean elements were prominent, but so too were elements culled from more recent styles – including actual Queen Anne – and the study of vernacular architecture of no very certain date. Frequently added to this, moreover, was a liberal dressing of Anglo-Japanese ornament.

Bedford Park, erected in West London in the 1880s, was a model suburb, built in the picturesque "Queen Anne" style by Richard Norman Shaw. It was in marked contrast to the surrounding rows of suburban terraces. W. B. Yeats, whose family lived there, recalled "the crooked ostentatiously picturesque streets with great trees casting great shadows", as well as the intentional nostalgia of some of the buildings: a co-operative store that looked like an old world village shop, and a pub named "The Tabard" after the inn in Chaucer's *Canterbury Tales*.

Garden Cities

The garden city was the culmination of the back-to-the-land movement, the vindication of its ideas and its aspirations. The impulse was not backwardly nostalgic, but forward-looking; not to repudiate the city, but to build a new society incorporating all the features of the good life.

The concept was rooted in a number of earlier visions that included Robert Owen's industrial villages at New Lanark and Saltaire; the sanitary reformer, Dr Ward Richardson's "City of Health", to be named Hygeia; and the model villages of Lord Lever at Port Sunlight and George Cadbury at Bourneville. The term was first used and the idea developed by Ebenezer Howard, an American journalist and inventor. In 1898, with the aid of a benefactor, he published *Tomorrow: A Peaceful Path to Real Reform*, reissued three years later as *Garden Cities of Tomorrow*.

The book argued that "there should be an earnest attempt made to organise a migratory movement of population from our overcrowded centres to sparsely settled rural districts". Howard's plan involved a garden city surrounded by farmland containing, amongst other things, cow pastures, allotments, an agricultural college, children's homes, fruit farms, asylums for the blind and a farm for epileptics. Inside the circular city, which is ringed by a railway line, is a layer of industry and commerce around concentric residential circles, pierced by boulevards and avenues leading to a central park, civic buildings and a cultural area. The total population was designed to be 32,000, the size of a small town.

Some thirty years later, Howard's biographer, Dugald MacFadyen, wrote:

The idea is nothing less than a vision of a transformed English industrial civilisation . . . There is no antagonism to any class . . . No abolition of anything in particular except slum dwellings and overcrowded industrial districts . . . Factories – no longer "dark Satanic mills" – have become sightly buildings, standing in gardens . . . Where foxes and partridges have been the principal occupiers of land in parks and preserves the land is carrying its complement of modest homes; red-cheeked children have taken the place of bright-plumaged birds . . . England is looking sober, prosperous, thrifty – as though the bad dream of the industrial revolution has somehow no more permanence . . . the dream is broken, the ugly nineteenth century has been wiped off the slate.

The idea was for the first garden city to be built as a model, with others following and clusters growing up around London. Eventually the whole population remaining in the capital would be temporarily rehoused while London itself was demolished and reconstructed as a garden city.

The publication of Howard's book stimulated the founding of the Garden City Association in 1899. A year later the Association formed the Garden City Ltd. and in 1901 the first garden city conference was organized at Bourneville. It was attended by 300 people from local authorities, churches, trade unions and co-operatives, who shared a common interest in the formation of new towns and estates.

The following year a second conference was held at Port Sunlight, attended by 1,000 delegates. The Garden City Co. purchased a site of 3,818 acres at Letchworth in Hertfordshire and appointed the Derbyshire firm of Raymond Unwin and Barry Parker as consultant architects.

Parker and Unwin were socialists. Inspired by the ideals of Ruskin and Morris and the Utopian community ideals of Edward Carpenter, they remained faithful to a simple vernacular style and made their aim to improve the houses of the working classes. In their writings, particularly in *The Art of Building a Home* (1901), they sought to popularize the Arts and Crafts Movement.

Construction began in the summer of 1904. Residential development was gradual. In the first year fifty plots were let alongside existing roads for the first houses. The Garden City Co. owned the land – houses and factories were erected by individuals and companies acting as leaseholders, and special regulations applied so that all plans were approved by Unwin and Parker. Sites varied in size, but nowhere was a density of more than twelve houses permitted to a single acre. Workmen's homes were built for rent by companies or housing associations.

174. (*above*) THE LIBRARY AT RAINHILL HALL, LIVERPOOL, *1890*. *This room is likely to be the work of A. H. Mackmurdo, and Herbert Horne, since the detailing on the furnishings, such as the arcaded bookshelves, is similar to features of the Century Guild's stand at the Liverpool Exhibition of 1886.*

175. (*below*) HALL AT 46 HOLLYCROFT AVENUE, HAMPSTEAD GARDEN SUBURB, *1906*.

The earliest houses, such as those built by Parker and Unwin for themselves and for Howard in 1904, set the standard, with roughcast walls, dormer windows and tall chimneys. They had "open plan interiors" based on the late medieval hall. A later feature of Parker's houses was a tower to provide balconies for sleeping out in fine weather.

In 1905 the *Spectator* magazine and the Country Gentleman's Association sponsored a Cheap Cottage Exhibition. Plots were allocated and competitors invited to construct dwellings suitable for farm labourers at a cost of no more than £150. Over a hundred houses were built by architects, builders and contractors to a variety of plans, some traditional and some experimental, such as the polygonal house made from Cubitt's prefabricated concrete parts. Baillie Scott, whose work will be discussed in the next chapter, entered the competition but was disqualified for exceeding the cost limit. The houses were let as soon as they were completed on the condition that they were opened to the public for three months. Over 60,000 visitors attended the exhibition.

By 1906 Unwin had transfered most of his work to the new Hampstead Garden Suburb in north London. The suburb was the brainchild of Henrietta Barnett, an enthusiastic social reformer, whose aim was to preserve the Hampstead area from the rapidly encroaching sub-

176. *C. R. Ashbee*, DESIGN FOR THE INTERIOR OF A FLAT AT SHREWSBURY COURT, CHELSEA.

urban developments and to create housing that would accommodate a socially mixed community in terms of income and occupation. The development epitomized the ideal suburb, with a variety of vernacular and Domestic Revival architecture, and was laid out in curved leafy streets. In order to plan the streets as he wanted, Unwin had to have an Act of Parliament passed to get local suspension of the 1875 Public Health Act.

This enabled him to design narrow streets in village style. The houses were quickly taken up, but their inhabitants were almost exclusively middle-class people, keen to acquire cottages close to London. The project failed in its social ambitions.

The Arts and Crafts Movement

The Arts and Crafts Movement gained its cohesion by following Ruskin's advocacy of the medieval guild system. Ruskin personally donated £7,000 in 1871 to found the Guild of St George, an organization whose achieve-

177. *C. R. Ashbee*, WRITING CABINET IN MAHOGANY AND HOLLY WITH METAL MOUNTS, *made by the Guild of Handicraft, 1898.*

to take the post. The Society held its first exhibition of members' work at the New Gallery in Regent Street in 1888. A headline-making reception was organized at which Isadora Duncan was invited to dance and William Morris gave demonstrations of weaving.

Whilst the New Gallery promoted public interest in the work of the Movement's leaders, the Home Arts and Industries Association, founded in 1884, provided an organizational base for the host of amateur craftspeople working at home. All their products, from lace collars to pokerwork tea caddies, were gathered at Carlton House Terrace in 1885 for the first of the Association's annual shows. In 1904 the first practical monthly manual, *Arts and Crafts* began publication.

The Century Guild

The first of the privately run guilds, The Century Guild, was established in 1882 by architects Arthur Heygate Mackmurdo and Herbert Percy Horne. Their ambitions were clearly stated in their magazine *Hobby Horse*:

The aim of the Century Guild is to render all branches of Art the sphere, no longer of the tradesman, but of the artist. It would restore building, decoration, glass-painting, pottery, wood-carving, and metalwork to their rightful place beside painting and sculpture.

The Century Guild operated as a design practice. Its members, amongst whom were Selwyn Image, Harold Rathbone and Clement John Heaton, worked solely to commission rather than offering a range of products for sale. As *The Builder* noted, The Century Guild was "a society of artists primarily, and a trading concern secondarily . . . an inversion of the ordinary trading methods". Their most substantial commission was for a modest "modernist" house in Enfield, built between 1886 and 1887. The group dissolved in 1888, although

ments were limited to the building of a cottage museum near Sheffield and a few "ideal" working men's cottages in Wales.

In 1884 the Art-Workers' Guild was formed by a group of eager young architects working in the office of Richard Norman Shaw. Encouraged by prominent painters such as Holman Hunt, they set up two years later the Arts and Crafts Exhibition Society to promote joint shows of fine and applied art. Walter Crane was voted President, a position he held until 1912, apart from a three year gap from 1893 to 1896 when the grand old hero of the Movement, William Morris, was persuaded

the partnership of Mackmurdo and Horne continued until 1890. The Library at Rainhill in Liverpool, the home of a local business man and politician, Philip Rathbone, although executed in 1890 after the break-up of the Guild, clearly bears the hallmarks of their style. Horne retired to Florence in 1900, and Mackmurdo spent most of the remainder of his long life studying baroque music and publishing esoteric tomes on Socialist reform.

C. R. Ashbee and the Guild of Handicraft

On the evidence of numbers alone, the most fanatical believer in the guild ideal must surely have been Charles Robert Ashbee, whose Guild of Handicraft, founded in 1888 in London's East End, at one time numbered 150 working men, women and boys. Ashbee was motivated primarily by social rather than aesthetic concerns. "Most people", he wrote, "are agreed that one of the greatest problems before the Country is the problem of unemployment." His solution, put forward in *Craftsmanship in Competitive Industry* (1908), was to free the craftsman from "the precarious weekly wage-dependence" and "to put his labour at the service of the community". He was bitterly critical of the education system and its administrative wastage. He called the new Board Schools, set up under the 1888 Education Act, "overgrown and ill-ornamented urinals". Ashbee was a great believer in the

benefits of physical exercise, organizing expeditions for his apprentices to swimming pools, gymnasiums and the countryside, where it was possible for these "young citizens" to "enjoy the use of naked limbs in air and water".

In workshops at Essex House, a ramshackle eighteenth-century building on the Mile End Road in East London, the Guild produced furniture and furnishings, which the *Studio* in 1897 criticized for their "simplicity carried dangerously near triteness". Their work became more confident and inspired after 1898, when Ashbee was commissioned by Baillie Scott to produce all the furniture for the Duke of Hesse's Palace at Darmstadt.

In 1899 the Guild launched the Essex House Press with much of the equipment from Morris's Kelmscott Press, which had been disbanded on his death in 1896. A small shop was run by the Guild in Dering Yard, near the retail warehouse of the successful metalwork firm of W. A. S. Benson. Ashbee also managed to maintain a small architectural practice, from which he designed a number of mildly eccentric houses in Chelsea, in one of which, named the Magpie and Stump after the sixteenth-century inn which once stood on the site, Ashbee lived himself with his mother and his wife.

In 1902 the Guild of Handicraft moved to the Cotswold village of Chipping Camden. One hundred and fifty men, women and children left the East End to start

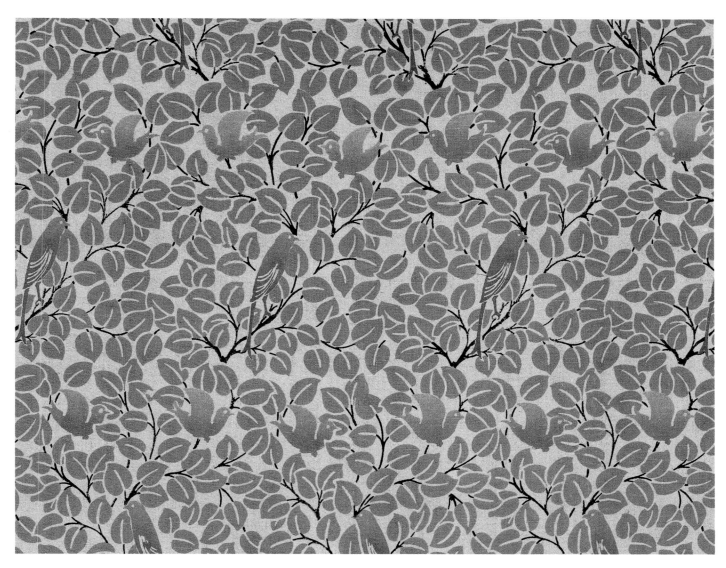

178. (*opposite*) LIVING-ROOM IN HOUSE AT SAPPERTON, GLOUCESTERSHIRE. *Home of Sydney Barnsley, the house was furnished with pieces from his and Gimson's workshops.*

179. (*above*) C. F. A. Voysey, HEDGEROW, *block-printed linen, manufactured by G. P. & J. Baker for Heal & Son, 1908.*

180. (*right*) C. F. A. Voysey, SALADIN, *roller-printed cotton, printed by Stead McAlpine for Warner & Sons, 1895.*

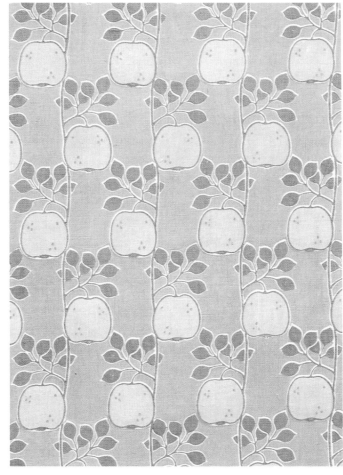

a new life in the country. The social achievements of the Guild were considerable, but financially the venture was a disaster. In London it had been possible for skilled craftsmen to obtain "inferior work . . . in the ordinary commercial shops" to tide them over hard times, but in Gloucestershire there was no alternative but to continue to produce goods which sold for less than they cost to make. In 1907 the Guild was disbanded, although many individuals stayed on to work independently. The Essex House Press survived for a few more years under the direction of Ananda Coomeraswamy. Disillusioned, Ashbee himself moved away from the Arts and Crafts Movement, leaving the field to the "lady amateurs" from the Home Arts and Industries Association, jokingly referred to among the Guild as the generic "Dear Emily", whose livelihood was not dependent on their labour.

Gimson and the Barnsleys

Privately run craft organizations had a high failure rate: the respected Kenton & Co. survived for barely two years after its formation in 1890. Its key founders were William Richard Lethaby and Ernest Gimson, together with Sydney Barnsley, Mervyn Macartney and Reginald Blomfield. In a mews workshop off Kenton Street in the Bloomsbury area of London's West End, they employed seven cabinet-makers to produce furniture designed by the five architect partners. Their first exhibition in 1891 was a critical and financial success, with sales of over £700.

The experiment folded due to the pressure of the partners' outside commitments. Lethaby had established his own architectural practice in 1898 and during the next five years produced amongst the best buildings of his career. In 1896 he co-founded the highly influential Central School of Art and Design. He was Principal of both the Central School and from 1900, the Royal College of Art, until 1914. Like Webb, he declined the RIBA Gold Medal, dismissing this coveted award as "a lot of nobodies giving themselves distinctions".

Ernest Gimson, with Sydney Barnsley and his brother Ernest, made the decision to move from London to the Cotswolds in 1893, where they shared workshops at Pinbury until 1902. Then their landlord, Lord Bathurst, moved them to Sapperton where they worked in a sixteenth-century manor, Daneway House. Here they produced work to commission as well as for direct sales.

C. F. A. Voysey

The last leading figure of the Arts and Crafts Movement, Charles Frederick Annesley Voysey, was "an intense visionary, whose chronic conviction of his own infallibility resulted in difficulties with clients and a tantalizingly small body of immensely impressive work". He always saw himself as an heir of Pugin rather than a founder of the Modern Movement, as was suggested by the many admirers of his work. In his last public lecture in 1934, he responded to his fellow architect, Lutyens's praise for the "absence of accepted forms" in his work:

Modern architecture is pitifully full of such faults as proportions that are vulgarly aggressive, mountebank eccentricities of detail and windows lying down on their sides . . . This is false originality, the true originality having been, for all time, the spiritual something given to the development of traditional forms by the individual artist.

Voysey's principles of domestic architecture were: "Repose, Cheerfulness, Simplicity, Breadth, Warmth, Quietness in a Storm, Economy of Upkeep, Evidence of Protection, Even-ness of Temperature and making the house a frame for its inmates". Like Webb, he designed every detail of the house, down to door hinges and window catches. His houses were rooted in the vernacular tradition. In a lecture to the Architectural Association in 1911 on "Patriotism in Architecture", he claimed that "the best architecture of the past has always been native to its own country and has grown out of a thorough knowledge of local requirements and conditions".

Voysey worked most consistently as a flat pattern designer. He produced his first wallpaper in 1883 for Jeffrey & Co. and was still well enough known in 1920 for Essex & Co to promote him in advertisements as "the Genius of Pattern". As well as wallpapers he designed tiles, carpets, rugs, curtains and furnishing fabrics.

Despite failing to secure a single public commission, Voysey designed, decorated and furnished five small houses, the best-known of which is The Orchard at Chorleywood in Hertfordshire, which he designed for his family in 1899. A committed architectural colourist, Voysey used startling yellows and blues for the exteriors of many of his buildings. Inside The Orchard, although the ground-floor woodwork and walls were enamelled white, he placed a peacock blue rug in the hall, a grey-green carpet up the stairs and hung bright red turkey-twill curtains throughout.

Mission Style

The Mission style, which has many similarities with Cottage style, had strong beginnings in upper New York State, but comparable designs were soon evident in the Midwest and California, especially in Pasadena and San Francisco. Two origins for the name have been suggested: one points to the similarity of Mission furniture to that of the Spanish missions in the West, while the other suggests that the style had a mission to perform – the transformation of earlier mistakes in decoration. The Mission style was one created largely by architectural detail, as well as by furniture and textiles; such detail showed the same angularity as was evident in the furniture – straight, long, vertical and horizontal lines gave even empty rooms a distinctive look. Typical overmantels had hoods, with the fireplace surrounded by tile or brick. Common in country houses were massive fieldstone fireplaces.

American Arts and Crafts organizations in the late nineteenth century were spurred into action by the Arts and Crafts Movement in Britain. Following the formation of the Arts and Crafts Exhibition Society in London in 1888, a similar body was established in Boston in 1897, as many American designers adopted the teaching of Ruskin, Morris and Eastlake.

Gustave Stickley was one of the early leaders of the movement. In 1898 he founded the Gustave Stickley Co. in Eastwood, a suburb of Syracuse, New York, to be distinguished from his brother's rival firm, I. and J. G. Stickley Co. Gustave Stickley used the trade name Craftsman for his products – furniture and work in metal, leather and linen – and in 1901, he started a monthly magazine to promote the new look. *The Craftsman* featured writings of the current art movement and showed ideal interiors adapted to either large homes or bungalows. Stickley's motives were financial as well as aesthetic, for the magazine carried yearly price lists of his products. In 1915 the firm went bankrupt, shortly after executive offices were opened in New York City. The magazine folded the following year.

Stickley's main rival as leader of the movement was Elbert Hubbard, who founded the Roycroft Shops in East Aurora, New York. Inspired by Morris's Kelmscott

181. (*above*) A "CRAFTSMAN" STYLE LIVING-ROOM WITH A RECESSED WINDOW-SEAT, *illustrated in the* Craftsman, *October 1905.*

182. (*below*) HALL BENCH IN HONDURAS MAHOGANY *designed by C. & H. Greene for Blacker House, Pasadena, California 1907–9.*

Press, Hubbard produced fine books as well as a range of decorative items; he established an apprenticeship system which attracted workers from all over the United States; and he also produced a small magazine, *The Philistine*. He died when the *Lusitania* went down, but the Roycroft Shops continued until 1938.

The Arts and Crafts Movement in both Britain and America was losing its momentum by the turn of the century. Its figure-head, William Morris, had died in 1896. The Arts and Crafts Exhibition Society shows of 1903 and 1906 were not successful. Commercial compitititon was undermining those who maintained their commitment to hand production. This came at a time of economic depression, and directly led to the final liquidation of several groups, notably Ashbee's Guild of Handicraft. The relationship between design and industry was being rethought all over Europe and North America by pioneers like Frank Lloyd Wright in Chicago and Josef Hoffmann and the Wiener Werkstätte in Vienna. The greatest contribution of the Arts and Crafts Movement in Britain was to design education. Its promotion of the interdependence of art and craft led to the reorganization and formation of design schools throughout the country, where students were taught by practising designers brought up in the Arts and Crafts tradition. Their direct influence lasted into the 1940s.

Progressive art and design in Britain was largely exemplified by the work of the Arts and Crafts Movement. Avant-garde designers in Britain had to look largely to America and to Continental Europe for recognition and support.

NEW ART

. . . absolute nonsense . . . [a] mud mountain of rubbish daily and yearly heaped up
by the incompetent, social, amateur ass.
(H. Binstead, The Furniture Styles, *1929)*

"NEW ART", "Art Nouveau", "Arte Nova", "Jugendstil" were among the terms that were applied to a style of architecture and decoration that developed in Europe around the turn of the century. These style labels all suggest a conscious effort to break away from the dominant revival styles and all that they represented. The progressive element of this style derived from many of the same sources as the Arts and Crafts Movement, which was developing simultaneously. Practitioners of both the Arts and Crafts Movement and Art Nouveau, as it is most commonly referred to now, made important contributions to the development of Modern architecture and decorative art, which compounds the difficulty of distinguishing between the two. Aspects of both movements have been identified by twentieth-century design historians as "proto-Modern". Designers in both idioms were committed to developing the relationship between architecture and interior decoration. The simplest way to analyse the two is to regard the Arts and Crafts Movement as an essentially ideological expression and Art Nouveau as a purely aesthetic manifestation. Whereas the Arts and Crafts Movement had its origins in the Gothic Revival, Art Nouveau developed from the Aesthetic Movement.

There were two main tendencies: an exuberant, sinuous, organic, asymmetrical, dynamic style, exemplified by the work of French and Belgian designers; and a more restrained, geometric, minimalist style, seen in the work of the Glasgow School and the Viennese Secessionists. Both share a common concern for aestheticism, rather than functionalism, which is the key tenet of the Arts and Crafts Movement. Both are characterized by a vigorously individual and innovative approach, which produced striking visual effects. These were partly created by the use of new materials such as iron and glass in architecture, and experimental techniques in the production of glass and ceramics. Symbolism, as in the Arts and Crafts Movement, was an important element in the application of decorative motifs, but whereas members of the Arts and Crafts Movement tended to invest their forms with moral and political meaning, the architects and designers working in the New style employed more poetic devices. Lilies, sunflowers, tree roots, the swan and the peacock were dominant motifs, symbolizing purity, freedom and promise. They were inspired by remote sources, primarily Japanese, Primitive and Celtic art.

There is sometimes a confusion between Art Nouveau and the Celtic Revival, which originated as a nationalist, literary movement amongst those poets and novelists in Britain who were searching for the roots of their culture in Welsh, Scottish and Irish history. The publication of W. B. Yeats's *Wanderings of Oisin and Other Poems* in 1889 marks the beginnings of this movement. By the 1890s the fashion for Celtic ornament was influencing the decorative arts. From 1899, Liberty's produced two highly successful ranges inspired by Celtic art: "Cymric" silverware and "Tudric" pewter, designed by, amongst others, Archibald Knox and Rex Silver.

The sinuous style, based on plant forms, which was known as Art Nouveau, was applied primarily to graphic design and some decorative art, notably metalwork, furniture and glass. The work of the Czech émigré Alphonse Mucha has come to epitomize the popular conception of Art Nouveau today. Best known for his posters and jewellery, which he made for,

183. *Alphonse Mucha,* DESIGN FOR WALLPAPERS, *published in* Documents Décoratifs, *1902.*

184. *Georges Remon,* DESIGN FOR A CABINET DE TOILETTE, *published in* Interieurs Modernes, *1900. Art Nouveau incorporated many of the key elements of the Aesthetic Movement, seen here in the elaborate working of peacock motif.*

amongst others, the actress Sarah Bernhardt, Mucha also produced designs for wallpapers, textiles and some furniture.

The term 'Art Nouveau' was first applied to progressive art in France in 1895 when the entrepreneur, Samuel Bing, opened a shop of that name at 22 rue de Provence, Paris. Three years later in 1898 the German art critic, Julius Meier-Graefe established its main competitor, La Maison Moderne. With its elaborately intricate detailing it was expensive to produce as so much hand-work was necessary. Its influence was therefore limited to a comparatively small circle of wealthy people who could afford to pay for one-off pieces. The Paris Exhibition of 1900 was at once the apogee and the finale of Art Nouveau. In 1902 Bing retired and his shop, L'Art Nouveau, converted back to a gallery of Far Eastern art and antiquities.

Art Nouveau can rarely be seen as a unified style in domestic interiors. It was used for some interior schemes, mostly shops and restaurants, the most famous of which was Maxim's in Paris, completed in 1899. Describing a salon which he had designed for a private house in the rue Villaret-Joyeuse, Paris, the architect Georges Farcy has explained how Art Nouveau was applied to domestic settings. He believed that the last vestige of artistic tradition had vanished by the time of the First Empire and that the showy styles of the Renaissance, Louis XV and Louis XVI were no longer suitable for modern life, which had been so radically altered by scientific discoveries. Consequently he demanded that a new architecture be developed:

. . . in the first place the rectilinear is only possible as a reminder of the law of gravitation. Objects may be fashioned on the square but every outline that shows visibly on the exterior surface must be full of life and motion so as to delight the eye by its diversity. Symmetrical ornament is out of place in the new art in which every line is supple and winding. The mouldings have been studied with a special view to avoid anything sharp or harsh. There is no straining for outlandish forms; rather the artist's object has been to avoid startling by any exaggeration of detail which is apt to arrest instead of attracting the attention. The colouring of the walls in shades of rose or tenderest green fascinates by its harmonious effect and imparts to the whole a note of warmth far more cheerful than the icy white tone in general vogue. The sight of the soft opalescent tints recalls visions of pale pastels. The new style is one in which women and flowers as being typical of all that is freshest and daintiest provide the principal motifs of decoration.

Most Art Nouveau decoration was a good deal more sober than is generally supposed, and most of the features in the style tended to be two-dimensional. Grey-green with a salmon colour formed an alternative colour scheme at this time to the ubiquitous white. Designs published in the Parisian magazine *Intérieurs Modernes* by the 'architecte-décorateur' Georges Remon demonstrate this approach.

There was an active interchange of ideas between France and Belgium, its north-eastern neighbour, Flemish-born Henri van de Velde was the most out-

185. *Georges Remon*, DESIGN FOR AN INTERIOR, *published in* Intérieurs Modernes, *1900. Most published designs for interiors in the Art Nouveau style were never executed. They exist merely as decorative doodles.*

standing designer in Belgium. A member of the pioneering group, "La Libre Esthetique", in the 1890s, he maintained a prime position in the development of modernism until the 1930s. His work was well represented in Paris through the shops L'Art Nouveau and La Maison Moderne. A spate of commissions from Germany prompted him to settle there in 1898. Although he worked in many parts of Europe, he has always been thought of primarily as a Belgian designer.

Van de Velde was concerned with the idea of a totally harmonious, organic environment. This resulted in the production of furniture, carpeting, embroidery, windows and interior wallcoverings. He even went so far as to design complementary clothing for his interiors (only his wife is known to have worn garments designed by him). This is exemplified in his best-known project, the design of his own home, Bloemenwerf, near Brussels. In 1901 van de Velde was offered an advisory past in Weimar, with the aim of improving the artistic and cultural life of the town. Here he went through several distinct stylistic phases. Influenced by Hoffmann and the Viennese Secessionists, he turned to a simpler, more austere, but lighter and more airy style.

Victor Horta was another Belgian architect-designer. Unlike his compatriot Henri van de Velde, he spent most of his working life in Belgium, designing fur-

nishings only for his own buildings. Horta created buildings that expressed a total, harmonious environment, both inside and out. His first major commission, the Tassel house in Brussels, erected in 1892–3, has often been taken to be the first fully developed Art Nouveau building. His work, which is characterized by exuberant ribbon-like loops, made a great impact on Parisian designers, notably Hector Guimard.

Jugendstil

"Jugendstil", which translated means "young style", was the term applied to progressive art and design in Germany and Austria. A proto-Modern style, which was characterized by stark, unadorned lines and skilful disposition, it was developed in Vienna at the turn of the century, under the influence of Otto Wagner. The best-known practitioners of the style were architect-decorators like Josef Hoffmann, Koloman Moser and other members of the "Secession" group. Although accepted in certain intellectual circles in Germany, particularly in Munich, Berlin and Darmstadt, it was not assimilated into popular culture until the 1920s when a diluted form became the basis for the "Art Deco" style.

The Secession was founded in 1897 by a group of progressive architects and designers who were disgruntled with the conservative academic style. Otto Wagner, who joined the movement in 1899, as former tutor of most of the group, took on the role of *éminence grise*. In 1895 he had published an influential book, *Moderne Architektur*, which provided the basis for the Secessionist aesthetic. Adolf Loos, having trained in Dresden and effect akin to the work of the British designers Charles Rennie Mackintosh and M. H. Baillie Scott.

Many British designers were enormously influential in Europe. In France, the term "Modern Style" had originally been applied to the work which came to be known as Art Nouveau, in acknowledgement of its origins. In Italy it was known as "Stile Liberty", after the London emporium. The flat patterns for wallpapers and textiles produced in the 1880s, notably by Voysey, Crane and Mackmurdo, were particularly influential in the development of modern styles in Europe. The reaction in Britain to Continental Art Nouveau was, however, hugely hostile.

British Reaction to Continental Art

The term "Art Nouveau" was not applied to British art at the time; it was reserved solely for Continental work. The collector and connoisseur, Charles Handley Read, once noted the differences between English and French furniture:

186. (*above*) *Alphonse Mucha*, PAINTED SCREEN.

187. (*right*) WOVEN COTTON FABRIC *designed in Britain and manufactured in Northern France. It was bought in Berlin in 1894.*

188. (*opposite*) *Georges de Feure*, WOVEN SILK, *made in France by Majorelle. It was bought from Bing's 'Maison de L'Art Nouveau' in 1906. One of the most stylish of Art Nouveau designers, de Feure's patterns show the unmistakable influence of British pattern designs, which were also on sale in Bing's shop.*

the United States, settled in Vienna in 1896. In an article published in 1908, he coined the aphorism "Ornament=Crime", which encapsulates the philosophy of the movement. He admired English and American Arts and Crafts designers, whose influence can be seen in his own designs for furniture and interiors. Josef Hoffmann and Koloman Moser were the two most distinctive designers of the Secession group. In 1903 they founded the Wiener Werkstätte (Viennese Workshops), modelled on C. R. Ashbee's Guild of Handicraft. Their object was to apply artistic design to a wide range of decorative products. Their early work was typically rectilinear in style, often ornamented with diaper patterns in black and white or silver. Joseph Olbrich, another founded member of the group, best-known for the design of their dramatic exhibition building in 1897, also worked in Darmstadt, to where he was invited in 1899 by the Grand Duke of Hesse.

Darmstadt attracted a colony of artists and designers from Austria, Germany and Britain. Peter Behrens, a prominent figure in the Munich circle, who was responsible for the formation of the Vereinigte Werkstätten für Kunst und Handwerk (United Workshops for Art and Handwork), was also called to Darmstadt. The dining-room he designed there in 1901 demonstrates an amalgam of straight lines and subtle curves. The furniture, which was all painted white, created a sparse, airy

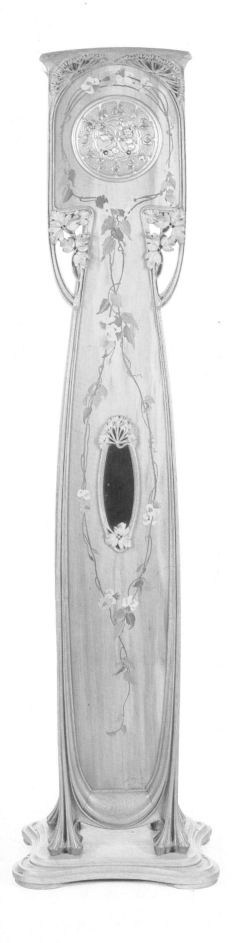

English furniture . . . is always symmetrical in overall shape. None is marked by its plasticity; its structural members never seem about to melt or deliquesce compared with the attenuated linearity of work by Gallé, Gaillard and others where structure and decoration including hinges and handles blend in a plastic, indivisible unity.

The Studio in 1902, whilst promulgating wariness of Continental work, made a plea for a more adventurous approach to design in Britain:

It would be hard to say which is the lesser evil in modern work – the copying of past styles at the expense of structural fitness and efficiency, or the deliberate effort of a self-conscious person "to do something original" . . . It seems clear enough that the vehemence with which "the new" is being encouraged on the Continent has begun to show itself in foolish ways, very well calculated to set a great many persons at odds with the progressive movement as a whole, thinking that imitations of the long-familiar old styles are more reputable . . . The followers of the artistic movement in England appear to have more discretion . . . England however might do better if her artworkers, while retaining their moderation, could be persuaded to adopt a more adventurous policy.

In 1901 George Donaldson presented a collection of modern French furniture to the South Kensington Museum. Donaldson had been on the selection committees for the 1889 and 1900 Paris Exhibitions. The gift was prompted by his desire to see "my countrymen to the front in the artistic and mercantile race which my special opportunities have shown me to exist". He believed that Art Nouveau was the emergent modern style, and proposed that the museum circulate his collection as widely as possible as an object lesson to designers and manufacturers. Condemnation came from all sides. The Arts and Crafts architects, Reginald Blomfield, John Belcher and E. S. Prior wrote in a letter to *The Times* that "the work is neither right in principle, nor does it evince a proper regard for the material employed". In 1903 *The Magazine of Art* ran a symposium on the subject, in which Voysey described it as "void of intuition" and showing "no sign of reverence", Crane condemned "the readiness with which its characteristic forms seemed to lend themselves to exploitation by commercialism", and another writer rejoiced that "hitherto our British solidity and self-sufficiency have saved us as a nation from the foreign contagion; notwithstanding, certain signs of its presence indicate that here and there some unfortunate has been infected with the hideous disease". The painter, George Frampton concluded, "I believe it is made on the Continent, and used by parents and others to frighten naughty children."

Despite the efforts of a small number of committed individuals to introduce Continental design to Britain, both the design profession and the public remained doggedly hostile. Much was written at the time about the

189. (*left*) *Louis Majorelle*, INLAID MAHOGANY LONGCASE CLOCK. *Trained as a painter under Millet, Majorelle returned to his home town Nancy in 1879 to take over the family cabinet-making business. By 1900 he had become the main producer of Art Nouveau furniture in France.*

search for a national style, which was best expressed by traditional forms of furnishing and decoration. Cottage style and neo-Georgian style were the most commonly employed. In characteristically xenophobic fashion, the British vehemently rejected foreign design and that of those of their compatriots who were seen to be working in a Modernist vein.

The Glasgow School

A recognizable style in interior design emerged in Glasgow in the mid-1880s with furniture designed by Charles Rennie Mackintosh and Herbert MacNair for the firm of Guthrie and Wells. The work was first seen in London at the Arts and Crafts Exhibition Society show of 1896, where a poster designed by Mackintosh for the Scottish Musical Review earned them the title 'the Spook School'.

Mackintosh and the other Glaswegian designers working in a similar Modernist mode, were hailed abroad but attacked and ridiculed in Britain. H. J. Jennings, illustrating in 1902 a room from Mackintosh's *House of an Art Lover*, described it as "Hooliganism . . , a blasphemy against art", that "the bones of men and animals have been pressed into degraded service, and a ghoulish sort of ornament has been founded on them", and warned that "the Scotto-Continental 'New Art' theorists, its delirious phantasies, threaten to make the movement for novelty a target for the shafts of scoffers, and a motive for the laughter of the saner seven-eighths of mankind". Only *The Studio* magazine defended the work of the Glasgow School in Britain.

The work of Scottish designers was best appreciated

190. (*above*) and 191. (*below*) ENTRANCE HALL AND WHITE BEDROOM AT HILL HOUSE, GLASGOW, *designed by Charles Rennie Mackintosh for the publisher Walter Blackie in 1902.*

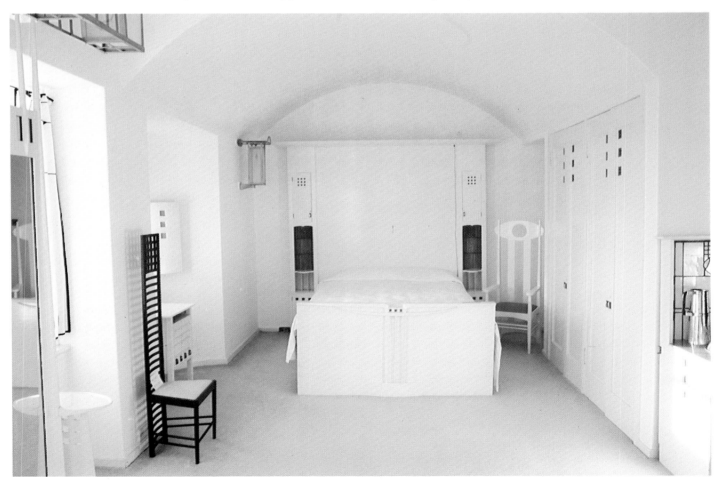

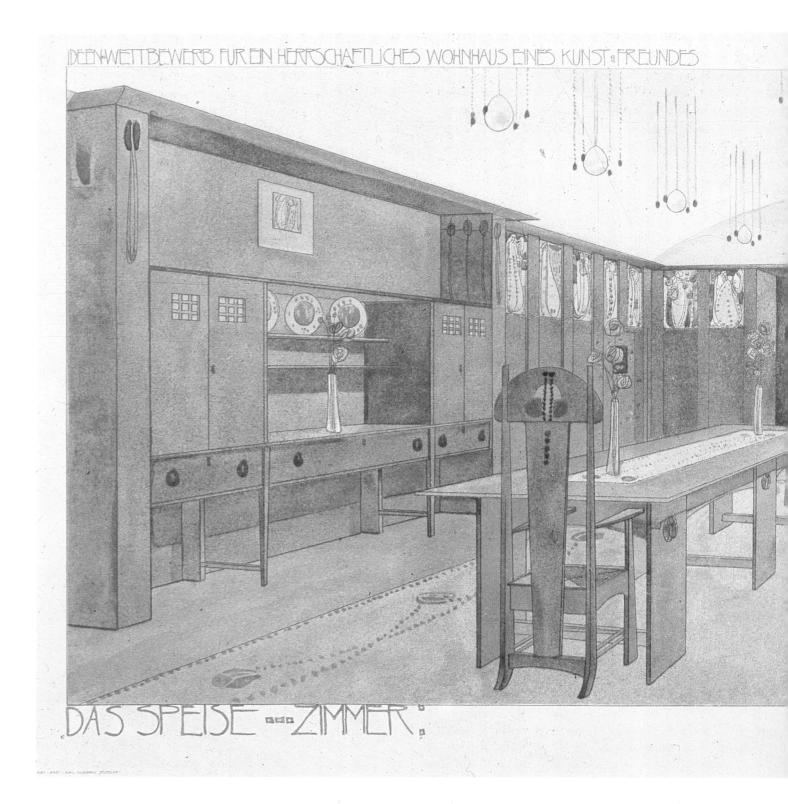

abroad, particularly in Germany and Austria, where their work found sympathy with groups like the Viennese Secessionists. "The Four" – Mackintosh, MacNair and the Macdonald sisters, Frances and Margaret, whom they later married – exhibited at the Vienna Secession in 1900. Herman Muthesius, who spent seven years with the German embassy in London and published on his return a three volume work on *Das Englische Haus* (1904–5), admired their work for its "lofty, rather mystical spirit" which conjured up "a lovely fairy-tale world".

In 1889 Mackintosh joined the firm of Honeyman and Keppie, where he remained until 1913, becoming a partner in 1904. His most important architectural and decorative work was carried out during this period. In 1896 he won a competition to build the new School of Art in Glasgow. From 1897 until 1906 he was occupied intermittently with designing and furnishing the chain of tea-rooms established in Glasgow by the Misses Cranston as part of a campaign to combat the widespread daytime drunkenness which was a scandal in the city. In spite of the provision of billiard-rooms, the original and elegant schemes seem to have done very little to wean hardened drinkers from their accustomed haunts, but they allowed Mackintosh to experiment with the possibilities of commercial production on a considerable scale.

Mackintosh's early style was characterized by its use of rectilinear black and white patterning, with points of colour used occasionally for effect. Following the example of Godwin's Anglo-Japanese furniture, he favoured

C. R. MACKINTOSH. GLASGOW. HAUS EINES KUNST-FREUNDES
VERLAGS-ANSTALT: ALEXANDER KOCH-DARMSTADT. - TAFEL XIV

192. (*left*) *Charles Rennie Mackintosh*, DESIGN FOR A DINING-ROOM FOR THE "HOUSE OF AN ART LOVER", *1901–2*.

193. (*above*) *Charles Rennie Mackintosh*, FABRIC DESIGN. *Natural forms of stems and tendrils have been stylized to the point where they almost lose their organic origins and simply become abstract patterns.*

the application of lacquer on oak surfaces.

In 1902 he received an important commission from the publisher Walter Blackie to build a house looking out on to superb views of the Firth of Clyde. The Hill House furniture, which has been described as "almost oriental in its refinement", is highly original.

In the early years of this century, Mackintosh and his wife, Margaret Macdonald, worked on a number of important commissions in Germany and Austria. By the outbreak of the First World War in 1914 he had left Glasgow and in 1916 settled in London, where he found it difficult to work. During this period he produced designs for textiles, some of which were made by the firms of Foxton's and Sefton's. In 1923 the couple went to live in France, where Mackintosh died of cancer five

years later.

Mackintosh has been credited with the creation of some of the most original furniture and interiors of his day. In retrospect his work has been seen as outstandingly progressive. His early furniture, however, owes much to the style of William Morris and his adherents. Unlike Morris, Mackintosh was not interested in craft *per se*, and much of his furniture was not only badly made, by a variety of Glasgow firms, but was also badly designed structurally. His success lay in an inspired use of organic form. His decorative schemes were often enlivened by the application of strongly coloured stained glass and prominent metalwork. His wife contributed bold gesso panels in Symbolist style and vases of flowers in wirework and linen. Interiors such as those designed for the Northampton model manufacturer, W. J. Bassett-Lowke, between 1916 and 1920, exemplify his later style, which is an expression of painterly concerns for naturalism and abstraction. Mackintosh's work is often compared with that of the Dutch painter, Piet Mondrian.

The great distinction of Mackintosh's interiors is their stylistic unity: furniture, fabrics, lights, architectural detailing and decoration were all conceived as a single whole. He favoured white painted woodwork very sparsely decorated in gem-like colours (sometimes incorporating pieces of amethyst glass) with intricate flat flower paterns which look like Japanese motifs, elaborated and entwined by a Celtic manuscript illuminator. Designs are based on a combination of straight lines and gentle curves. Chairs have tall, attenuated backs; tables have spindly supports; cupboards are topped with wide

194. *Charles Rennie Mackintosh*, FABRIC DESIGN. *Mackintosh used a stylized rose motif from early on in his career. This design is probably the most elaborate rendering of the theme.*

projecting cornices. In his room schemes he emphasized the subtlety of special effects by rather scanty furnishing, striving to create a poetic atmosphere. The German critic, Julius Meier-Graefe called them, "chambers garnies pour belles âmes" (rooms decorated for beautiful souls). His last years, beset by financial difficulties and ill-health were devoted mainly to painting.

A memorial exhibition held in Glasgow in 1933 stimulated interest in his work and from the mid-1930s the writings of Nikolaus Pevsner credited Mackintosh with a key role in the development of modernism.

M. H. Baillie Scott

The only English designer working in a Modernist idiom who had a great reputation on the Continent, comparable to that of Mackintosh, was Mackay Hugh Baillie Scott, who from 1889 set up his practice in Douglas, Isle of Man. Here he collaborated with the designer Archibald Knox on the production of stained glass and fire grates to embellish the houses he was building on the island. His early work was in a red brick, half-timbered style derived from the vernacular architecture of southern England. Scott was strongly influenced by American architecture, particularly in his approach to planning, where he adopted a much more open-plan arrangement than his contemporaries were using, with spaces flowing together between rooms.

His first foreign commission, from the Grand Duke of Hesse in 1897, was to design new furniture for the dining-room and drawing-room in the ducal palace at Darmstadt. The furniture was made by C. R Ashbee and the Guild of Handicraft. Baillie Scott felt dubious about

---

195. *George Logan,* DESIGN FOR ROSE BOUDOIR, *published in the* Studio, *1903. Logan, a member of the Mackintosh circle in Glasgow at the turn of the century, favoured a slightly less attenuated style than Mackintosh. The rose motif, the ovoid shapes and the white paint are all characteristics of the Glasgow School.*

the commission since he had always insisted that interior design was a complete fusion of architecture and decoration. He was unable to create the kind of spatial effects that he liked, so had to rely entirely on the colour scheme for effect, which he described as follows:

In the sitting room at Darmstadt the panelling is ivory white and above this the wall is orange. The central electric light fittings, designed by Mr Ashbee, are grey pewter and the furniture is chiefly in tones of green and blue. And this arrangement of white, orange, grey, green and blue is supplemented by touches of brilliant pink in the flowers. In the dining room a more sober colour scheme prevails, the wall above the panelling being covered with embossed leather.

Largely as a result of this project his work was published in a number of German magazines on interior design. In addition to other German commissions, he decorated the forest retreat of Queen Marie of Romania.

In 1901 Baillie Scott gave up the practice in Douglas and moved to Bedford, where he was within easy reach of John P. White, the furniture manufacturer for whom he had been designing since 1898. By 1901 White was able to produce a catalogue which itemized 120 pieces of furniture designed by Baillie Scott, most of which was sold either through their own showrooms in Bond Street, or through Liberty's. In a passionate preface, clients were advised to throw out all the furniture of the previous generation and to "not perpetuate the memory of the departed in preserving these gloomy and silent witnesses of their bad taste".

Scott applied this rational approach to furnishing in his designs for cottages at Letchworth in 1905 and in Hampstead Garden Suburb in 1908. In his book *Houses and Gardens*, published in 1906, he set down his ideas on planning:

The house rationally planned should primarily consist of at least one good-sized apartment, which, containing no furniture, but that which is really required, leaves ample floor space at the disposal of its occupants . . . In this way, even the labourer's cottage retains its hall, which has now become the kitchen, dining room and parlour.

Baillie Scott's designs for interiors were praised by Muthesius for their stylistic unity, often expressed in the application of a simple leitmotif, such as the daisy inlay of a Baillie Scott dresser, repeated in the wallpaper, the carpet, and even the tablecloths. Much of the advertised appliqué work was executed by his wife Florence Baillie Scott. Despite his preference for painted furniture, most of the pieces made at White's Pyghtle Works were of inlaid oak. Muthesius has described the work of Baillie Scott as "tender and intimate but refreshingly healthy pastoral poetry".

Omega Workshops

A very different approach to interior design was practised by members of the Bloomsbury set, a group of artists and intellectuals who lived in this fashionable area of London's West End. The critics Roger Fry and Clive Bell, influenced by the paintings of Cézanne and the Post-Impressionists, developed a modernist aesthetic which was strikingly different to the craft-oriented philosophies of the Arts and Crafts Movement, so dominant in the British design profession in the early part of this century. Clive Bell anticipated the thinking of Le Corbusier in the 1920s when he wrote of Edwardian architecture in 1914:

Walk the streets of London; everywhere you will see huge blocks of ready-made decoration, pilasters and porticoes,

---

196. *H. M. Baillie Scott*, DESIGN FOR DINING-ROOM AT GLEN FALCON, DOUGLAS, ISLE OF MAN, *published in* Houses and Gardens, *1906. Cottage style is the starting-point for this scheme, which incorporates elements of Art Nouveau such as the obtrusive frieze and the organic forms of the inglenook.*

friezes and façades, hoisted on cranes to hang from ferro-concrete walls. Public buildings have become public laughing-stocks. They are senseless slag-heaps, and far less beautiful. Only where economy has banished the architect do we see masonry of any merit. The engineers, who have at least a scientific problem to solve, create, in factories and railway bridges, our most creditable monuments. They at least are not ashamed of their construction, or at any rate they are not allowed to smother it in beauty at thirty shillings a foot. We shall have no more architecture in Europe till architects understand that all the tawdry excrescences have got to be simplified away, till they make up their minds to express themselves in the materials of the age – steel, concrete and glass – and to create in these admirable media, vast, simple and significant forms.

In 1913 Roger Fry founded the Omega Workshops with the twin aims of improving the standard of decorative design in England and promoting young artists such as Duncan Grant, Vanessa Bell, Wyndham Lewis, Henri Gaudier-Breszka and himself. Fry also designed his own house of which he wrote: "So far there has been no question of architecture; it has been merely solving the problem of personal needs and habits, and of cost, and if architecture there is to be, it should, I think, come directly out of the solution of these problems."

The functionalism of Fry's approach to the design of houses was not apparent in most of the products of the Omega Workshops. Textiles, ceramics and furniture were all made with decorative motifs inspired by the Cubist painters. Roger Fry's "Giraffe" Cupboard, illustrates the way in which Cubism was interpreted for surface decoration and form. Functional qualities were secondary to aesthetic qualities and much of the furniture and pottery was actually made quite badly. Amateurism characterized the whole operation, which, unlike Morris & Co., was not a financial success. The workshops folded in 1920, seven years after opening.

Modernism in America

Americans had the opportunity to see illustrations of both Modernist tendencies – the opulent, sinuous style of the French and Belgian designers and the stark, rectilinear style of the Glasgow School and the Viennese Secessionists – in the magazine *International Studio*, which appeared in 1897. Although the sinuous Art Nouveau style was known to American designers through such publications and also through exhibitions such as the 1904 St Louis Exposition, where an "Art Nouveau" interior was shown in the French pavilion, this style was rarely applied in American homes. The Northern European proto-Modern style was more prominent. The early work of Frank Lloyd Wright in the Midwest, the Californian houses of the brothers Henry Mather and Charles Sumner Greene and the designs Will Bradley produced for the *Ladies Home Journal* in 1901 and 1902 all show highly individual interpretations of this progressive European style.

Will Bradley's decorative schemes published in New York at the beginning of this century, are often cited as examples of the influence of the British designers Baillie Scott and Mackintosh on American design. The rectilinear quality of Mackintosh's work is evident in these designs, as is the sparse planning of Baillie Scott. There is, however, a profusion of decorative motifs and a richness in the colouring which make his work quite distinctive. Although the designs published in the *Ladies Home Journal* were never executed, they exerted a considerable influence on European designers, following their subsequent publication in the German Journal *Moderne Bauformen* in 1906.

Chicago became the focus for progressive architecture and design. Frank Lloyd Wright, one of the most influential American designers, began his career in Chicago as chief draughtsman in the firm of the pioneering architect, Louis H. Sullivan. He set up on his own soon after and developed a highly personal style of

197. (*above*) *H. M. Baillie Scott*, DESIGN FOR A MUSIC-ROOM AT CROWBOROUGH, SUSSEX, *published in the* Studio, *1902.*

198. (*below*) *Roger Fry*, GIRAFFE CUPBOARD, *1915–16. Originally designed for Lady Tredegar, this was later sold through the Omega Workshops.*

199. *Will Bradley*, DESIGN FOR A BEDROOM IN CONCORD, MASS., *published in* Documents d'Architecture Moderne, *1906.*

architecture and decoration, first for what he termed the "prairie house", the most notable example of which is the Robie House, built in Chicago in 1907, then later for buildings on a grander scale, culminating in the Imperial Hotel in Tokyo, built between 1913 and 1920.

He wrote in 1908 that "the most satisfactory apartments are those in which most or all of the furniture is built in as a part of the original scheme. The whole must always be considered as an integral unit."

His first experiments in this approach to interior design were in his own home, Oak Park, Chicago, where he modified and expanded some rooms around 1895. The forms of this early work, simple and rectilinear, emphasized both the means of production and the materials. Wright was greatly influenced by the writings of William Morris and the work of the Arts and Crafts Movement in England. Recalling the 1890s, some sixty years later, he wrote that "good William Morris and John Ruskin were much in evidence in Chicago intellectual circles at the time". He was committed to making his furniture affordable.

Unlike Morris, who had been unable to make his work available to anyone other than the "swinish rich", Wright had some measure of success in promoting well designed, mass-produced furniture. Looking forward to the technological advances of the twentieth century, rather than backward to pre-industrial times, he advo-

cated machine production wherever it was appropriate. In a talk to the Chicago Society of Arts and Crafts in 1901 on "The Art and Crafts of the Machine", he declared that he designed for machines, and that machines were only to be avoided for non-mechanical tasks such as carving. His later designs became increasingly eccentric, for example, circular chairs with segmental arms for a circular-plan house and even polygonal chairs and beds for a hexagonal-plan house. Several of his clients found his furniture so uncomfortable that they disposed of it.

Wright was a seminal influence on architecture and design in Europe as well as America. He had many contacts with European designers, in particular C. R. Ashbee, who visited him in the States three times between 1898 and 1908. Wright made a return visit to Chipping Camden in 1911, when Ashbee was developing his ideas about machine production, which he set down in *Should We Stop Teaching Art?*. The same year, Ashbee wrote an introduction to the German edition of the writings of Frank Lloyd Wright.

One of Wright's key statements was his lecture to the Chicago Society of Arts and Crafts, mentioned above. In this he castigated "the theatrical desire on the part of fairly respectable people to live in Chateaux, Manor Houses, Venetian Palaces, Feudal castles, and Queen Anne Cottages":

Look within all this typical monotony-in-variety and see there the machine-made copies of handicraft originals; in fact, unless you, the householder, are fortunate indeed, possessed of extraordinary taste and opportunity, all you possess is in some degree a machine-made example, of vitiated handicraft, imitation antique furniture made antique by the machine, itself of all abominations the most abominable... Here we have the curse of stupidity – a cheap substitute for ancient art and craft which has no vital meaning in your own life or our time.

Modernism was not a style favoured by the rich. It was more at home in the bungalows of the Midwest and the far West. George W. Maher, a Chicago architect, observed in *Architectural Record* in 1907 that Eastern work was stultified by tired copying of historical European models. New art had made little progress there. An editor responded that Eastern architects build what clients wanted, houses that were "big, bold and stunning and redundant". In the Midwest, he continued, "the state of mind which is too big and overflowing for anything but a baronial hall is not so frequent as in the East", and "the successful Western businessman is usually satisfied with something simpler and more genuinely domestic, but it is not anything less traditional". Even in the West, the editor held, "the client's basic preference was for the Colonial, Jacobean or Elizabethan styles, and only a persuasive architect could bring about anything else".

The Practical Book of Home Decoration by H. D. Eberlain, A. McClure and E. S. Holloway, published in Philadelphia in 1919, identified two main preferences for American homes: the first, "English Cottage" style, was sometimes referred to as "Peasant Style", while the harmonious amalgam of old styles taken from the "Beaux-Arts" tradition, Colonial style and "Empire" Revival, came to be termed the "International Interperiod" style.

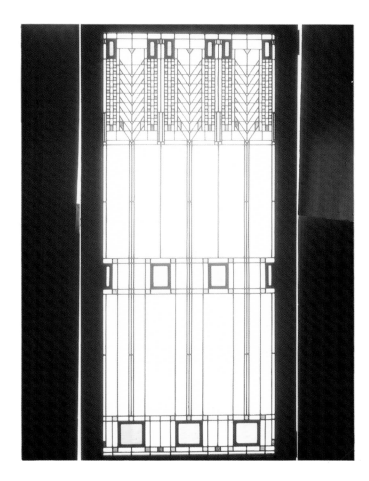

200. (*above*) *Frank Lloyd Wright,* LEADED GLASS TREE OF LIFE DOOR, *1904.*

201. (*below*) DESIGN FOR "QUAINT FURNITURE FOR THE BEDROOM" *published in the* Cabinet Maker, *August 1897.*

202. THE DRAWING-ROOM, NAVARINO, SUTTON COLDFIELD, *1901*.

203. THE SMOKING-ROOM, THE KNOWLE, HUDDERSFIELD, *1904*.

The Modern Home

It is important to realize that these advanced ideas were favoured by a tiny minority; few of the designs for decorative schemes produced by those working in the new style were actually executed. They made little impression on the domestic interior until after 1920. The majority of middle-class people all over Europe and America chose to live in more conventional surroundings based on either interpretations of classical styles or vernacular traditions such as the "Free English" style.

A reaction is however discernable in both middle-class and aristocratic homes, where the fashionable decorators' mania for excessive ornament and elaborate drapery had reached its zenith in the late 1880s. During the 1890s it became quite usual to combine traditional-style furnishings with a more "modern" manner of decorating and arrangement. The "great clean up", which some writers claimed was taking place around the turn of the century, can be seen in some ways as an expression, by those with informed yet conventional taste, of the main tendencies in the emergent Modern Movement. As W. R. Lethaby, Principal of the Central School of Art and Design from 1896–1911 later stated in *Form and Civilization* (1922):

The house of the future will be designed as a ship is designed, as an organism which has to function properly in all its parts. Style . . . is clearness, effectiveness, mastery; often it is simplification.

192

Drapery became simpler and flounces less pronounced, ornaments were thinned out and an overall effect of lightness and airiness was created by the application of whites and creams. White schemes could be seen in *fin-de-siècle* rooms of all sorts, from Frank Lloyd Wright's Robie House in Chicago to the British royal family's house at Sandringham. White painted furniture became fashionable, usually in Adam or Louis Seize style, often with gilded detailing. White painted woodwork was *de rigueur* for discerning home-makers in the Edwardian era. The plain forms, clean lines and sturdiness of furniture produced from about 1790 to 1830 – Regency, "Empire" and "Biedermeier" – fulfilled the taste for simpler furnishings and was collected by people in both progressive and traditionalist circles.

"Quaint" style was a popular alternative to the equally fashionable "Chippendale" or "Louis XVI" styles. The uncluttered look of the modern style was adapted by the mass market and made more comfortable and homely by the addition of bold patterned wallpapers and occasional furniture – small tables and cabinets that provided ideal forms for the application of intricate fretwork. Green-stained furniture, with applied copper decoration and spade-shaped cut-outs, was ubiquitous in trade magazines at the turn of the century. At around the same time, a change can be seen in flat pattern designs, produced to complement these goods. The complicated, swirling motifs and deep colours of the 1890s gave way to simpler, more formally organized patterns and much lighter colours; soft blues, greens, mauves and pinks on pale grounds became popular.

The term "Quaint" appeared in many advertisements for what Pauline Agius has described as "feebly designed pieces encumbered with curly laths and other irrelevances". Many pieces by designers such as Voysey, Baillie Scott and Ashbee were more or less closely copied and from the early 1890s labelled and sold as "Quaint" style. Reviewing the Arts and Crafts Exhibition Society show of 1896, *The Furnisher and Decorator* praised some hall chairs by Voysey, but warned that "before the year is out, a great many house furnishers will be offering travesties of this idea to the ease-loving public". In the same year it was observed that "the middle-class and lower middle-class furnishing firms have begun to harp largely on the 'inexpensive art furniture' string, and to stock stained green cabinets and chairs as if their very trade depended on this style of goods". Features of the style included a minimum of mouldings, novel and often eccentrically shaped chair-backs, arms and cabinet shelves, and an overemphasis on the qualities of materials, for instance an exaggerated thickness of wood and oversized hinges.

"Extravagancies of quaintness" were condemned by H. J. Jennings in his book *Our Homes and How to Beautify Them*. He saw this style of furnishing as a reworking of the Aesthetic Craze, which by the turn of the century had long since ceased to flourish. He was critical of Continental designers in their "insane race after novelty" and their "grotesque conventionalism" of Japanese art:

If there be one thing more certain than another it is that the employment of Japanese or quasi-Japanese ornament has already been overdone. A few years ago, one of those waves of absurdity which occasionally sweep over communities, carried many people to the Japanese shrine . . . We all lived amidst fabulous vegetation and impossible monsters. However appropriate these fanciful conceptions may be in an oriental scheme, they can have no place in western art.

In England the Modern idiom found little acceptance until after the First World War. The dominant ideas in domestic decoration in the early years of this century fell broadly into the categories of Cottage style and neo-Georgian. These forms continued to influence decoration in Europe until well into the 1920s. In 1919, only a few months after the Armistice, a German magazine published an English design for a drawing-room.

REVIVALISM REVISITED

This is the age of old furniture. It is the pride and joy of the fortunate possessor, and is secretly desired by the many who have none. For even the man who lacks interest in it for artistic or sentimental reasons can appreciate its solid financial worth.
(*J. H. Elder Duncan,* The House Beautiful and Useful, *1907*)

LATE VICTORIAN and Edwardian domestic interiors were mainly decorated and furnished in a plethora of period styles. The Modern Movement made little impact on most homes. Throughout the British Empire and right across North America traditional values were paramount. A new attitude to the use and to the meaning of "old things" in the home and to the interpretation of revival styles can be seen in the later decades of the nineteenth century, and had become firmly established by the beginning of the present century. The "Antiques Movement" represents the culmination of Victorian interior design.

In the early years of the nineteenth century, collecting was practised mainly by wealthy connoisseurs and restricted to the rare and ancient; by the 1870s there was a new emphasis on the amateur collector and collecting was extended to more commonplace objects, "those excellent ordinary works of art" as Mrs Orrinsmith described them in her popular publication, *The Drawing Room* (1878). The new vernacular revival meant that the "genuine" did not have to be searched for in remote periods; things surviving from the past could be found in rural areas. Enthusiasts of the Gothic and the Elizabethan declared old furniture superior in its emotional appeal but not as regards practicality. Now many old objects seemed eminently "serviceable", as Mrs Orrinsmith put it. There was a feeling of "completeness", of "comfort", even a "sort of companionship" when old furniture was used. This was also linked to the stress on

permanence in the home, in opposition to the seemingly ever greater pace of change outside. The concept of permanence additionally implied social status. Old families had old things. Heirlooms were of the highest value. "Home" and the look of the old became almost synonymous. The chief characteristic of the new home movement, which popularized the concerns of the design reformers, was the way in which moral and quasi-religious values were extended to the criticism of design. Much was written about the appropriateness of style.

It has been suggested that it was perhaps Ruskin's outcry at the furniture in Holman Hunt's *The Awakening Conscience* in *The Times* in 1854 which stimulated the thinking that linked older, simpler environments, with the virtues of home. The whole interior, from the "terrible lustre" on the rosewood of the furniture to the manufacture of the textiles, all smacks of "fatal newness; nothing there has the old thoughts of home upon it". The appropriateness of traditional furnishings for the home was as much bound up with notions of the family in the past, as with criticism of modern manufacturing techniques. J. H. Elder Duncan writing in 1907 on Early English design claimed that,

"home", as we now understand it, was then assuming a definable shape. The family was beginning to associate itself, as a detail of the national habit, with a common domicile. Note the vast importance given to the chimney-piece in Elizabethan and Jacobean times. The ingle was the focussing point of the family life, the hallowed spot where old and young met in quiet restfulness after the day's labours, and to which the memories of the children tenderly flew back in after years.

Towards the end of the nineteenth century Britain experienced a surge of nationalism. The application of historic, and in this case, specifically British styles, was imbued with nationalist overtones. When William

204. HALL AT MANDERSTON, BERWICKSHIRE, *completed around 1910. The house was rebuilt in Adam style by the Scottish architect, John Kinross, for the* nouveau riche *baronet, Sir James Miller. Kinross was inspired by Adam interiors at Kedleston Hall, where Lady Miller was brought up, and where Sir James proposed to her.*

Whiteley displayed a Chippendale dining-room in the window of his London department store in 1882, *The Cabinet Maker and Art Furnisher* reported: "In looking at such a picture in its entirety it is easy to understand how that period of our national furniture history has taken such a hold upon society of late. It is so homely, unaffected and thoroughly national." neo-Georgian and neo-Tudor styles have remained popular since the beginning of this century. These styles emerged and remained favourites because they were national, they represented tradition, and they evoked imagined virtues of Old England. The furniture of these periods seemed solid and workmanlike, and its decoration unaffected. And while both satisfied national sentiment, the Georgian met the need for order as well. Just as Georgian buildings were designed according to rules of proportion and a classical "grammar" whose rules were unchangeable, so the decoration and furniture of the period associated naturally with its architecture and followed many of the same rules.

Old furniture not only fulfilled a need to proclaim personal, social, and national affiliations. The collecting of it was a pleasurable pastime and the arrangement of pieces a creative activity, especially for women. The countless publications on the subject of home-decorating and furnishing that appeared during this period all offered extensive advice on how to identify, purchase and use antiques. They also had romantic appeal, as H. J. Jennings, in *Our Homes and How to Beautify Them* (1902), explained:

Fashions have changed, beliefs have broadened, intellectual revolutions have taken place; yet the old chairs and cabinets and commodes remain to remind us . . . *Vita brevis, Ars longa.* What stories they might tell us could they but speak, what gossip of long-ago romances and intrigues, of jealous quarrels, of tipsy, hot-blooded revels ending in tragedy, of elopements to Gretna Green, of all-night carousals, of high and reckless gaming, of all the excitement and stress and turmoil of a life and society that have passed away!

The "Antique Movement"

Antique furniture had long been sought by people with antiquarian leanings, especially if they lived in neo-Gothic or neo-Elizabethan surroundings. Old furniture had otherwise never held much appeal for those building "modern houses" in the past. In a modern house everything had to look smart, unworn and unfaded. Tattered covers, signs of repair and patina were not at all desirable in such surroundings. But with the advent in the 1870s of the "Queen Anne" fashion, with its stress on informality, its love of irregularity and asymmetrical arrangements, antiques came into widespread demand.

205. *(opposite, above) B. O. Corfe,* WATERCOLOUR OF CANON VALPY'S DRAWING-ROOM, WINCHESTER, *1900. Quintessential English style with mid-Victorian upholstery and Georgian furniture.*

206. *(opposite, below)* BEDROOM AT EAST 122ND STREET, NEW YORK CITY, *1895. This room demonstrates a not uncommon mixture of revival styles, in this instance, French eighteenth-century, merging with Art Nouveau.*

207. PARLOUR AT GEORGE GREY RESIDENCE, STOCKTON, CALIFORNIA, *1890. Elaborate drapery and soft furnishings expressed opulence and comfort. Around 1890 the fashion for draping almost everything in a room reached its peak.*

If they were faded, they blended nicely with the muted colour schemes that were then admired.

The craze was current on both sides of the Atlantic. Clarence Cook declared in his well-known book, *Artistic Houses* (1883), that the interest in "old furniture" was "a fashion, that has been for twenty years working its way down from a circle of rich, cultivated people, to a wider circle of people who are educated, who have natural good taste, but who have not so much money as they could wish".

Sources for antique furniture were plentiful. J. Elder Duncan, in *The House Beautiful and Useful* (1907), recommended "the quaint little second-hand furniture shops in Wardour Street and elsewhere" as useful places, but had to point out that "ten or twenty years ago, before old furniture was as much sought after and as highly prized as it is now, it might have been possible to secure bargains, but your second-hand dealer of today knows to the last penny what the value of his stock is". The painter Dante Gabriel Rossetti was a well-known customer of these shops and one of the first people to start collecting the new antiques. He greatly admired English eighteenth-century furniture for its simplicity and craftsmanship. As H. Treffry Dunn wrote in his *Recollections of Dante Gabriel Rossetti and His Circle* (1904), he "delighted to take an evening's walk through Leicester Square, visiting the various curiosity shops in that neighbourhood, or through Hammersmith, a district where many a Chippendale chair or table could be met with and bought for next to nothing, such things not being then in the repute that they have become since the taste for Queen Anne houses and fittings sprang up". What distinguished Rossetti's interiors from the earlier antiquarian ones was that there was no precise historical theme. Gothic preferences were now supplemented by new likings for later objects, including many from the eighteenth century. There was no evocation of any one period, just a generally old atmosphere, using "all conceivable superannuated designs".

The term "Antique Dealer" first appeared in London trade directories in 1886. By the turn of the century there were over 200 "Antique Dealers" listed for central London alone and in 1918 the British Antique Dealers Association was established. Most large retail shops like Waring & Gillow's and Heal's had antique departments. A great deal of publicity was given to this type of furniture. Articles were regularly published in both the trade press and in fashionable magazines.

Antiques were soon in short supply. Ella Rodman Church, writing on the situation in America in *How to Furnish a Home* (1883), wanted her readers to fill the many shelves of their artistic chimneypieces with bric-à-brac including "one's own or someone else's great-grandmother's candlesticks", and she spoke of how "every one's eyes are opened to the advantages of having had great-grandfathers" on account of the "trea-

208. (*opposite*) *J. Eastman Johnson*, NOT AT HOME, *mid 1870s. A view from the hall into the drawing-room of a typical nineteenth-century middle-class American home. There is a mixture of reproduction furniture in Northern Renaissance style and eighteenth-century furniture. The artist was evidently interested in antiques.*

209. (*above*) DRAWING-ROOM IN EMPIRE STYLE FOR MRS R. E. SCHROEDER, NEW YORK, *1903.*

sures" that had in many cases come down from them. If these were lacking, one had to visit "the Broadway bazaar, filled with antiques and supercilious clerks, with fabulous prices for the simplest articles". When the dealers in turn could not produce the genuine article, ingenuity was needed. By 1884 the American magazine *Cabinet-Making and Upholstery* told its readers that "there is little doubt but the manufacture of antiques has become a modern industry".

The first serious book on furniture history in Britain, *An Illustrated History of Furniture* was produced by a Wardour Street dealer, Frederick Litchfield, in 1892. The new kinds of book helped to assess authenticity; the new kind of dealer had to guarantee it. As Litchfield wrote in 1904, "Be prepared to pay a good price to a man of reputation for a really good article". "Authenticity" or "genuineness" are polite formulations of what had become the chief issue, the chief problem in collecting antiques: how to avoid fakes.

Early faking of old furniture, from the beginning of

the nineteenth century onwards consisted chiefly of making new pieces by reassembling old pieces of timber, or by carving plain old pieces. By the 1870s this was already ridiculed, as was the buying of "family portraits from Wardour Street". Eastlake condemned the application of thick varnish with the aim of making furniture look old. In the 1880s one hears of the creation of worm holes by "specialist craftsmen". Stories abound amongst old cabinet-makers in London's East End, once the centre of the furniture trade in Britain, about faking and the dealers who came from West End showrooms to purchase fakes. J. H. Elder Duncan summed up the situation in *The House Beautiful and Useful* (1907):

Beyond a few dozen pieces of furniture made for royal households or ennobled families, where their history is preserved or known, it is unsafe to proclaim a single article that comes into the market as the authentic work of any known master . . . apart from the British delight in labelling things, there would be little reason for saying more concerning an antique piece other than it was "Georgian", or appeared to be early, or late eighteenth century work, as the case might be . . . For those who desire old furniture, it is only sound advice to say, never worry about the maker. Satisfy yourself that the piece is really old . . . ; satisfy yourself that it is really beautiful; see if its beauty and utility is sufficient recompense for the price you are called upon to pay for it, and if so, buy it. All else is chimera or supposition.

The commentators of the 1870s were fully aware that theirs was a new movement in collecting. The protagonists saw themselves opposed to the collector of the older

kind, the collector of the rare and the very old; hence they could formulate the demand, "collecting and furnishing must be kept strictly separate". Secondly there was a reluctance to get too involved in the new professional art-historical rigour of distinguishing between the many historical styles. Eastlake in 1868 was already reviling the nineteenth-century custom of giving the main reception rooms different styles: "With amateur furnishers there is the danger that their rooms might become an incongruous medley." Some advocated slow buying in order to find the right pieces for the right context. It was only after 1900 that these contradictions and problems seemed resolved and art-historical knowledge, serious, even professional collecting and the creation of a "comfortable" home of a unified design, worthy of artistic consideration, could be combined.

There were fluctuations amongst collectors of antiques regarding the choice between the rougher, archaic furniture and the later refined styles. After 1900 this dichotomy appeared to be less problematic as certain kinds of style were assigned to certain kinds of environment: Old Oak to the cottagely interior, eighteenth-century to the more formal urban interior.

Furnishing Practice

Jacob von Falke, whose *Art in the House* was published in English in Boston in 1878, observed in connection with the International Exhibition held in Vienna in 1873 that, "In so far as style is concerned the modern Frenchman dwells in the eighteenth century, he sleeps in that century likewise, but he dines in the sixteenth, then on occasion he smokes his cigar in the Orient, while he takes his bath in Pompeii, in Ancient Greece."

In many middle-class homes rooms were furnished in different styles according to prevailing fashions. Vast catalogues of period styles were produced by the furniture trade, promoting different styles for different rooms. Halls were typically decorated in Renaissance (Italian/Flemish/French) styles, dining-rooms in Early English (Elizabethan/Jacobean) styles, drawing-rooms in English or French eighteenth-century styles

210. (*above*) Ogden Codman, SCHEME FOR FURNISHING WITH ANTIQUES, *1900. Where an owner did not already possess old furniture in the required style, Codman was quite prepared to have accurate reproductions specially made. Antique furniture had to be in mint condition for schemes such as these.*

211. (*opposite, above*) DRAWING-ROOM AT GLEN ROY IN MOSELEY, BIRMINGHAM, *1881. A prosperous middle-class home decorated in an imaginative mix of revival styles: 'Adams', Queen Anne and French rococo.*

212. (*opposite, below*) DESIGN FOR A DINING-ROOM IN RENAISSANCE STYLE *published in a Hampton & Sons catalogue, 1900.*

(Chippendale/Adams/Louis XV or XVI), and bath-rooms in Pompeian style.

Writers on home-furnishing in books and magazines produced lengthy texts on the appropriateness of particular periods for specific settings. H. J. Jennings in *Our Homes and How to Beautify Them* (1902) advocated:

For the dining room, you may have it Italian Renaissance, François Premier, Elizabethan, Jacobean, eighteenth century English or modern English Renaissance. French styles may be put on one side for an English dining room; so may the Gothique Anglais . . . For the drawing room there are available the whole range of the French styles, from Louis XIV to the Empire, also the English Chippendale to Adam period, and, if these give not enough scope, the English Renaissance as practised by the English school. A breakfast or morning room . . . is essentially of the national character . . . There is one thing about the English styles that recommend them – they are expressive of a certain national sentiment which finds its strongest note in a family circle when gathered round the table at the evening meal.

While it was widely accepted that different styles might be appropriate to different rooms in the house, the result was often deplored. Mrs Panton, for instance, in *Suburban Residences and How to Circumvent Them* (1896) attacked "the jumble of styles made by having an eastern-looking hall, an Old English dining room, a Queen Anne drawing room, and Moorish landing, which is inexpressibly dear to the would-be artistic decorator".

The aristocracy were more likely to furnish in a

historically consistent manner, often to provide a setting for their collections of art and antiques. One example was Baron Ferdinand de Rothschild's massive English home, Waddesdon Manor in Buckinghamshire, which although built in French Renaissance style was furnished and decorated in French eighteenth-century style, to complement his family's fine collection of works of art of that period. Many of the interiors were designed to incorporate elaborately carved Rococo "boiseries" taken from houses in France.

It is difficult to distinguish the precise characteristics of all the period styles employed by the Victorians to furnish and decorate their homes, because the terms used to describe them vary from one firm and from one writer to another. The way in which furniture was designed and manufactured created a profusion of hybrid styles, which are impossible to disentangle.

213. (*left*) THE HALL AT WICKHAM HALL, KENT, *1897. Set in the heart of the English countryside, this house has been described as a "rambling, mid-century 'Renaissance' pile".*

214. (*below*) BILLIARD-ROOM AT THE ELMS, HAMPSTEAD, *1899. The Elms was typical of many houses at the time in the selection of different styles for different rooms in the house.*

There were also trans-Atlantic crossings, such as Heal's "Colonial Adam" range. When viewed through the perspective of another hundred or more years of period furnishings, the task becomes even more complicated. What follows is an attempt to define the characteristics of the chief styles that were current in the last decades of the nineteenth century and the early years of the twentieth century.

"Free Renaissance" Style

Robert Kerr, author of *The Gentleman's House* (1864), wrote an essay in 1884 entitled "English architecture thirty years hence", in which he insisted that architecture was always bound to return to "the universal European Renaissance" which, while created long before in Italy, was also "a Modern European style . . . a universally accepted mode of building . . . that . . . has been maintained in use ever since, and is still maintained for all ordinary purposes without a question being raised". The term "Free Renaissance" is sometimes applied to this central tradition, which developed during the middle decades of the nineteenth century. Based on neo-Classicism, it evolved within the academic framework of the Ecole des Beaux-Arts in Paris, from which it spread all over the Western world. It embraced much more than variations of the Renaissance styles: it took in all shades of Classicism, including "Louis Quinze" Rococo which was seen as an extension of "Louis Quatorze" Baroque, and it could happily assimilate fresh revivals of Pompeian, Grecian and "Empire". It could even encompass Turkish and Egyptian.

Since the middle of the century many features of Italian and French fifteenth- and sixteenth century Renaissance and Mannerist work had been incorporated into exhibition pieces and quality furniture. These consisted of architectural forms such as pilasters and pediments, sculptural figures of classical gods, caryatids, grotesques, masks and animal supports, and elaborate inlays of woods, stones, metals and ivory, variously known as intarsia or certosino work. The Renaissance work of the 1880s and 1890s employed much of this decorative vocabulary and there was much enthusiasm for inlaying.

The New York architects Arnold W. Brunner and Thomas Tyron, in their *Interior Decoration* (1887), noted that "The various periods of French Renaissance have long been favorites for parlor decoration . . . The Italian Renaissance . . . is perhaps, the better for inspiration, and certainly less hackneyed." Renaissance styles were especially popular in Germany and America. Von Falke strongly advocated the Renaissance style:

Our merchant princes, our large manufacturers, our money-coining miners, railway magnates, and financiers of all kinds are much more disposed to emulate the expenditures of the Medici of the old Italian republics than to conform to the habits of their thrifty forefathers.

Some of the most notable expressions of palatial building in America are Richard Morris Hunt's amazing châteaux at Newport, Rhode Island, of the late 1880s and early 1890s. After 1900 a more reticent style came

215. *Owen Jones,* ETRUSCAN, *silk, woven by Benjamin Warner, Spitalfields, 1870–80. Patterns based on Italian Renaissance designs, examples of which could be studied at the South Kensington Museum, were often used to compliment Renaissance-style furnishings.*

to prevail. H. G. Croly noted in *Architectural Record* (September 1915):

The reaction against building palaces has won a complete triumph, and the good American, no matter how wealthy he may be, is now content to live in a comparatively modest and unpretentious house . . . the feeling for style has . . become very much finer and more delicate . . . and at the same time more distinguished . . . The gibe, which had a certain measure of truth in it twenty years ago, that American architecture was either bizarre or Beaux-Arts, is no longer true.

An interest in post-Renaissance styles, notably the Baroque, began to arise about 1875. Neo-Georgian and, in America, the Colonial Revival were aspects of this.

"Tous-les-Louis"

The history of French decoration as a fashion in England goes back to the patronage of the Prince Regent, and by the middle years of the century a free interpretation of French Rococo was employed in a number of grander homes. The styles was seldom reproduced correctly. A more authentic approach was developed

THE VERSAILLES SUITE. Superior Carved Dark Mahogany 5ft. Cabinet, with shaped shelves, and bevel-edged mirror in back .... Handsomely Carved Dark Mahogany Settee, stuffed best manner, upholstered in Silk Tapestry or Brocatelle .... Handsomely Carved Dark Mahogany Gentleman's Easy Chair, covered to match ....

216. (*above*) DESIGN FOR THE "VERSAILLES SUITE" *published in a Story & Triggs catalogue around 1900.*

217. (*opposite, above*) BEDROOM IN LOUIS QUINZE STYLE IN NEW YORK, *1905.*

218. (*opposite, below*) DRAWING-ROOM AT 5 HAMILTON PLACE, WESTMINSTER, *1890. Leopold Rothschild's London home was the apogee of 1890s conspicuous consumption. He installed a hydraulic lift of legendary cost and also employed two Italian carvers for two years on a staircase of sumptuous intricacy.*

through individual collections of antique furniture and "boiserie" (wood panelling). Important collections were formed by the Marquis of Hertford and Sir Richard Wallace, Lord Pembroke and certain members of the Rothschild family. French taste had finally "arrived" by the middle of the 1880s.

Louis Quinze (XV) Rococo scrolls were high fashion for drawing rooms and boudoirs from before 1840 until well into the twentieth century. Louis Seize (XVI) came into favour from around 1855 when Jackson & Graham won a Paris exhibition for a satinwood, ormolu-mounted, marquetry cabinet in that style. Queen Victoria bought a Louis XVI-style table and cabinet at that exhibition. Many "French" pieces were exhibited by British firms at the 1862 exhibition. Leading firms specializing in the style, who often employed French workers, were Wright & Mansfield, Holland & Sons, Jackson & Graham, Shoolbred & Co., Hindley & Wilkinson, Waring & Gillow. Waring & Gillow devoted twenty-seven pages of their 1908 catalogue to French furniture. "Our Exhibition of French furniture is not surpassed even in Paris and is the result of many years search through Museums and Private Collections for the finest models and the means of reproducing them . . . The work is carried out by *ébénistes* of the highest reputation with whom we enjoy the closest relations."

The most fashionable interiors at the turn of the century were decorated in the style of Louis XVI. Baron Ferdinand de Rothschild considered that:

it is not classical, it is not heroic, but does it not combine, as no previous art did, artistic quality with practical usefulness? . . . French eighteenth century art became popular and sought for,

because of that adaptability which more ancient art lacks . . . Fashions will fluctuate, but French eighteenth century art seems destined to maintain its spell on society, and tighten its grip on the affection of the collector, so long as the present social, economic and political conditions prevail.

Gladstone's daughter, Mary, found Waddesdon hideously vulgar. Her diary noted: "Felt much oppressed with the extreme gorgeousness and luxury . . . The pictures in his sitting room are too beautiful, but there is not a book in the house save 20 improper French novels." And Lady Frances Balfour, whose husband was a practising architect, wrote on her visit to another Rothschild house in Buckinghamshire, Halton House: "Yesterday we went to see the new house that Alfred de Rothschild is building for himself. I have seldom seen anything more terribly vulgar . . . Oh! but the hideousness of everything, the showiness! the sense of lavish wealth thrust up your nose!"

In America, the French Revival was promoted by the publication of Edith Wharton and Ogden Codman's *The Decoration of Houses* in 1897. The book was criticized for

219. (*above*) BOUDOIR AT 17 GROSVENOR PLACE, WESTMINSTER, *1890. The boudoir also served as an ante-room to the ballroom: it was probably useful for sitting out at dances.*

220. (*opposite*) DINING-ROOM AT THE ANCHORAGE, SUTTON COLDFIELD, BIRMINGHAM, *1900. Home of the architect, Edmund Butler, this room shows the fusion of Early English style with the Arts and Crafts Movement.*

its insidious advice, its execrable taste and for encouraging a return to the standards of decorating that were current in the days directly following the Civil War. One critic expressed the hope that the price would deter many from buying it, who might otherwise be misled.

In its combination of comfort and opulence and its association with aristocratic ease, the style recommended itself not only to the nobility, but also to anyone with aristocratic pretensions. Hampton & Sons' catalogue recommended the style as "one of the most exquisitely beautiful in existence," but suggested that "for this very reason, it is particularly desirable that a room treated after that period be dealt with by those whose taste and experience fully qualify them to undertake the duty". It was thought to be particularly appropriate for drawing-rooms or boudoirs. Hampton & Sons' catalogue concluded that "nothing could be more suggestive of refined taste than the form and colour, the one so elegant, the other so rich and glowing, which were popular in France in the days of its greatest brilliance".

The cost of French furniture was high. In 1881 it was reported in *The Cabinet Maker* that "it was, indeed, the cost of the cabinet work of the latter [Louis XVI] period which has driven manufacturers to reproduce sideboards, cabinets, chairs and tables of the Stuart or Flemish styles".

Early English Styles

In 1902 the famous English architect Norman Shaw gave an interview in which he stated that "the Gothic Revival, for all practical purposes, is dead, and the tendency of late years has been to return to the English Renaissance". The Gothic Revival had paved the way for some of the most creative and original interior design of the last decades of the nineteenth century. As Morris's pupil, John Sedding, wrote in an essay on "Our Arts and Industries" in *Art and Handicraft* (1893): "Our Gothic Revival . . . has enriched the crafts by impetus and imitation. It has imbued two generations of art-workers with passion. It has been the health-giving spark – the ozone of modern art."

A mixture of sixteenth- and seventeenth-century features thought to be Elizabethan had been popular since the 1830s. It was not one of the most popular styles after 1880, but it appeared in many trade catalogues and was specially favoured for billiard-rooms and dining-rooms. Hampton & Sons, illustrated a scheme for a dining-room in their lavish catalogue captioned:

There is something essentially English about the Elizabethan style, and no style of furniture and decoration could be more appropriate for a dining room than this, which takes us back at once to an era when hospitality was a stately . . . part of life, and "Merrie England" something more than a mere name.

Jacobean, which embraced early and late seventeenth-century features, was one of the most popular styles of the period, especially for dining-rooms. Waring & Gillow's were credited by *The Cabinet Maker* in 1880 with "taking the lead in Jacobean". Bulbous-legged tables, court cupboards, panel-back chairs and cane seated high-back chairs were all reproduced in great quantities. Jacobean style inspired much good quality if dull furniture for several decades.

"Queen Anne" Style

The writer H. J. Jennings summed up the problem of defining this style in his book *Our Homes and How to Beautify Them* (1902): "if one had to write about 'Queen Anne style', it would be like writing about 'Snakes in Ireland'. Strictly speaking there is no Queen Anne 'style' . . . Up to a certain time . . . everybody called everything English that was at all antique 'Queen Anne'."

Mrs Haweis, illustrated the confusion with her story: "Only the other day I was shown a French mirror (Louis XIV) by some really cultivated folks as: 'Queen Anne – Empire you know – genuine Chippendale'." The name was applied indiscriminately to furniture which adapted elements of the architectural style – often based on classical forms as reinterpreted in the early eighteenth century – such as pillars, pilasters, broken pediments, cornices, dentils and urns. "The Curator", a column in *The Cabinet Maker* advised in 1882:

In designing modern Queen Anne . . . study the lines of the architects rather than those of the furniture makers; not by any means making . . . furniture architectural in character but picking from old sources . . . mouldings, enrichments and carvings . . . In this way furniture may be designed and legitimately called Queen Anne without having any resemblance to the article actually made from 1702–14.

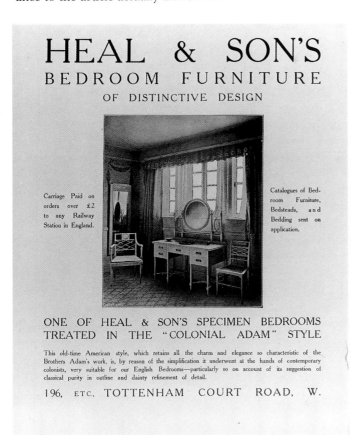

HEAL & SON'S
BEDROOM FURNITURE
OF DISTINCTIVE DESIGN

Carriage Paid on orders over £2 to any Railway Station in England.

Catalogues of Bedroom Furniture, Bedsteads, and Bedding sent on application.

ONE OF HEAL & SON'S SPECIMEN BEDROOMS TREATED IN THE "COLONIAL ADAM" STYLE

This old-time American style, which retains all the charm and elegance so characteristic of the Brothers Adam's work, is, by reason of the simplification it underwent at the hands of contemporary colonists, very suitable for our English Bedrooms—particularly so on account of its suggestion of classical purity in outline and dainty refinement of detail.

196, ETC., TOTTENHAM COURT ROAD, W.

Queen Anne style was above all associated with homeliness, cosiness and comfort, as the copy for a Hampton & Sons' scheme for a Queen Anne morning room suggests:

The general effect aimed at is to produce a comfortable and homelike room, which is made cheerful by its white panelling, its recessed cupboards and chimney-piece, its comfortable Mother Hubbard and other chairs, its convenient hob stove, and bright-looking fender of pierced brass. The china cabinet is in the old Dutch style, and the tall chairs and the round table are made to match; the handsome screen gives the finishing touch to a room entirely suggestive of comfort.

The style quickly found favour in the United States, most notably in the work of McKim, Mead and White and gave impetus to the nascent "Shingle" style with its Picturesque planning and detailing. This last had "old Colonial" connotations as well; indeed, Americans sometimes equate their Colonial Revival style with "Queen Anne".

Colonial Revival

The American Colonial Revival began about the time of the Philadelphia Centennial Exposition of 1876 and reached full development in the 1880s. Although a small number of individuals had collected American furniture and decorative arts since the 1800s, popular interest in the seventeenth and eighteenth centuries had remained dormant. At the Centennial Exposition, visitors could see the New England Kitchen or "Log Cabin in 'Ye Olden Times' ", which showed the development of domestic technology over the past century. It was furnished with a mix of old tables, cradles, Windsor chair, and a spinning wheel. Hostesses in colonial costume served a boiled dinner with beans, brown bread, and old-fashioned pudding.

Rhoda and Agnes Garrett's *Suggestions for House Decoration* was published in America in 1877. This book was one of the first to advocate mixing contemporary designs with antiques. Clarence Cook likewise recommended good early furniture to complement modern pieces. Several publications were brought out in the late 1880s and 1890s on the subject of Colonial architecture and interiors. *The Decorator and Furnisher* reproduced many designs in, what by 1889 was termed, "revived colonial style".

Not everyone could find antiques. By the 1880s, the Paine Furniture Co. of Boston was manufacturing what it called "Colonial Furniture". Generally this type of furniture was found in modest houses; it never gained much popularity amongst those who lived in magnificent villas and palaces.

Neo-Georgian Style

Enthusiasm for later eighteenth-century styles was encouraged by the development of the Queen Anne Revival which demanded the use of lighter and more delicate furniture. Regency, "Empire" and neo-Biedermeier styles also provided the basis for a lighter, less cluttered look. As Peter Thronton has pointed out in *Authentic Decor* (1984), neo-Georgian was "more for-

221. (*opposite*) ADVERTISEMENT FOR HEAL & SON'S "COLONIAL
ADAM" BEDROOM FURNITURE, *1908*.

222. (*above*) *Paul Stosseck*, DESIGN FOR A YOUNG GIRL'S ROOM,
published in Moderne Bauformen, *1912. Traditional styles of
furnishing in Britain were as influential abroad as progressive
designs, especially in Northern Europe and the United States.*

223. (*right*) *Andrew F. Brophy*, ADAM, *wallpaper for Arthur
Sanderson & Sons Ltd., 1903.*

mal and Classical than pure 'Queen Anne' and thus
converged stylistically with the main classical tradition".

From the 1830s there had been signs of a revival of
eighteenth-century styles. As early as 1834, there had
been sufficient interest in the work of Chippendale and
his contemporaries for the speculative publisher, John
Weale, to begin reprinting their designs. Eighteenth-
century styles were further promoted by the design
reformers of the middle years of the century. Up to the
1870s however, Georgian furniture was considered
"clumsy" by most observers.

By the early 1860s there is evidence of a popular
interest in the work of Adam, Hepplewhite and Sheraton. The "Adam's" style was sufficiently topical for
Messrs Wright and Mansfield, a well-known firm of
cabinet-makers, to show furniture at the 1862 International Exhibition, which according to the *Art Journal
Illustrated Catalogue of the International Exhibition 1862* was
"gleaned from the work of Messrs Adam" which "may
be considered as indicating a style of English decorative

furniture of the eighteenth century". Wright and Mansfield were described by *The Cabinet Maker and Art Furnisher* in 1886 as "the leaders of that pleasing fashion which has happily brought back into our houses many of the charming shapes of the renowned eighteenth century cabinet makers". At the sale of their stock in 1886, caused by the dissolution of the partnership, the South Kensington Museum bought several pieces, all said to be in the style of Sheraton.

Eastlake had claimed that eighteenth-century joinery was "sound"; by 1874 *The Builder* called workmanship of the eighteenth century "first rate". A strong wave of the revival of eighteenth-century forms had set in during the 1870s, to some extent driving out neo-Gothic and Japanese, the "Aesthetic" styles which could possibly be considered more modern or avant-garde. From the 1890s there seemed to be widespread agreement that English workmanship of the eighteenth century was unsurpassed.

Writers on decorating and furnishings now stressed that medieval furniture was not really practical. It was held that prior to the eighteenth century there was generally only very ornate, stately furniture made for the few, while that used by most people was very primitive. Only in the eighteenth century did more elaborate furniture begin to be within reach of a wider public. It was eighteenth-century English furniture which provided the mass of objects for the amateur

222. (*above*) DESIGN FOR DINING-ROOM IN SHERATON STYLE, *published in Story & Triggs catalogue, 1900.*

225. (*opposite*) DESIGN FOR A DINING-ROOM IN EIGHTEENTH-CENTURY STYLE, *published in H. P. Shapland's* Schemes in Antique Furnishing, *1909. Neo-Georgian schemes of this kind were widely admired throughout Britain and North America. A few rooms of this sort were furnished with real antiques; most people made do with reproductions. The density of furnishing is characteristically Edwardian; not at all Georgian. It was the effect that mattered.*

collector, for the comfort of the new kind of home. It had the additional advantage that many pieces could be labelled with the name of a designer. Chippendale was probably the best-known name and the most misused. As H. J. Jennings in *Our Homes and How to Beautify Them* (1902) explained:

It may be taken for granted that a vast deal of the so-called "Chippendale" furniture was not manufactured by Chippendale at all — was not even designed by him. And here it is permissible to say a word concerning the ignorance with which a great many people talk about this interesting but rather vague personality of the eighteenth century. When a few years ago the beauty and refinement of old cabinet-work came into more general recognition, they caught up the name of Chippendale, and have been repeating it, they and their parrot-like successors — with the persistency of Poe's Raven ever since . . . They prate about Chippendale, and fly into noisy raptures over any article, no matter how devoid of taste, that goes by his name.

Chippendale's own designs were influenced by the French style of Louis XV. There was therefore a great tendency to mix Chippendale with Tous-les-Louis, resulting in intricate and ornate forms which were considered to be well suited to the decoration of drawing-rooms. A scheme for a drawing room in the Chippendale style published in Hampton & Sons' catalogue was captioned: "So well-proportioned are all Chippendale designs, and so gracefully conceived, that the general effect is always suggestive of that air of refinement which distinguishes the best class of English homes."

Chippendale style was also popular for dining-rooms, "the splendid chairs offering prestige and comfort", in the words of one manufacturer. Quality pieces were produced by the West End firm of Edwards & Roberts and cheaper versions by firms such as Messrs North of High Wycombe. Sometimes the name merely implied "mahogany".

The "Adams" style was a popular, prestigious style throughout the period. Gillow's exhibited Adam interiors at the Paris Exhibition of 1878 and at the Fine Art and Industries Exhibition in Manchester in 1882. Batsford published a reprint of *The Architecture, Decoration and Furniture of R & J Adam* in 1881. The *Cabinet Maker and Art Furnisher* in 1881 commented on "how admirably the Adams' style lends itself to the chaste decoration of bedroom furniture". The mode lent itself to the vogue for painted bedroom furniture in the 1880s and 1890s. It was also popular in drawing-rooms. Many pieces were copied from the domesticated 'Adam' of Hepplewhite but, strangely, his name does not seem to have had the sales appeal of the other eighteenth-century designers.

Some of the Adams' decorative designs were taken to America, where they were fused with the more informal Colonial Revival style. The classical strictness of the decorations was modified with certain concessions to quaintness, a more vigorous treatment, and a less mathematically rigid attention to form. In the towns of the eastern coast this modified Adams style made headway and was largely employed in the decoration of the better class of home. It was known as "Colonial Adams", and came into vogue after it had been employed by the decorators of the King's yacht.

In 1883 *The Magazine of Art* noted: "In recent years a fashion for Sheraton's furniture has sprung up and has so widely spread that modern cabinet makers have found it worth their while to reproduce many specimens and even to attempt original work in the same style". It was especially popular for bedrooms and drawing-rooms. Sheraton's *Drawing Book* was reprinted in 1895. H. J. Jennings in *Our Homes and How to Beautify Them* (1902) described this style as rather austere, attributing to it "a cold virginity". His view was that "however admirable may be their proportions, and however delicate their inlays, a reception room furnished entirely in this manner is not to everyone's taste".

Empire style

The interest in Empire as well as Regency styles was an extension of the eighteenth-century revival. The *Cabinet Maker* noted in 1884 that "the rage for reproducing late eighteenth century work is creeping on into this century". Designs for Empire furniture taken from the books of Thomas Hope and Percier and Fontaine were

226. *Paul Ludwig Troost*, DESIGN FOR A DINING-ROOM, *published in C. H. Baer's* Farbige Raumkunst, *1911. The furniture in this design demonstrates a not uncommon fusion of revival styles, in this case Sheraton, with progressive developments, in this case Secessionist.*

included by Robert Brook in *Elements of Style in Furniture and Woodwork* (1889), in which he referred to the availability of Napoleonic relics for further inspiration in Madame Tussaud's Exhibition in Baker Street.

By the 1890s the growing enthusiasm for the Napoleonic period had become firmly established. *The Furnisher and Decorator* reported in 1895 that, "from wallpapers and tapestry hangings to dress goods, and even patterns of women's clothes, all have shown a tendency to imitate the fashions of France in the days of the First Empire".

The Empire Revival of the 1880s to 1890s was the least copied French style. The trade press often referred to the style as offering possibilities for designers but stated that it was underused. Edwards & Roberts of Wardour Street, however, specialized in high-quality Empire-style furniture and Alexander Henderson of Buscot Park did commission furniture for some Empire rooms from Robert Christie of George Street.

Britain was not the only country to experience a revival of interest in Regency and Empire styles. America was also interested and, according to *The Cabinet Maker* "greedily adopted the style of the 'Empire' as soon as they saw public opinion was ripe for it . . . ", while England had been toying with the style, "our more courageous relations have filled their showrooms with revivals".

Revivalism Survives

Throughout the twentieth century, designers and consumers on both sides of the Atlantic have continued to revisit the past in search of inspiration. The pace of stylistic recycling has quickened.

Some of the styles admired in the nineteenth century – Gothic, for instance – have faded from popularity. Others have found new contexts; the 1930s 'Jacobean' dining-room suite shares many features with Victorian 'Elizabethan' furnishings; 'Louis' styles have continued to signify glamour, particularly in films. Many of Morris's principles, and those of the Arts and Crafts Movement have survived as tenets of architectural and design training and have regularly resurfaced in different forms, from wartime 'Utility' through to the stripped pine and cottage style furnishings of the 1970s and 1980s. Of all revivalist styles, the Georgian and Colonial have proved the most enduring; Queen Anne chairs, Chippendale occasional tables, even new neo-Georgian style homes still sell in their thousands.

Nineteenth-century homes, furniture and furnishings are now valued in their own right. Victorian buildings are protected, Victorian fabrics and wallpapers reproduced, Victorian furniture restored, to a degree that the Victorians themselves could never have predicted. In 1911 H. G. Wells posed the question: 'Will anyone a hundred years from now consent to live in the houses the Victorians built, travel by their roads or railways, value the furnishings they made to live among or esteemed except for curious or historical reasons . . .' Today the answer is unequivocally 'yes'.

BIBLIOGRAPHY

Primary Sources

Ackermann, R., *Repository of Arts, Literature, Commerce, Manufactures, Fashions and Politics*, London, 1809–28.

Adams, M. B., *Artists' Homes*, London, 1883.

Arrowsmith, H. W. and A., *The House Decorator's and Painter's Guide*, London, 1840.

Arrowsmith, J., *The Paper Hanger's and Upholsterer's Guide*, London, 1854.

Ashbee, C. R., *Craftsmanship in Competitive Industry*, London, 1908.

Baillie Scott, M. H., *Houses and Gardens*, London, 1906.

Barrington, R., *The Life, Letters and Work of Sir Frederic Leighton*, 2 vols., London, 1906.

Batley, H. W., *A Series of Studies of Domestic Furniture*, London, 1883.

Bridgens, R., *Furniture with Candelabra and Interior Decoration*, 1825–6.

Brunner, A. W., and Tyron, T., *Interior Decoration*, New York, 1887.

Burne-Jones, G., *Memorials of Sir Edward Burne-Jones*, 2 vols., London, 1904.

Carr, J. Comyns, *Coasting Bohemia*, London, 1914.

Church, E. R., *How to Furnish a Home*, New York, 1883.

Collinson & Lock, *Sketches of Artistic Furniture*, London, 1871.

Conway, M., *Travels in South Kensington*, London, 1882.

Cook, C. *Artistic Houses*, New York, 1883.

—— *The House Beautiful*, New York, 1878.

Crane, W., *William Morris to Whistler: Papers and Addresses on Arts and Crafts and the Commonweal*, London, 1911.

Day, L. F., *William Morris and his Art*, London, 1899.

Downing, A. J., *The Architecture of Country Houses*, New York, 1850.

Eastlake, C. L., *Hints on Household Taste in Furniture, Upholstery and Other Details*, London, 1868; Boston, 1872.

Edis R., *Decoration and Furniture of the Town House*, London, 1881.

—— *Healthy Furniture and Decoration*, London, 1884.

Elder Duncan, J. H., *The House Beautiful and Useful*, London, 1907.

Falke, J. von, *Art in the House*, Boston, 1878.

Garrett, R. and A., *Suggestions for House Decoration*, London, 1877.

Haweis, M. E., *Art of Decoration*, London, 1876.

—— *Beautiful Houses*, London, 1882.

Hole, J., *The Homes of the Working Classes with Suggestions for their Improvement*, London, 1866.

Hope, T., *Household Furniture and Interior Decoration*, London, 1807.

Hueffer, F. M., *Ford Madox Brown: A Record of his Life and Work*, London, 1896.

Jennings, H. J., *Our Homes and How to Beautify Them*, London, 1902.

Jones, O., *Plans, Elevations, Sections and Details of the Alhambra*, London, 1836–45.

—— *The Grammar of Ornament*, London, 1856.

Kerr, R., *The Gentleman's House*, London, 1864.

King, T., *The Modern Style of Cabinet Work Exemplified*, London, 1829 (and later editions).

Lethaby, W. R., *Philip Webb and his Work*, London, 1935.

Loudon, J. C., *An Encyclopaedia of Cottage, Farm and Villa Architecture*, London, 1833 (and later editions).

Mackail, J. W., *The Life of William Morris*, 2 vols., London, 1906.

Morris, W., *The Collected Works of William Morris*, 24 vols., London, 1910–15.

Muthesius, H., *Das Englische Haus*, Berlin, 1904 (English edn. 1979).

Nicholson, P. and M. A., *The Practical Cabinet Maker, Upholsterer and Complete Decorator*, London, 1826.

Orrinsmith, Mrs, *The Drawing Room*, London, 1878.

Panton, J. E., *Surburban Residences and How to Circumvent Them*, London, 1896.

Parker, B. and Unwin, R., *The Art of Building a Home*, London, 1901.

Parkes, F. B., *Domestic Duties: or Instructions to Young Married Ladies*, New York, 1825.

Pugin, A. W. N., *Contrasts: or a Parallel between the Architecture of the 15th and 19th Centuries*, London, 1836.

Repton, H., *Observations on the Theory and Practice of Landscape Gardening*, 1803.

Ruskin, J. R., *The Stones of Venice*, London, 1851–3.

Select Committee Report on Arts, Manufactures and Principles of Design, London, 1836.

Shaw, H., *Specimens of Ancient Furniture*, 1836.

Smith's Art of Housepainting, London, 1821.

Smith, G., *A Collection of Designs for Household Furniture and Interior Decoration*, London, 1808.

Smith, J. Moyr, *Ornamental Interiors, Ancient and Modern*, London, 1887.

Sparrow, W. S., *Flats, Urban Houses and Cottage Homes*, London, 1906.

—— *Hints on House Furnishing*, London, 1909.

Stephens, F. G., *Artists at Home*, London, 1884.

Stirling, A. M. W., *William de Morgan and his Wife*, London, 1922.

Talbert, B. J., *Gothic Forms Applied to Furniture*, London, 1868; Boston, 1873.

The Upholsterer's Accelerator, being rules for Cutting and Forming Draperies, Valances, &c, London, n.d.

Throop, L. A., *Furnishing the House of Good Taste*, New York, 1890.

Vallance, A., *William Morris*, London, 1897.

Walsh, J. H., *A Manual of Domestic Economy suited to families spending from £100 to £1,000 a year*, London, 1857.

Watts, M. S., *George Frederick Watts, The Annals of an Artist's Life*, London, 1912.

Webster, T. and Parkes, F. B., *An Encyclopaedia of Domestic Economy*, London, 1844.

Wharton, E., and Codman, O., *The Decoration of Houses*, New York, 1897.

Wheeler, G., *Rural Homes, or Sketches of Houses Suited to American Life*, New York, 1851.

Whittock, N., *The Decorative Painter's and Glazier's Guide*, London, 1827.

Wolfe, E. de, *The House of Good Taste*, New York, 1913.

Secondary Sources

Adburgham, A., *Liberty's: A Biography of a Shop*, London, 1975.

Agius, P., *British Furniture 1880–1915*, Woodbridge, 1978.

Anscombe, I., and Gere, C., *Arts and Crafts in Britain and America*, London, 1978.

Arts Council, *Edward Burne-Jones*, London, 1975.

Arts Council, *Morris & Co. 1861–1940*, London, 1961.

Aslin, E., *E. W. Godwin: Furniture and Interior Decoration*, London, 1986.

—— *Nineteenth Century English Furniture*, London, 1962.

—— *The Aesthetic Movement: A Prelude to Art Nouveau*, London, 1969.

Banham, J. and Harris, J. (eds.), *William Morris and the Middle Ages*, Manchester, 1985.

Barrett, H., and Phillips, J., *Suburban Style: The British Home 1840–1960*, London, 1987.

Billcliffe, R., *Charles Rennie Mackintosh: The complete Furniture, Furniture Drawings and Interiors*, London, 1979.

Brandon-Jones, J. et al., *C. F. A. Voysey: Architect and Designer 1857–1941*, Brighton, 1978.

Blunt, W., *England's Michelangelo*, London, 1975.

Collins, J., *The Omega Workshops*, London, 1984.

Comino, M., *Gimson and the Barnsleys*, London, 1984.

Cooper, J., *Victorian and Edwardian Furniture and Interiors*, London, 1987.

Cooper, N., *The Opulent Eye: Late Victorian and Edwardian Taste in Interior Design*, London, 1976.

Crawford, A., *C. R. Ashbee*, London, 1985.

Denvir, B., *The Late Victorians: Art, Design and Society, 1852–1910*, London, 1986.

Design Council, *William Morris & Kelmscott*, London, 1981.

Dixon, R., and Muthesius, S., *Victorian Architecture*, London, 1978.

Forty, A., *Objects of Desire: Design and Society 1750–1980*, London, 1986.

Gaunt, W., *Kensington and Chelsea*, London, 1975.

—— *Victorian Olympus*, London, 1975.

Gere, C., *Nineteenth Century Decoration: The Art of the Interior*, London, 1989.

Girouard, M., *Sweetness and Light: The "Queen Anne" Movement 1860–1900*, Oxford, 1977.

—— *The Victorian Country House*, Oxford, 1971.

Harrison, M., and Waters, B., *Burne-Jones*, London, 1973.

Hyde, S., and Smith, G., *Walter Crane*, London, 1989.

Jervis, S., *High Victorian Design*, London, 1983.

Kirkham, P., *The London Furniture Trade 1700–1870* (Furniture History Society), Leeds, 1988.

—— Mace, R., and Porter, J., *Furnishing the World: The East London Furniture Trade 1780–1980*, London, 1987.

Maas, J., *The Victorian Art World*, London, 1984.

Marsh, J., *Back to the Land: The Pastoral Impulse in Victorian England from 1880–1914*, London, 1982.

Mayhew, E., and Myers, M., *A Documentary History of American Interiors*, New York, 1980.

Metropolitan Museum of Art, *In Pursuit of Beauty*, New York, 1986.

Muthesius, S., *The English Terraced House*, New Haven and London, 1982.

Ormond, L. and R., *Lord Leighton*, New Haven and London, 1975.

Parry, L., *William Morris Textiles*, London, 1936.

Pevsner, N., *Pioneers of Modern Design*, London, 1960.

Richardson, M., *Architects of the Arts and Crafts Movement*, London, 1983.

Schoeser, M., and Rufey, C., *English and American Textiles from 1790 to the Present Day*, London, 1989.

Service, A., *Edwardian Interiors*, London, 1982.

Swanson, V., *Sir Lawrence Alma-Tadema*, London, 1977.

Thornton, P., *Authentic Decor: The Domestic Interior 1620–1920*, London, 1984.

Turner, M., and Hoskins, L., *Silver Studio of Design: A Design Source Book for Home Decoration*, London, 1988.

Wainwright, C., *George Bullock: Cabinet Maker*, London, 1988.

Watkinson, R., *Pre-Raphaelite Art and Design*, London, 1970.

—— *William Morris as Designer*, London, 1967.

Periodicals

The Art Journal, 1839–1911

The Artist, 1880–1902

The British Architect, 1874–

The Builder, 1843–

Building News, 1855–1926

The Cabinet Maker and Art Furnisher, 1880–

The Cabinet Maker's Monthly Journal of Design, 1856–

Cassell's Household Guide, 1875–

The Journal of Decorative Art, 1881–1937

Journal of Design and Manufactures, 1849–52

The Magazine of Art, 1878–1904

The Studio, 1893–

SELECTED BIOGRAPHIES

Aitchison, George, (1825–1910)

Aitchison was trained by his father, an architect, and became his partner in 1859. Between 1853 and 1859, he travelled around Italy with William Burges. He worked mainly as an architect but also designed the decorations for a number of interiors. His most famous work was for Leighton House, begun in 1864, notably the design of the Arab Hall (1877–9). Aitchison was professor of architecture at the Royal Academy from 1887.

Alma-Tadema, Sir Lawrence (1836–1912)

Alma-Tadema was born in Holland and in 1852 entered the Antwerp Academy. He moved to London in 1870 and in 1879 was elected to the Royal Academy. He lived both at Townshend House and at 34 Grove End Road where, between 1884 and 1885 he redecorated and designed his own furniture. One of his couches, with one side Pompeian and the other Egyptian, was shown at the London 1893 Arts and Crafts Exhibition. Alma-Tadema was knighted in 1899.

Ashbee, Charles Robert (1863–1942)

Ashbee studied at Oxford and in 1883 went into the office of the architect G. F. Bodley. After this he moved to the East End of London and set up the Guild of Handicrafts, which was inaugurated in 1888. The Guild designed leatherwork, metalwork, woodwork and jewellery and showed at the Arts and Crafts Exhibitions from 1890 onwards. In the 1890s Ashbee designed several houses in Cheyne Row. He was elected to the Art-Workers' Guild in 1897 and in the same year visited America, where he met Frank Lloyd Wright. The Guild of Handicrafts became a limited company in 1898 and Ashbee was commissioned to make some of the furniture designed by Baillie Scott for the Grand Duke of Hesse's palace at Darmstadt. The Guild also showed at the Vienna Secession Exhibition in 1900 and the following year were given a warrant to design jewellery for Queen Alexandra. In 1902 the Guild moved from London to the Cotswolds before finally collapsing in 1905 despite the praise that Ashbee's individual work had been receiving. In 1917 he was involved in town-planning in Jerusalem and in Egypt but returned to England in 1924.

Baillie Scott, Mackay Hugh (1865–1945)

In 1886, Baillie Scott was articled to E. Davis, the city architect of Bath. After marrying, he settled in Douglas on the Isle of Man. The first work of his architectural practice owes much to Voysey. He was a regular contributor to *The Studio* from 1895. Two years later he was commissioned by the Grand Duke of Hesse to decorate a dining-room and a drawing-room in his palace at Darmstadt. Many of his designs were executed by Ashbee's Guild of Handicraft. In 1901 he won first prize for designing a house for an art lover in the 'Zeitschrift fur Innen-Dekoration' competition and in the same year moved to Bedford. From about this time until 1914 Baillie Scott designed furniture, interiors and tapestries for the Deutsche Werkstätten, and for Wertheimer in Berlin. Muthesius's *Das Englische Haus* did much to promote Baillie Scott's international influence and from 1907 his English architectural practice took off. He retired in 1939.

Behrens, Peter (1869–1940)

Behrens studied painting from 1886 to 1889 at the Karlshruhe School of Art, moving to Düsseldorf after this. In 1896 he became one of the founders of the Munich Vereinigte Werkstätten. The 1901 house that he designed for the Darmstadt Exhibition received a great deal of praise. In 1902 he designed the German Entrance Hall at the Turin Exhibition. Between 1903 and 1907 he was director of the Düsseldorf School of Applied Arts, also in 1907 he became a founder member of the Deutsche Werkbund and was appointed architect of the AEG electrical company in Berlin. Behrens remained there until 1914 designing buildings, kettles, electric fans and lamps. In 1910 Gropius, Van der Rohe and Le Corbusier all worked in his office. From 1922 to 1936 he taught architecture at the Vienna Academy and in 1936 conducted masterclasses in architecture at the Berlin Academy.

Benson, William Arthur Smith (1854–1924)

Benson was educated at Oxford and worked in an architect's office up until 1880. After this, having met William Morris and Burne-Jones, he was inspired to set up a metalwork workshop, which survived until 1920, and in 1887, a shop in Bond Street. He was an active member of the Art-Worker's Guild from 1884 and a founder member of the Arts and Crafts Exhibition Society. He became chairman of Morris & Co. on Morris's death in 1896 and continued to design furniture and wallpapers for them. In 1914 he was involved with the setting up of the Design and Industries Association. Benson retired in 1920.

Bradley, Will (1868–1962)

Bradley was the son of a cartoonist and began work in about 1879 as a wood engraver in Chicago, where he also opened a studio in 1893. He designed covers for the trade magazine *The Inland Printer* from 1894. In 1897 his furniture designs were exhibited at the Boston Arts and Crafts Exhibition. Between 1901 and 1902 he published designs for interiors and furniture in the *Ladies' Home Journal*. From 1915 he was art director for the Hearst publishing and film corporation. Bradley retired in 1930.

Bridgens, Richard (1785–1846)

From about 1810 Bridgens was in contact with George Bullock, designing furniture in collaboration with him. From around 1819 to 1824 he designed Elizabethan furniture and interior schemes for Aston Hall in Birmingham, a view of the East Front of which he exhibited at the Royal Academy in 1826. Following a seven-year trip to the West Indies, he worked as a draughtsman on Henry Shaw's 'Details of Elizabethan Architecture'. Bridgens's main importance was as a pioneer of the Victorian Elizabethan revival.

Brown, Ford Maddox (1821–1893)

Brown studied painting in Bruges and Ghent and travelled to Paris and Rome in the 1840s. Back in London in 1848, he became very closely associated with the Pre-Raphaelites although he never joined them. In 1861 he became a founder member of the Morris firm for which he designed wallpaper, stained glass and furniture, pioneering the firm's rush-seated furniture in 1865/6. Also in 1861 he helped to decorate a cabinet by Seddon, later shown at the 1862 London Exhibition along with a bookcase designed by himself. Between 1878 and 1893 he worked on decorations for Manchester Town Hall. In 1890 furniture by Brown was shown at the Arts and Crafts Exhibition. His role as a pioneer design reformer has been widely acclaimed.

Bullock, George (1778–1818)

Bullock was President of the Liverpool Academy from 1810 to 1811 having been a partner in a cabinet-making firm from 1805. In about 1813, he moved to London, six plates of his work appearing in Ackerman's Repository in 1816 and 1817. Between 1814 and 1819 he supplied furniture to Blair Castle. His work was mainly in the neo-classical style but he also pioneered the Elizabethan and Gothic Revivals.

Burges, William (1827–1881)

Burges studied engineering at King's College but started work in Matthew Digby Wyatt's office in 1859. His furniture designs received their first public showing in 1862 at the International Exhibition in London. He was strongly influenced by the Japanese Court at that exhibition and was an early collector of Japanese prints. His lectures to the Royal Society of Arts on 'Art applied to Industry' were published in 1865. Burges was not prolific, much of his work being in the Gothic Revival style. He concentrated on restoration (such as Cardiff Castle from 1869, and Castle Coch from 1875) rather than completely new design work.

Burne-Jones, Sir Edward (1833–1898)

In 1853 Burne-Jones went up to Oxford where he met William Morris with whom he travelled around France in 1855. Returning to Oxford the following year he met Rossetti and became his pupil. Having decorated some of Morris's and Philip Webb's furniture he designed a stained-glass panel in 1857 for Powell's of Whitefriars and continued stained-glass designing for William Burges for Waltham Abbey in 1859. He also designed for Morris's Red House at this time and in 1861 was involved in the foundation of Morris & Co. Later work included embroidery designs for the Royal School of Needlework, founded in 1872. In 1891 he designed the illustrations for the Kelmscott Chaucer and was made an honorary member of the Vienna Secession in 1897.

Butterfield, William (1814–1900)

Butterfield studied architecture from 1833 to 1836 and set up office as a Gothic Revival architect in London in 1840. Between 1843 and 1847 he designed a number of plates of church fittings published in *Instrumenta Ecclesiastica*. He won a medal for the church plate he showed at the 1851 exhibition in London. Butterfield also designed medieval style furniture.

Cole, Sir Henry (1808–1882)

Cole started his career in the government service but became increasingly interested in the arts. In 1843 under the pseudonym Felix Summerly, he published the first Christmas card. He launched Felix Summerly Art Manufactures in 1847 and, as Summerly, won an award from the Society of Arts for a tea-service in 1846. He became the Chairman of the Society of Arts in 1851. Working closely with Prince Albert, he organized the 1851 London Exhibition and was general advisor to the 1862 International Exhibition in London. In 1852 he was appointed Secretary to the Department of Practical Art. Founded at his suggestion, this department administered the School of Design and created what was to become the Victoria and Albert Museum. He retired in 1873.

Crane, Walter (1845–1915)

Crane was apprenticed to the wood engraver William Linton in 1859 and trained as a draughtsman on wood. From 1870 onwards his work concentrated upon innovative book illustrations mainly for the publishers Routledge. He met Morris, De Morgan and Webb in 1871, and at about this time produced some designs for Wedgwood's. During the 1870s he began to design wallpapers, working for the firm of Jeffrey & Co. from 1874. In this year he also designed embroideries for the Royal School of Needlework. In 1880 he became the Art Superintendent for the London Decorating Co., which made tiles, having worked on mosaic designs for Leighton House in 1877–9. In 1884 he became a founder member of the Art-Worker's Guild. Under Morris's influence he became a committed socialist from the mid-1880s, drawing cartoons in support of the cause. In 1898 he became Principal of the Royal College of Art, his European reputation having become established earlier that decade. He exhibited a large amount of work in 1902 in Turin. His last major scheme was the planning of the 1914 Exhibition in Paris, some of his decorations being used again in Paris in 1925.

De Morgan, William Frend (1839–1917)

De Morgan studied painting at the Royal Academy Schools from 1859. He began to design stained glass and tiles for Morris in 1863, and six years later began to decorate pottery. He was running a successful pottery by 1873 selling his tiles through Morris and Co. Some of his tiles were used to decorate the Arab Hall at Leighton House. In 1888 he was involved with the first Arts and Crafts Exhibition and set up a new factory in Fulham. De Morgan spent much of his time in Italy from the mid-1890s, designing for the Cantagalli factory in Florence. He also experimented with lustre-ware and glasses and was influenced by Parisian styles which were the forerunners of Art Nouveau.

Dresser, Christopher (1834–1904)

Dresser entered the government School of Design at Somerset House in 1847, where his interest in botanical studies quickly developed. He established himself as an important commercial designer in the 1860s and published his first book *The Art of Decorative Design* in 1862. In 1875 he started to design plate and silverware for Elkington & Co., for Hukin & Heath from 1878 and for James Dixon & Sons from 1879. Dresser judged the wallpaper designs for the Paris 1878 Exhibition and became Art Editor of the *Furniture Gazette* in 1880. Two years later he published his major work *Japan, its Architecture, Art and Art Manufactures*. Dresser died whilst on a trip to France in 1904.

Eastlake, Charles Locke (1836–1906)

Eastlake began his career studying architecture at the Royal Academy Schools but decided to become a journalist, although he was in fact appointed Secretary of the Institute of British Architects in 1871. In 1878 he resigned from this post to become Keeper of the National Gallery. His most influential book, *Hints On Household Taste*, was published in 1868. This book was hugely successful in America as well as Britain, so much so that it generated a type of design which became known as the "Eastlake style" although it in fact owed little to any of his precepts.

Edis, Robert William (1839–1927)

Edis began to work as an architect in 1861. He promoted the Queen Anne style through the 1870s and was knighted in 1919. His book *Decoration and Furniture of the Town House* was published in 1881 and included interiors by Walter Crane and Jeckyll amongst others. The book was hugely influential, helping to popularize the Queen Anne style and also sanitarian views on cleaner homes.

Faulkner, Kate (Dates uncertain)

Kate Faulkner was the sister of Charles Faulkner, one of the founding partners of Morris & Co., and her best-known work was for the firm, for which she painted tiles. She also decorated some pieces of furniture, notably pianos and settles with designs executed in gesso, some of which were shown at the first Arts and Crafts Exhibition of 1888. Faulkner also designed a number of wallpapers for Morris & Co. as well as for Jeffrey & Co.

Fry, Roger Elliot (1866–1934)

Fry read natural sciences at Cambridge between 1885 and 1888 but after this point became more and more interested in art history, helping to found the *Burlington Magazine*. In 1905 he became director of the Metropolitan Museum in New York and remained there until 1910. Back in London in 1913 he set up the Omega Workshops with the painter Wyndham Lewis. The workshops, which made ceramics, textiles and furniture, continued until 1919 and during this time produced the work of a number of well-known artists, Duncan Grant, Vanessa Bell and Dora Carrington amongst others.

Gimson, Ernest (1864–1919)

Gimson was articled to an architect's office in Leicester in 1881 and went to London to practise in 1886. Here he met Morris and also Sidney Barnsley. Two years later he left to study other crafts and became skilled in furniture-making and plasterwork, both of which he showed at the Arts and Crafts Exhibition. In 1893 he moved with the Barnsley brothers to the Cotswolds, where Gimson concentrated for the moment on plasterwork. By 1901 he had taken up furniture design again, and although the partnership with the Barnsleys ended in 1905 Gimson continued working in this field alone, mounting a huge exhibition of his designs at Debenham and Freebody's, the London shop, in 1907. In 1916 he designed two room settings for the Arts and Crafts Exhibition.

Godwin, Edward William (1833–1886)

Godwin set up as an architect in Bristol in 1854. He won his first major competition in 1861 with a design for Northampton Town Hall. This success was followed in 1864 with Congleton Town Hall, and in 1867 he expanded his practice and moved it to London. In that same year Godwin travelled to Ireland with his friend William Burges, where he received the commission to build Dromore Castle. Having become increasingly interested in furniture design, Godwin set up his own company, Art Furniture. In 1878 in collaboration with Whistler, Godwin worked on the British stand at the Paris Exhibition. Godwin was a prolific designer and one of the leading exponents of the Aesthetic Movement, producing textiles, wallpapers, tiles, ceramics and interior schemes.

Heal, Sir Ambrose (1872–1959)

After serving an apprenticeship as a cabinet-maker, Heal went into the family business. He designed furniture for Heal's from 1896, became a partner two years later, managing director in 1907 and chairman in 1913. A member of the Art-Workers' Guild, Heal became a founder of the Design and Industries Association in 1915. He was knighted in 1933 and continued designing, at first in an Arts and Crafts style and then from the 1930s in a style influenced by the Modern Movement. Heal retired in 1953.

Hoffmann, Josef (1870–1956)

Hoffmann studied architecture in Munich and in Vienna, where he became a pupil of Otto Wagner, working in Wagner's studio until 1897. In 1899 Hoffmann was appointed professor of architecture at the School of Applied Arts. In 1902 he was involved with the Vienna Secession Exhibition. Following this he visited England

and inspired by Ashbee's Guild of Handicrafts, two years later Hoffmann co-founded the Wiener Werkstätte with Koloman Moser. Hoffmann continued to design for the Werkstätte until 1931 but also worked on Austrian pavilions at a number of the International Exhibitions, Paris 1925 and Stockholm 1930 for example.

Hope, Thomas (1769–1831)

Hope was born in Amsterdam. The son of a wealthy banker, he was able to undertake an extensive Grand Tour, during which he studied and collected. In 1799 he moved into an Adam house in London and began to convert it to the then more fashionable neo-classical style. Hope became increasingly interested in design, the silversmith Paul Storr executing some of his work. In an early attempt to improve standards of design, he wrote *Household Furniture and Interior Decoration Executed from Designs by Thomas Hope*, which was published in 1807. In the same year Hope bought a country house, The Deepdene in Surrey, and became actively involved in remodelling it. The sale of this house in 1917 was a significant source for the twentieth-century Regency Revival.

Horne, Herbert Percy (1864–1916)

Horne trained as a surveyor from 1880 but entered Mackmurdo's office to become an architect in 1883, going into partnership in 1885. A member of the Century Guild, Horne co-edited the Guild's journal *Hobby Horse* with Mackmurdo. Horne also designed a number of wallpapers for the Guild, many of them printed by Jeffrey & Co. He moved to Florence in 1900 and left his house to the city.

Horta, Victor (1861–1947)

Horta studied drawing and architecture at the Ghent Academy but left the city to work in Paris in 1878. He stayed there for three years and went to the Brussels Academy in 1881. Horta's first buildings date from 1885 and in 1893 he designed the first full Art Nouveau building for the engineer Emil Tassel in Brussels. Horta's reputation was then firmly established by the Maison du Peuple, built in 1895, also in Brussels. In 1897 he designed a pavilion for the Val Saint Lambert glass factory at the Brussels Exhibition and in 1902 the Belgian pavilion for the Turin Exhibition.

Hubbard, Elbert (1856–1915)

Hubbard, originally a salesman in Illinois, travelled to England in 1894. On his return, having been strongly influenced by Morris and the Kelmscott Press, he set up his own Roycroft Press. The press became the centre of a very busy artistic community, which also began to produce leatherwork and Arts and Crafts style furniture known as "Aurora Colonial Furniture". By 1900 there were 175 "Roycrofters", the Roycroft shops surviving until 1938, although both Hubbard and his wife were lost on the *Lusitania* in 1915.

Jack, George Washington (1855–1931)

Born in New York, Jack was brought to Glasgow when young and then articled to a local architect. He came to London in about 1875 and by 1880 had entered Philip Webb's design and architectural practice, taking over on Webb's retirement in 1900. Between 1880 and 1896 he designed furniture for Morris & Co. He also executed a number of carvings in wood and designed stained glass, mosaics and cast-iron work.

Jones, Owen (1809–1874)

Jones attended the Royal Academy Schools from 1829. Following this he embarked on a Grand Tour, which sparked off his fascination with pattern and colour. On his return to England he lectured and wrote on these themes and was also an active member of the Architectural Society through the 1830s. During the 1840s, Jones' main reputation was as a tile and mosaic designer, although he also began to produce a number of books for publication at this time. In 1851, under Henry Cole's influence, Jones was appointed joint architect for the 1851 London Exhibition, and in 1852 he became Director of Decorations for the Crystal Palace. In the 1860s Jones began to design wallpapers for commercial production; his most elaborate works were his interiors, however, examples being Fishmongers' Hall (1865–6) and 16 Carlton House Terrace, London, for Alfred Morrison (from 1863). Jones' most influential work was his book *The Grammar of Ornament*, published in 1856, which illustrated more than 100 designs and became internationally successful as a repertoire of ornament.

Knox, Archibald (1864–1933)

Knox was born on the Isle of Man where he studied at Douglas School of Art probably moving to Baillie Scott's office in 1892 and then to London in 1897. The following year he began to design metalwork, chiefly pewter, for Liberty's. He was back on the Isle of Man between 1900 and 1904 but returned to London after this date to teach at a number of art schools there. He stopped working for Liberty's in 1912 (although he was to design Sir Arthur Liberty's tomb in 1917) and travelled to Philadelphia, where he designed carpets for Bromley & Co. returning once more to the Isle of Man in 1913.

Lethaby, William Richard (1857–1931)

Having been apprenticed in an architect's office in Devon, Lethaby went to work in Richard Norman Shaw's office in 1879. He helped to found the Art-Workers' Guild in 1884, becoming its master in 1911. Lethaby was also actively involved with setting up the Arts and Crafts Exhibition Society, established in 1887. In 1889 he set up practice independently and the following year, with Gimson, founded Kenton & Co., furniture designers. He was appointed as one of the first art inspectors for London County Council Technical Education Board in 1894 and from this, two years later, became joint director of the Central School of Arts and Crafts and sole Principal in 1900. From 1900 to 1918, Lethaby was professor of ornament and design at the Royal College of Art. He was also instrumental in the creation of the Design and Industries Association in 1915.

Liberty, Sir Arthur Lasenby (1843–1917)

The son of a draper, Liberty was apprenticed to a London draper in 1859. In 1862 he moved to Farmer and Rogers' Great Shawl and Cloak Emporium in Regent Street. He quickly became one of the managers of the Emporium's Oriental Warehouse but moved on in 1875, to open his own shop in Regent Street, selling silks, Japanese porcelain, screens and so on. As well as writing papers on Japanese art, Liberty published a book, *Japan, A Pictorial Record*, in 1910, which was based on his travels there. Liberty's enjoyed a very successful international reputation and in Italy Art Nouveau was in fact sometimes referred to as "Stile Liberty".

Loudon, John Claudius (1783–1843)

Loudon was apprenticed to a number of landscape gardeners from 1789. In 1803 he moved to London where he began to write articles on garden design. After travelling in Northern Europe, he returned to London in 1817, where he began to design conservatories. In 1822 he published *An Encyclopedia of Gardening*, which was followed in 1833 with his *Encyclopedia of Cottage, Farm and Villa Architecture and Furniture*. Loudon's influence was also strong in America.

Macdonald, Margaret (1865–1933)

Margaret Macdonald was a painter and textile designer. She married Mackintosh in 1900. Between 1916 and 1923 she designed textiles for Foxton's and Sefton's.

Mackintosh, Charles Rennie (1868–1928)

In 1899 Mackintosh joined the architectural firm of Honeyman and Keppie, but left them to travel around Europe in 1901, having designed the Scottish stand at the Vienna Secession Exhibition in 1900. In 1903 his work was shown in Moscow. The famous Willow Street tea-rooms in Glasgow were designed in 1904 and the School of Art Library in 1909. Mackintosh moved to London in 1916, but left for France in 1923, remaining there until his death. Although he has been hailed as a precursor of the Modern Movement, Mackintosh was much better known by his contemporaries as a designer of jewellery, cutlery, stained glass and lettering.

Mackmurdo, Arthur Heygate (1851–1942)

Mackmurdo began to study architecture in 1869 and is known to have attended Ruskin's drawing classes. In 1874 he travelled to Italy with Ruskin. In 1882 he founded the Century Guild with Herbert Horne who joined his practice in 1883. He showed at the Liverpool 1886 Exhibition and two years later dissolved the Century Guild. He continued to practise as an architect up until 1906, but after this concentrated on publishing theories on social reform.

Morris, May (1862–1938)

Taught by her father William Morris, May designed embroideries, wallpapers and fabrics. She took over the embroidery department of Morris & Co. in 1885 and later taught embroidery at the Central School of Arts and Crafts in London.

Morris, William (1834–1896)

Born the son of a wealthy London stockbroker, Morris went to Oxford intending to become a clergyman, but turned to architecture as the result of the influence of his friend Burne-Jones and of reading Ruskin's works during the 1850s. In 1856 he entered the office of the Gothic Revival architect G. E. Street and began studying architecture, although his attention was diverted when Rossetti encouraged him to turn to painting. Having decorated the Red House, built for him by Philip Webb, Morris followed Ford Madox Brown's suggestion to establish a co-operative firm to produce well-designed decorative work. Morris, Marshall, Faulkner & Co. was set up in 1861 and by the mid-1860s Morris, who financially underpinned the company, had assumed greater control, taking over the company in 1875. Morris & Co. were responsible for a number of decorative schemes, including Queens' College Hall (1875) and Jesus College Chapel (1867–74) in Cambridge. Between 1872 and 1876, he designed a large number of wallpaper patterns. He set up his own press, the Kelmscott Press, which closed in 1898 having produced fifty-three books. His greatest influence was as a teacher and he was to have a considerable international impact both in this capacity and as a designer. In particular, Morris's talents lay in the area of flat pattern designing. His advocation of and admiration for traditional modes of manufacturing textiles, furniture and printed work were to be of enormous influence on design in both Britain and America.

Moser, Koloman (1868–1918)

Moser was born in Vienna and entered the Academy there to study painting, moving on to the School of Applied Arts to study design. He designed postcards for the first Secession Exhibition in 1898, and the following year took up a teaching post at the School of Applied Arts, becoming professor in 1900. Some of Moser's furniture was shown at the Secession that year and during 1900 he also worked on the Austrian stand for the Paris Exhibition. In 1903 Moser founded the Wiener Werkstätte with Hoffmann and the financier Fritz Warndorfer. He left the venture in 1907, however, having fallen out with Warndorfer. From 1908 he worked mainly as a painter.

Pugin, Augustus Welby Northmore (1812–1852)

Pugin trained as a draughtsman with his father, who was himself an architect and designer. In 1827 he received his first commissions, to design Gothic furniture for Windsor Castle and to design the Coronation Cup and plate in St George's Chapel, Windsor, for the silversmiths Rundell and Bridge. In 1829 Pugin set up a decorating firm in Covent Garden where he was already working very successfully as a theatrical designer. Pugin's firm failed in 1831, but, unperturbed, he began to study architecture. This interest brought him into contact with the architect Charles Barry, whose work in collaboration with Pugin won the competition to design the new Palace of Westminster in 1835. During the second half of the 1830s Pugin became increasingly interested in Gothic forms. Associated with this was his conversion to Catholicism, a connection made apparent in his book *Contrasts; or a Parallel between the Architecture of the 15th and 19th Centuries*, which presented Catholicism and its architecture, that is Gothic architecture, as being wholly good, and anything opposed to this, namely, Protestantism and its architecture, as bad. In 1836 Pugin received his first major architectural commission, to build Scarisbrick Hall for a wealthy Catholic. Pugin's work for the Palace of Westminster continued through this period and he designed textiles, wallpapers and carpets for the new building. This job seems virtually to have exhausted him and although he was responsible for the organization of the Medieval Court at the 1851 London Exhibition, it is claimed that the stresses of his involvement at Westminster brought about his early death.

Repton, Humphry (1725–1818)

Repton was born in Bury St Edmunds but moved to Norwich with his family as a child. When he was 12, Repton was sent to Holland to continue his education. Returning to Norwich when he was 16, he was apprenticed in the textile trade and then at 21 set up in business by his father. He seems to have taken the earliest opportunity to move out into the Norfolk countryside, however, and here decided to establish himself as a landscape gardener. Repton's first commissions came from friends, but his reputation grew quickly, partly as a result of his representations of schemes in his *Red Books* which illustrated the 'before and after' effects of his work. Repton also gained a good reputation as an architect, working with John Nash between 1796 and 1800. After his death Repton's work was continued by his son J. A. Repton.

Rosetti, Dante Gabriel (1828–1882)

Rossetti studied painting at the Royal Academy between 1845 and 1847 and then as Ford Madox Brown's pupil in 1848. During that year he shared a studio with Millais and Holman Hunt, with whom he founded the Pre-Raphaelite Brotherhood. He met Morris in 1856, and in 1861 became involved in the setting up of Morris & Co., designing some stained glass and decorations for painted furniture for the firm from this date. A sofa designed by Rossetti was shown at the 1862 London Exhibition and he also designed a lyre-back chair which was part of the firm's Sussex Range, in about 1865. Between 1861 and 1871, Rosetti mainly designed bindings. His collaboration with Morris & Co. came to an end in 1875.

Ruskin, John (1819–1900)

Ruskin was up at Oxford from 1837. His influential books, *The Seven Lamps of Architecture* and *The Stones of Venice*, were written in 1849 and 1851–3 respectively. These were both a validation of Gothic architecture and forms, and in 1878 he founded the Guild of St George, which represented his dream that society return to a medieval state. Although his vision failed, Ruskin did prove to be of great significance to the Arts and Crafts Movement, many of the proponents of which had come into contact with him in Oxford where Ruskin held the post of Slade Professor of Art, or through his writings.

Seddon, John Pollard (1827–1906)

Seddon was apprenticed to an architect between 1848 and 1851, and in 1852 went into a ten-year partnership with John Pritchard in Llandaff. That same year he published *Progress in Art and Architecture with Precedents for Ornament*, which advocated the use of Gothic ornament. In 1857 he became a member of the Medieval Society. He moved to London in 1862, and some of his work, a roll-top desk and the "King Rene's Honeymoon Cabinet", was included at the London Exhibition of that year. Also during that year Seddon became secretary to the Institute of British Architects. He continued to practise architecture throughout his career, his pupils including Voysey.

Shaw, Richard Norman (1831–1912)

Shaw was articled to an architect in 1849. Ten years later he became G. E. Street's chief assistant. In 1862 a desk designed by Shaw was shown at the London Exhibition. That same year he set up his own architectural practice, developing his style from Old English to Queen Anne and then classicism. From the mid-1870s Shaw designed furniture, which was made by W. H. Lascelles and some of which was shown at the Paris Exhibition in 1878. Shaw's pupils were to form the Art-Workers' Guild although he himself never became attached to any particular movement.

Spofforth, Harriet Prescot (1835–1921)

Spofforth was born in Calais but moved with her family to Massachusetts. She was a prolific author of stories, articles and poems, although she received little attention until 1859. In 1878 she wrote *Art Decoration Applied to Furniture*, which connects her firmly with the Aesthetic Movement. The book became a vehicle for popular ideas on decoration and contributed to the Aesthetic mania which took hold of America in the 1870s and 1880s.

Stickley, Gustav (1857–1946)

Stickley trained as a stonemason in 1869 but moved to Massachusetts to work in a chair factory. In 1883 he set up a furniture store in Binghampton, New York, which manufactured Colonial-style chairs. The company moved to Syracuse in 1891. Seven years later, Stickley travelled to England where he met Voysey. Back in America Stickley showed some Arts and Crafts-style furniture at the Pan-American Exhibition in 1902. The following year he set up several workshops as the Craftsman Building, which he organized on a guild basis. This venture was very successful for the first decade or so of its existence but went bankrupt in 1915.

Street, George Edmund (1824–1881)

Street took articles with a Winchester architect in 1841–4 but moved to London to join Gilbert Scott's office. In 1850 he became diocesan architect of Oxford, similar appointments following through the 1850s so that his practice was very large by the end of the decade. From 1868, Street was sole architect of the Law Courts. He also designed church plate, wrought iron and brasses. His pupils and assistants included Philip Webb, William Morris and Richard Norman Shaw.

Talbert, Bruce J. (1838–1881)

Talbert initially trained as a wood carver but then went into an architect's office. Having moved to Glasgow in 1856, he won a medal for architectural design from the Edinburgh Architectural Association in 1862, although he became increasingly interested in furniture design after this. About four years later he moved to London. One of his furniture designs was shown at the London 1873 Exhibition and another piece was included five years later in the Paris Exhibition. In addition to furniture, Talbert designed ecclesiastical metalwork and wallpapers.

Tiffany, Louis Comfort (1848–1933)

The son of Charles Louis Tiffany, the founder of the famous New York jewellers. Tiffany visited Europe in 1865, studying painting in Paris for a while in 1868–9. Back in New York, in 1877 he co-founded the Society of American Artists but became increasingly interested in the decorative arts after this date. In 1879 he founded the decorating firm Louis C. Tiffany and Associated

Artists. Works executed by the firm included the Veterans' Room of the Seventh Regiment Armoury (1879), Mark Twain's House (1880–1) and several rooms in the White House, all of which were in an extravagant Art style. From the late 1870s Tiffany also took an interest in stained glass. He founded the Tiffany Glass Co. in 1885, and his work became a very successful Art Nouveau product. Tiffany also designed jewellery, ceramics, lighting and textiles and won the Grand Prix at both the Paris 1900 Exhibition and the Turin Exhibition two years later. He became artistic director of the family firm in 1902.

Van de Velde, Henri (1863–1957)

Having studied painting in Antwerp (1881–4) and then Paris (1884–5), Van de Velde was elected a member of the advanced Post-Impressionist group "Les Vingt" in 1886 but gave up painting for design in 1892, stimulated by Ruskin and Morris. His interests were quite broad, ranging from embroidery design and bookbindings to designing four rooms for Samuel Bing's gallery L'Art Nouveau. In 1897 his furniture was exhibited in Dresden and in 1898 at the Hague Arts and Crafts Exhibition. At the same time he founded his own decorating firm and factory near Brussels. In 1900 he moved his office to Berlin. The decoration at the Folkwang Museum in Hagen represented the culmination of his early Art Nouveau style. In Berlin his field of design extended to include silver, cutlery, porcelain, jewellery and textiles. He was appointed an artistic adviser in Weimar in 1902 and subsequently the professor of the new school of applied arts there. In 1907 he was a founder member of the Deutsche Werkbund. Criticizing standardization and the machine as too restrictive a discipline for the individual designer, Van de Velde resigned his post in Weimar in 1914, although he was influential in the appointment of his successor, Walter Gropius, who was instrumental in the advent of the Bauhaus movement. He moved to Holland in 1920 to become architect to Muller & Co., for whom he designed the Kroller-Muller Museum, from 1937–54. Between 1926 and 1936 he was professor of architecture at the University of Ghent. His work at this time reflected a modern approach to design, and he was to emphasize his role in the creation of the Modern style with the publication of his memoirs in 1957.

Voysey, Charles Francis Annesley (1857–1941)

In 1874 Voysey was articled to the architect J. P. Seddon. Having joined the office of George Devey in 1880 he set up as an independent architect in 1882. Through A. H. Mackmurdo he received commissions to design wallpapers for Jeffrey & Co. from 1883 onwards. The following year he joined the Art-Workers' Guild. In 1888 Voysey showed some of his wallpaper and fabric designs at the first Arts and Crafts Exhibition. In the same year he built the first house of an architectural practice which was to continue until 1920. Voysey's main interests, however, remained with flat pattern design although he attempted furniture design in the mid-1880s. His work enjoyed considerable international influence.

Webb, Philip (1831–1915)

Following an apprenticeship in Reading, Webb joined Street's office in Oxford in 1854. Two years later he met Morris who became a lifelong friend, the two moving to London with Street in 1856. Webb became a member of Morris & Co. in 1861 and in that year designed furniture which would be shown at the London 1862 Exhibition. During 1866–7 Webb worked on the Green Room at the Victoria and Albert Museum. Webb's architectural practice seems not to have been where his main interests lay, although it remained open until his retirement in 1900. Webb was responsible for a number of major commissions in the English vernacular style, for example, Great Tangley Manor, Surrey and notably the Red House for Morris, with whom he shared socialist beliefs. He was much admired abroad and by the next generation of architect-designers such as Lethaby.

Whistler, James Abbott McNeill (1834–1903)

Born in Lowell, Massachusetts, Whistler was a painter, etcher and lithographer. He was educated at West Point Military Academy from 1851 but left for Paris in 1855, arriving in London four years later. He moved to Chelsea in 1863 where he met Rossetti. Whistler's most famous work, his portraits, were mainly executed in the 1870s. He also advised on interior schemes, helping to create the famous Peacock Room for F.R. Leyland's house, and collaborated with Godwin in designing furniture for the 1867 Paris Exhibition. In 1897 he became President of the International Society of Sculptors, Painters and Gravers and between 1898 and 1901 ran his own art school, the Académie Carmen in Paris.

Wright, Frank Lloyd (1867–1956)

Wright began his career in the Engineering School of Wisconsin University but from 1888 spent the next five years as a draughtsman for the architect Louis Sullivan. Wright's architectural career took off in 1889 when he built his own home in Oak Park, Illinois. His early career as an architect was very successful; he had designed over fifty houses by 1900. During these early years he also became increasingly interested in furniture design and was a founding member of the Arts and Crafts Society of Chicago. For some of his later work, for example, Fallingwater, Bear Run, Pennsylvannia, he was both architect and furniture designer. Wright's love of Japanese art, which was sparked off by the 1893 Chicago World Columbian Exposition led to several exhibitions of Japanese prints, in 1906, 1908 and 1917.

Wyatt, Sir Matthew Digby (1820–1877)

Wyatt trained as an architect under his brother Thomas Henry Wyatt from 1836. He travelled through Europe between 1844 and 1846, and on his return to England became involved with drawing medieval mosaics for a book *Geometrical Mosaics of the Middle Ages*, which was published in 1848. From 1850 he began designing tiles for Maw & Co., his work including a fireplace which was shown at the 1862 London Exhibition. Wyatt was involved with the building of Crystal Palace and, as superintending architect, designed the Pompeian, Byzantine, English Gothic and Italian Rennaissance Courts there when the building was removed to Sydenham. During this time Wyatt met Owen Jones, and this led to his contributing to Jones' influential book *The Grammar of Ornament*. In 1852, Wyatt designed the ironwork for Paddington Station and in 1865 the Islamic tiled billiard-room at Kensington Palace Gardens. His Italian Renaissance courtyard for the India Office, built in 1868, is one of the best examples of the High Victorian Renaissance style.

INDEX

Numbers in italic refer to the illustrations

Abbotsford, 57, *57*
Aberdeen, Earl of, 121
Abney Hall, Cheshire, *66*
Ackermann's *Repository*, 56
Adam style, 209–10, 211; *204*
Adams, Maurice, 131; *151*
Aesthetic Movement, 107–29, 140, 154, 177; *22, 110–35*
Aitchison, George, 138, 140, 145; *18, 146, 147, 150*
Albert, Prince Consort, 51, 70–2; *15, 34, 47*
Alcock, Sir Rutherford, 111–12, 120, 149
Alhambra, Granada, 49
Alma-Tadema, Anna, *136*
Alma-Tadema, Lawrence, 135; *136, 144*
Amsterdam Exhibition (1883), 122
Anglican Church, 89
Annual Furnishing Trades Exhibition and Market, 21
antique dealers, 59, 60, 198
antiques, 57–60, 164–5, 195, 197–200; *210*
Arab rooms, 142–5; *147*
Arbuthnot, Mrs, 47
architects, 75, 158
Arrowsmith, H.W. and A., 45, 48, 51, 53, 57
Arrowsmith, James, 14–16, 19, 28, 36, 37–8, 41, 42
Art Deco, 179
"Art" furnishings, 124–9
Art Manufactures, 68–70
Art Needlework, 86
Art Nouveau, 9, 129, 161, 177–87; *95, 183–96, 206*
Art-Workers' Guild, 171
artists' houses, 131–55; *136–60*
Arts and Crafts Exhibition Society, 171, 174, 175, 183, 193
Arts and Crafts Movement, 9, 12, 74, 81, 92, 103, 120, 146, 154, 157–61, 170–1, 173, 174–5, 177, 180, 188, 190, 212; *161, 220*
Ashbee, C.R., 172–3, 175, 180, 187, 190, 193; *176, 177*
Audsley, W. & G., *20*
Austria, Jugendstil, 179–80
Aynhoe, *33, 35*

Baillie Scott, Florence, 188
Baillie Scott, M.H., 169, 172, 180, 187–8, 189, 193; *196, 197*
Baker, G.P. & J., *179*
Baker, Tommy, 84
Balfour, Lady Frances, 204
Ballantyne, John, *2, 138*
Balmoral, *34*
bamboo furniture, 120

Barnett, Henrietta, 169–70
Barnsley, Ernest, 174
Barnsley, Sydney, 174; *178*
Bassett-Lowke, W.J., 185
Bates, Dewey, *141*
Batley, H.W., 117–19; *122*
Bauhaus, 79
Bazin, Monsieur, 93
Beale, James, *101*
Beckford, William, 54
Bedford Park, London, 96, 108, 168; *171*
bedrooms, 33, 42–3, 211
beds, 42
Beebe, James M., *48*
Beerbohm, Max, 113, 125
Behrens, Peter, 180
Belcher, John, 182
Belgium, Art Nouveau, 178–9
Belgravia, 51
Bell, Ada Phoebe, *88*
Bell, Clive, 188
Bell, Florence, *88*
Bell, Sir Isaac Lowthian, 85
Bell, Margaret, *88*
Bell, Vanessa, 188
Belter, John Henry, 61
Benson, W.A.S., 93, 172; *109*
Berlin woolwork, 59, *25*
Bernhardt, Sarah, 178
Best, Mary Ellen, *26, 32*
Bing, Samuel, 95–6, 178; *188*
Binyon, Brightwen, 101
Birmingham, 65
Blackie, Walter, 185; *190, 191*
Blomfield, Reginald, 174, 182
Bloomsbury group, 188
Blount, Godfrey, 161; *163*
Boehm, Edgar, 145
bookcases, 38
books, 23–4, 47–8, 60
Boston, 74
boudoirs, 33, 41; *50, 219*
Bourneville, 168
Bradley, Will, 189, *199*
breakfast-rooms, 33
Bridgens, Richard, 57–8
Brighton Pavilion, Sussex, 49
Britton, John, 57
Brook, Robert, 212
Brophy, Andrew F., *223*
Brown, Ford Madox, 82, 89, 90, 92, 158–61; *92, 94*
Brown, Richard, 49, 54
Brunner, Arnold, W., 203
Bullock, George, 53–4, 57
Burd, James, *51*
Burden, Elizabeth, 85
Burden, Jane, 83–4, 85
Burges, William, 75, 91, 112, 168; *63, 78*
Burne-Jones, Edward, 82–5, 87, 89, 90, 99–100, 108, 112, 116, 137, 150, 158; *86, 88, 90, 91, 102, 108*
Burne-Jones, Georgiana, 85; *90*
Burnham, John A., *83*

Burton, Decimus, 52, 66
Burton, Sir Richard, 142
Bute, Marquis of, 75; *63*
Butler, Edmund, *220*
Butterfield, William, 75, 91, 92
Byron, Lord, 57

Cadbury, George, 168
Caldecott, Randolph, 145
Cardiff Castle, 75; *63*
Carlisle, George Howard, 9th Earl of, 99–100; *102*
Carlyle, Thomas, 83, 137, 147
carpets, 95; *36, 55, 99*
Cartwright, Lili, *33, 35*
cast iron furniture, 14
Castell Coch, 75
Castle Howard, Yorkshire, 100
catalogues, 21, 53, 54
Catholic church, 67
Celtic Revival, 177
Century Guild, 166, 171–2; *174*
ceramics, 13–14
Cézanne, Paul, 188
Chelsea, 147–55, 172
Cheltenham, 52
Chicago, 74, 189–91
children's bedrooms, 43
Chinese style, 45, 49; *45*
chintz, 42, 94; *71*
Chippendale, Thomas, 60, 93, 197, 209, 210–11, 212
Chipping Camden, 172–3, 190
Christianity, 56
Christie, Grace, *165*
Christie, Robert, 212
Church, 56, 75, 89
Church, Ella Rodman, 198–9
Church, Frederick, 131
Cobbe, Frances Power, 27
Cockerell, F.P., 138
Codman, Ogden, 24, 204–7; *210*
Cole, Henry, 68–73, 75, 81, 111; *71*
Colefax, Sybil, 12
Collcutt, T.E., 125; *131*
Collinson & Lock, 115, 119, 125; *14*
Colonial Revival, 208, 211, 212; *221*
colours, *21*; Aesthetic Movement, 126, 154, 155; Art Nouveau, 178; for different rooms, 33–4; in dining-rooms, 35; drawing-rooms, 38; Grecian style, 53; for libraries, 37–8; Morris & Co., 94; theories, 70
Compton Bassett, Wiltshire, *42*
Concanen, A., *112*
Conishead Priory, 58
Conway, Moncure, 96–7, 151
Cook, Clarence, 79, 197, 208
Coomeraswamy, Ananda, 173
Cooper, H. & J., 121
Le Corbusier, 188
Corfe, B.O., *205*
Cotehele, Cornwall, 58

cottage style, 157–75, 183, 193; *75, 161–82, 196*
cotton fabrics, 31, 42; *56*
Country Gentleman's Association, 169
Cowtan & Tout, 96
Crace, J.G., 14, 52, 166; *64, 67*
Crace, John Diblee, *49*
Cragside, Northumberland, *132*
Crane, Walter, 81, 82, 99, 110, 122, 128, 145, 146–7, 157, 161, 171, 180, 182; *12, 111, 147, 152, 164*
Croly, H.G., 203
Crystal Palace, London, 72
Cubism, 188
Cubitt, Thomas, 51, 169
curtains, 39–41, 42

dados, 126–8
Daily Mail Ideal Home Exhibition, 21
Dalby, Elizabeth Pearson, *42*
D'Arcy, William Knox, 101, 103
Darmstadt, 180, 187
Davies, Owen W., *121*
Davis, Alexander Jackson, 79; *52*
Davis, John Scarlett, *59*
Day, Lewis Foreman, 11, 16; *104*
De Morgan, William, 87, 140, 151; *146*
De Wolfe, Elsie, 12
Deanery Garden, Berkshire, 164; *167, 168*
Dearle, John Henry, 85, 95, 102; *100, 106, 108*
decorators, 14–16, 19
The Deepdene, Surrey, 31; *43, 50*
department stores, 16, 21
Deptford Furnishing Co., 21
Derick, J.M., 101
design reform movement, 63–79
desks, 38, 75
Dickens, Charles, 27, 72–3, 137
dining-rooms, 33, 35–7, 38, 41
Dolmetsch, Heinrich, 47
Donaldson, George, 182
Downing, Andrew Jackson, 42, 48, 49, 52–3, 56, 60, 79; *82*
D'Oyle Carte, Mrs 153
drawing-rooms, 33, 38–41
Dresser, Christopher, 23, 117; *81*
Dromore Castle, Eire, 114; *115*
Du Maurier, George, 126
Duncan, Isadora, 171
Dunlop, Walter, 90
Dunn, Henry Teffry, 149–50, 197–8; *153*
Duret, Theodore, 153
Dyce, William, 72, 153

Early English style, 207–8; *220*
East London Working Men's College, 74
Eastlake, Charles Locke, 24, 77–9, 95, 124, 126, 174, 199, 200, 210; *79*

Eaton Hall, Cheshire, 47; 6, 76
Eberlain, H.D., 191
Ecclesiological Society, 75
Edis, Sir Robert, 91–2, 166
Edwards & Roberts, 211, 212
Egg, Augustus, 74
Egyptian style, 45, 52; 44, 50
Elder Duncan, J.H., 165, 195, 197, 199
Elizabethan style, 38, 57–60, 61; 58, 59
Elmore, W.T. and Son. 120
embroidery, 59, 85–6, 103; 25, 87, 163, 165
Empire style, 211–12
encyclopaedias, 47–8
Essex & Co., 16, 174
Essex House Press, 172, 173
exhibitions, 21–3, 70–2
Eyles, Henry, 15

fabrics see textiles
fakes, antiques, 199
Falke, Jacob von, 200, 203
"fancy work", 30
Farcy, Georges, 178
Farmer & Roger, 120
Faulkner, Charles, 82, 87
Faulkner, Kate, 99; 105
Feure, Georges de, 188
Field, Erastus Salisbury, 36
Fildes, Luke, 145–6; 151
Fine Art and Industries Exhibition, Manchester (1882), 211
fireplaces, 39
Firth, Ray & Prosser, 134
Fleetwood, 52, 66
Flemish Renaissance style, 51
Flower, Wickham, 100
Fontaine, Pierre, 211–12
Fonthill Abbey, 54
Forbes Robertson, Sir Johnston, 116
Fortier, Ursin, 120
Foster, Birket, 89: 91
Foxton's, 185
Frampton, George, 182
France, 63, 72, 178, 180, 203–7
"Free English" style, 192
"Free Renaissance" style, 203
French Renaissance style, 51
French Revolution, 59
French styles, 60, 65–6
friezes, 126–8, 164; 20, 27, 81
Frith, W.P., 12, 132; 138
Fry, Roger, 188; 198

Gandy, J.P., 52
garden cities, 168–70
Garnett, Edward and Constance, 164
Garrett, Rhoda and Agnes, 208
Gaudier-Brzeska, Henri, 188
Gell, William, 52
George IV, King, 49
George, Ernest, 166
German Renaissance style, 51
Germany, 72, 179–80
gilding, 14, 16
Gillow's, 79, 115, 166, 211; 61, 132
Gimson, Ernest, 174; 162, 178
Girouard, Mark, 131, 132, 153
Gladstone, Mary, 204
Glasgow School, 177, 183–7, 189; 190–5
glass, 14; stained glass, 87–90, 91; 92
Gobelins tapestry works, 103
Godley, G.F., 89
Godwin, Edward William, 110, 113–17, 120, 122, 126, 145, 153–4, 184; 17, 93, 115, 116–20, 156, 157
Gothic style, 38, 47, 52, 54–7, 63, 66–8, 73–5, 77, 79, 92, 158, 177, 207, 212; 54–6, 65, 76, 80, 82–3

Government Schools of Design, 51, 65, 72, 73
Grand Rapids, 61
The Grange, Fulham, 86, 90, 150; 90
Grant, Duncan, 188
Great Exhibition, London (1851), 21, 49, 51, 61, 68, 72, 145; 15, 67, 70, 71
Grecian style, 36, 37, 39, 45, 52–4, 66; 43, 50, 52
Greenaway, Kate, 135
Greene, Charles Sumner, 189; 182
Greene, Henry Mather, 189; 182
Griggs, F.L., 162
Grogaert, Georges, 127
Guild of Handicraft, 161, 172–3, 175, 180, 187; 177
Guild of St George, 74, 170–1
Guimard, Hector, 179
Guthrie and Wells, 183

Hackney Furnishing Co., 21
Haddon, 58
Haghe, Louis, 70
Haig, Axel, 63
Halifax, 33
halls, 34–5
Hampstead Garden Suburb, 169–70, 187; 175
Hampton & Sons, 21, 207, 208, 211; 212
Harrison, Robert, 166
Hatch, Alfrederick Smith, 8
Hatfield House, Hertfordshire, 37
Haweis, Mrs, 24, 145, 208
Hayllar, Kate, 110
Heal, Ambrose, 92, 166
Heal's, 21, 165–6, 198, 203; 169, 179, 221
Heaton, Clement John, 171
Heckmondwike Manufacturing Co., 95
Heinemann, William, 153
Henderson, Alexander, 212
Hepplewhite, George, 209, 211
Herculaneum, 52
Herkomer, Hubert, 135
Hertford, Marquis of, 204
Hesse, Grand Duke of, 180, 187
Heywood, Higginbottom & Smith, 72
Hicks, George Elgar, 30
High Church Movement, 89
Hill House, Glasgow, 185; 190, 191
Hindley & Wilkinson, 204
hire purchase, 23
Hoffmann, Josef, 175, 179, 180
Hogarth Club, 75
Hokusai, 110
Hole, James, 33
Holland & Sons, 51, 79, 93, 166, 204; 80
Holland Park, London, 100, 136–46; 104
Holloway, E.S., 191
Homann, W.H., 47
Home Arts and Industries Association, 161, 171, 173
Hope, Thomas, 31, 52, 53, 54, 211; 43, 50
Horne, Herbert Percy, 171–2; 174
Horsfall Museum, Manchester, 75
Horta, Victor, 179
The House Decorator's and Painter's Guide, 14–16
Houses of Parliament, 67–8; 64
Howard, Ebenezer, 168–9
Hubbard, Elbert, 174–5
Hudson, Edward, 164; 167, 168
Hunt, Charles, 53
Hunt, Leigh, 147
Hunt, Richard Morris, 203
Hunt, Thomas, 58
Hunt, William Holman, 74, 132, 171, 195; 73

Hunter, Colin, 146

Image, Selwyn, 171
Indian style, 45, 49; 3, 46
International Health Exhibition (1884), 166
Ionides, Alexander, 100, 117
Islamic decoration, 121
Italian Renaissance style, 51; 47
Italy, 64, 180

Jack, George, 93, 103
Jackson & Graham, 19, 21, 51, 119, 166, 204; 16
Jacobean style, 208, 212
Jacoby, Julius, 124
Jacquard looms, 13
Japanese influences, 45, 49, 77, 110–20, 125, 154–5, 193; 12, 114–19, 121, 122, 159, 160
Jeckyll, Thomas, 117; 123
Jeffrey & Co., 93, 128, 174; 116
Jennens & Bettridge, 64
Jennings, H.J., 183, 193, 197, 200, 208, 210, 211
Jervis, Simon, 9
Johnson, J. Eastman, 8, 208
Johnson, Thomas, 60
Jones, Owen, 47, 48, 49, 70, 72, 73, 94, 121, 135, 145, 158; 44, 69, 215
Jonquet, A., 119, 125
Jugendstil, 179–80

Kelmscott House, London, 95, 97, 103; 103
Kelmscott Manor, Oxfordshire, 86, 92, 97; 89
Kensington, 136
Kenton & Co., 174
Kerr, Robert, 35, 37, 45, 166–8, 203
Kidderminster carpets, 55
Kimbel & Cabus, 79
King, Thomas, 39, 41, 42, 54, 57, 60
Kinross, John, 204
Kipling, Lockwood, 46
kitchens, 27, 33
Knight, Charles, 30
Knight, T. & Sons, 19
Knox, Archibald, 177, 187

Langtry, Lily, 21
layouts, houses, 31–3
leather, 37, 38; 125
Lee, Daniel, 111
Leighton, Frederic, 112, 138–42, 149
Leighton House, London, 136, 138, 140–5, 149; 146–50
Letchworth, 168–9, 187; 172, 173
Lethaby, W.R., 82, 103, 132, 158, 163, 174, 192; 107
Lever, Lord, 168
Lewis, Wyndham, 188
Leyland, Frederick, 114, 117, 153; 123
Liberty, Arthur Lasenby, 110, 120
Liberty's, 16, 21, 120–2, 177, 180, 187; 13, 110, 113
libraries, 33, 37–8
"La Libre Esthetique", 179
Light, C. & R., 39, 41, 54; 28, 39
Linley Sambourne, Edward, 4, 23, 130
Linley Sambourne House, London, 4, 23
Litchfield, Frederick, 199
Little Holland House, London, 136–8
Locke, Matthias, 60
Logan, George, 195
London: artists' houses, 131–55; 136–60; exhibitions, 21; flats, 11; furniture retailers, 21; government school of design, 65; population, 10; speculative housing, 51
London International Exhibition

(1862), 49, 75–7, 91, 111–12, 149, 204, 209–10
London Transport, 161
Loos, Adolf, 179–80
Loudon, J.C., 33, 35, 37, 48, 49, 51, 52, 56, 57, 59, 60, 61, 66
"Louis" styles, 39, 60–1, 65–6, 72, 178, 203–7, 211, 212; 60, 61, 216–18
Lutyens, Edwin, 164, 174; 167, 168

Macartney, Mervyn, 93, 174
McClure, A., 191
Macdonald, Frances, 184
Macdonald, Margaret, 184, 185
MacFadyen, Dugald, 168
McKim, Mead and White, 208
Mackintosh, Charles Rennie, 180, 183–7, 189; 190–4
Mackmurdo, Arthur Heygate, 155, 161, 171–2, 180; 159, 160, 174
Maclise, Daniel, 70, 153
MacNair, Herbert, 183–4
Macrea, M.C., 93
Maher, George W., 191
Majorelle, Louis, 189
Manchester, 10, 65, 74, 92
Manderston, Berwickshire, 204
Maple's, 21
Marks, Henry Stacy, 116
Marks, Murray, 113
Marlborough House, London, 72, 73
Marshall, Peter Paul, 82
Martin, John, 147, 153
Martin, Leopold, 147
mass-production, 45, 61, 77–9
Maugham, Syrie, 12
May, Phil, 146
Mayhew, Henry, 10, 21
Mayor, A., 40
mechanization, 12–13, 29–30
Mediaeval Society, 75
Meier-Graefe, Julius, 178, 187
Melrose Abbey, 57
Menpes, Mortimer, 153, 154–5; 159, 160
Meyrick, Sir Samuel Rush, 58; 58
Middleton Park, Oxfordshire, 45
Mikado Bamboo Co., 120
Miles, Frank, 154; 157
Millais, John Everett, 132
Miller, Sir James, 204
mirrors, overmantel, 28; 53
Mission style, 174–5; 181, 182
Mitchell & Rammelsburg, 79
"Modern Gothic" style, 79
Modern Movement, 79, 189–93, 195
Modern style, 39, 52–4, 66
Moorish style, 47, 49, 121, 145; 126, 147
Morant, George, 65–6
Moreau, Gustave, 131
Morley, Henry, 73
Morris, May, 86; 89
Morris, William, 79, 81–105, 114, 146, 150, 157–8, 161, 163, 168, 171, 172, 174–5, 185, 190, 212; 75, 84–109, 115, 130
Morris & Co., 74, 75, 81–105, 117, 150, 164, 166, 188; 84–109
Morrison, Alfred, 135
Morrison, T.E., 48
Moser, Koloman, 179, 180
Mucha, Alphonse, 177–8; 183, 186
Muthesius, Hermann, 93, 129, 184, 188

Napoleon I, Emperor, 52, 53
Napoleonic Wars, 53, 63
Nash, John, 49, 51
National Association of Retail Furnishers, 19
Needham, William Frederick, 120
Neo-Classicism, 52, 203
neo-Georgian style, 93, 183, 193,

197, 203, 208–10, 212; *225*
neo-Tudor style, 197
"New Art", 177-93; *183–202*
"New Lifers", 161–3
New York, 21, 79
New York Exhibition (1853), 61
Newcastle, 65
Newhouse Park, Hertfordshire, *126*
Nixon & Son, 60
North, Messrs, 211
novelty, 30, 45
nurseries, 43

Oetzmann's, 21
Olbrich, Josef, 180
"Old French" style, 60–1; *59–61*
Old Swan House, Chelsea, 100–1; *105*
Omega Workshops, 188; *198*
Oriental rugs, 95
Orrinsmith, Mrs, 39–41, 195
Osborne House, Isle of Wight, 51; *46, 47*
overmantel mirrors, 28; *53*
Owen, Robert, 168

Pabst, Daniel, 79
Paget, H.M., *171*
Paine Furniture Co., 208
Palace Green, London, 99–100; *102*
panelling, 57
Panton, Mrs J.E., 12, 24, 200
papier-mâché, 14, 61; *74*
Papworth, John Buonarotti, 52, 64
Parian ware, 13
Paris, 21
Paris Exhibitions: *1849*, 72; *1855*, 51, 61; *1867*, 125; *80*; *1878*, 115, 211; *1900*, 166, 178, 182
Parker, Barry, 168–9
Parker, Charles, 51
Parkes, Frances Byerly, 35, 48, 49, 52
parlours, 28, 33, 41–2
pattern books, 48, 49, 60
Peasant Arts Society, 161; *163*
Pellegrini, Carlo, 154
Penshurst Place, Kent, 58; *58*
Percier, Charles, 211–12
Persian style, 45
Pevsner, Nikolaus, 9, 187
Philadelphia Centennial Exposition (1876), 79, 208; *14*
"picturesque" planning, 33
plywood furniture, 61
Pompeian style, 51, 52; *49*
Pompeii, 52, 65
porcelain, 13–14
Port Sunlight, 168
La Porte Chinoise, Paris, 110–11, 120
Post-Impressionism, 188
pottery, 13–14
Pottier & Stymus, *22*
Powell & Sons, 89
Pre-Raphaelites, 74, 84, 91, 147–51, 158
Price, Henry, 84
Prignot, Eugène, 51
Prince's Gate, London, *123*
Prinsep, Sarah, 136–8
Prinsep, Thoby, 136–8
Prinsep, Val, 145
printing: tablewares, 14; textiles, 13; wallpaper, 14, 30
Prior, E.S. 182
privacy, 33
propriety, 31, 61
Public Libraries and Museums Act (1845), 65
Puckler-Muskau, Prince, 60
Pugin, A.C., 66
Pugin, A.W.N., 66–8, 70, 72, 73, 75, 77, 79, 81, 85, 158, 174; *64–8*

"Quaint" style, 193

Queen Anne style, 89, 145, 146, 151, 154, 166–8, 197, 208, 209, 212; *19, 111, 142*

Rainhill Hall, Liverpool, 172; *174*
Raphael, 65
Rathbone, Harold, 171
Rathbone, Philip, 172
Rayner, Samuel, *31*
Read, Charles Handley, 180–2
Red House, Bexleyheath, 82–7, 89–90, 91, 95, 103, 145, 150, 163
Redgrave, Richard, 70, 72, 81, 111
Remon, Georges, 178; *184, 185*
Renaissance styles, 51, 200, 202, 203; *47, 212, 213, 215*
Repton, Humphry, 51, 52, 54; *38*
retailers, 16, 21–3
revivalism, 195–212; *204–26*
Reynolds, Sir Joshua, 131
Rickman, Thomas, 47, 56
Roberts, David, *2, 57*
Roberts, James, *34*
Robertson, J.C., 64
Robinson, George, *154*
Rockefeller House, New York, *22*
Rococo style, 203–4
Rooke, Thomas Matthew, 86; *90, 140*
Ros, Olivia de, *37*
Rossetti, Dante Gabriel, 82, 83, 84–5, 89, 90, 92, 97, 108, 112–13, 137, 149–51, 158, 197–8; *153, 154*
Rothschild, Alfred de, 204
Rothschild, Baron Ferdinand de, 202, 204
Rothschild, Leopold, *218*
Rottmann, Strome & Co., 121; *125*
Rounton Grange, Northallerton, 85, 94–5; *88*
Royal School of Needlework, 86
Royal Wilton Carpet Works, 95
Royal Windsor Tapestry Works, 103
Roycroft Shops, 174–5
rugs, 95
Ruskin, Effie, 19
Ruskin, John, 19, 63, 73–4, 81, 83, 107, 108, 153, 157, 158, 168, 170–1, 174, 190, 195
Rutter, John, *54*

St James's Palace, London, 92
St Louis Exposition (1904), 189
Sanderson, Arthur & Sons, *223*
Scott, G., 85
Scott, Samuel, *64*
Scott, Sir Walter, 57, 83; *57, 68*
Scott, William Bell, 84, 151; *155*
second-hand furniture, 31
Sedding, John, 207
Seddon, Charles & Co., 92
Seddon, John Pollard, 75; *77*
Sefton's, *185*
Select Committee Report on design reform, 63–5, 66, 68, 70
Semper, Gottfried, 51
servants, 27, 42, 43
Shakers, 74
Shannon, Sir James, 146
Shapland, H.P., *225*
Shaw, Henry, 57, 58–9; *58*
Shaw, Richard Norman, 75, 77, 96, 100, 145–6, 168, 171, 207; *132, 142*
Sheffield, 65, 74
Shepherd, T.H., 52
Sheraton, Thomas, 93, 209, 210, 211; *226*
Shiplake Court, Oxfordshire, *166*
Shoolbred, James, 117–19, 125
Shoolbred, James & Co., 16, 21, 204; *121*
shops, 16, 21
Sickert, Helena Maria, *103*

sideboards, 37; *48, 80*
Silver, Arthur, 122; *128*
Silver, Rex, 177
Singh, Bai Rham, *46*
Smallhythe Place, Kent, 165; *169*
Smee, W. & A., 115
Smith, George, 54, 56
Smith, J. Moyr, 79
Smith family, *36*
Smith's Art of Housepainting, 23–4
Snell (upholsterer), 19
Society of Arts, 68, 70–2
Society for the Protection of Ancient Buildings, 163
soft furnishings, 28–9, 39–41, 42
South Kensington Museum, London, 72, 73, 90, 92, 95, 111, 150, 158, 182, 210; *93*
Southey, Robert, 56
Soye, Madame de, 110–11
Spence, Charles, 5
Spofforth, Harriet Prescott, 79
sprung upholstery, 14, 29
Squire, Alice, *41*
stained glass, 87–90, 91; *92*
staircases, 35
Standen, Sussex, 93, 95; *101*
Stanmore Hall, Middlesex, 101–3; *106–8*
Stead McAlpine, *180*
Stevens, Alfred, 51
Stevens (John Cox) House, *52*
Stickley, Gustave, 174
Stirling, Mrs A.M.W., 136–7
Stone, Marcus, 135, 145–6; *142*
Story & Triggs, *216, 224*
Stosseck, Paul, *222*
Street, George Edmund, 75, 83–4
Stuart-Wortley, Stuart, 154
studies, 33; *26*
studio houses, 131–55; *136–60*
Sullivan, Louis H., 189
Summerly, Felix, 68–70
Swaby, John, 57

tablewares, 14
Tait, Robert, *29*
Talbert, Bruce James, 23, 77–9, 117, 128; *16, 80, 129, 130, 133*
tapestries, 103–5; *108*
Taylor, Warrington, 91; *96*
technology, 12–13
Tennyson, Alfred, Lord, 137
Terry, Daniel, 57
Terry, Ellen, 21, 113, 114, 165; *169*
textiles: Art Nouveau, *187, 188, 193*; durability, 31; Elizabethan style, 59; Liberty's, 121–2; *128*, mechanization, 13; Morris & Co., 93–6; *84, 97*; Renaissance style, *215*; Voysey, *179, 180*
Thackeray, William Makepeace, 137
Thornton, Peter, 9, 208–9
Thornycroft, Hamo, 146
Tiffany, Louis Comfort, *124*
Tiffany & Co., 119
tiles, 87, 142–3; *77, 135*
Times Furnishing, 21
Tissot, James, 135; *143*
Tite Street, London, 151, 153–5
Tottenham, *59*
Tous-les-Louis style *see* Louis styles
Townshend House, *136*
Trollope & Co., 166
trompe l'oeil, 30–1; *27, 51, 72*
Troost, Paul Ludwig, *226*
Tudor House, Cheyne Walk, 149–51, 155; *153, 154*
Turner, J.M.W., 147
Twain, Mark, *9*
Tyron, Thomas, 203

United States of America: bedrooms, 42; Colonial Revival, 208, 211; Empire

style, 212; French Revival, 204–7; Gothic style, 56, 79; Grecian style, 52, 53; house layouts, 31–3; Mission style, 174–5; *181, 182*; Modernism, 189–91; parlours, 41–2; plywood furniture, 61; Shakers, 74; women interior decorators, 12
Unwin, Raymond, 168–70
Upholsterer's Accelerator, 28, 39
upholstery, 14, 19, 28–9, 31, 37, 38, 39

Van de Velde, Henri, 178–9
veneers, 14
vernacular tradition, 163–8, 195
Versailles, 66
Victoria, Queen, 140, 204; *34*
Victoria and Albert Museum *see* South Kensington Museum
Vienna Secession, 177, 179–80, 184, 189; *226*
villas, 51
Vivant Denon, 52
Volck, A.J., *24*
Voysey, C.F.A., 23, 161, 174, 180, 182, 193; *179, 180*

Waddesdon Manor, Buckinghamshire, 202, 204
Wagner, Otto, 179
Walker, Emery, *85*
wallpaper, 14, 16–19, 30, 42, 93–4, 96, 114; *1, 12, 27, 60, 61, 64, 69, 72, 98, 116, 117, 133, 134, 183, 223*
Walpole, Horace, 54
Walsh, J.H., 31, 42
Wardle, Thomas, 122
Waring & Gillow, 21, 198, 204, 208
Warndrop, J. & Sons, *11*
Warner, Benjamin, *215*
Warner & Sons, *180*
Waterhouse, Alfred, *76*
Watt, William, 115; *120*
Watts, George Frederick, 137–8; *140, 145*
Weale, John, 60, 209
Webb, Philip, 75, 82, 83–4, 87, 90, 92–3, 99–100, 117, 145, 158, 163, 174; *86, 91, 93, 96, 98, 101–3*
Webster, Thomas, 48, 49, 52
West Hill Park estate, Halifax, 33
Westminster, Duke of, 47; *6, 76*
Wharton, Edith, 24, 204–7
Wheeler, Gervase, 35, 38, 41
Whistler, James McNeill, 107, 108, 110, 112–17, 151, 153–4, 155; *113, 120, 123, 156, 158*
White, John P., 187, 188
The White House, Tite Street, 153, 155; *156*
Whiteley's, 21, 195–7
Whittock, Nathaniel, 24, 48, 49, 51
Wickham Hall, Kent, *213*
Wiener Werkstätte, 175, 180
Wightwick Manor, Staffordshire, *100*
Wilde, Oscar, 108–10, 113, 154
Wiley, Samuel, 64
Wilkins, William, 47
Windsor Castle, 66
Winston, Charles, 90
wood, 14, 54
Wood, Esther, 161
Woollams, William & Co., *27*
woolwork, Berlin, 59; *25*
Wright, Frank Lloyd, 79, 175, 189–91, 193; *200*
Wright & Mansfield, 204, 209–10
Wyatt, Matthew Digby, 72
Wyburd, Leonard, 121; *137*

Yeats, W.B., 168, 177
York, 65

Zahn, Wilhelm, 52